SELLING SOCIAL

Procurement, Purchasing, and Social Enterprises

Edited by Jennifer Sumner, Andrea Chan, Annie Luk, and Jack Quarter

Since the 2010s, all levels of governments in Canada have gradually initiated social procurement as a policy tool to further their social values and political agendas. Social enterprises of various shapes and sizes across the country have served as partners in the execution of those agendas. *Selling Social* examines the experiences of these enterprises in social procurement and social purchasing.

Selling Social presents the findings of a three-year Canadian research project detailing experiences of work integration social enterprises (WISEs) selling their goods and services to organizational purchasers, including governments, businesses, and non-profit organizations. Drawing on survey findings and interviews, the book explores a diverse group of social enterprises from across Canada, showcasing their successes and their challenges based on real-life examples to aid social enterprises that are considering this path. The book emphasizes the importance of including social and environmental considerations in procurement and purchasing decisions, particularly at larger scales and through public policy. In doing so, *Selling Social* extends the understanding of social enterprises beyond their social and economic outcomes and into the broader movement towards responsible procurement and purchasing.

JENNIFER SUMNER teaches in the Department of Leadership, Higher and Adult Education and is coordinator of the Adult Education and Community Development Program at the Ontario Institute for Studies in Education at the University of Toronto.

ANDREA CHAN is a research associate at the Troost Institute for Leadership Education in Engineering at the University of Toronto.

ANNIE LUK is a sessional instructor at the Ontario Institute for Studies in Education at the University of Toronto.

JACK QUARTER was a professor at the Ontario Institute for Studies in Education at the University of Toronto.

Selling Social

Procurement, Purchasing, and Social Enterprises

EDITED BY JENNIFER SUMNER, ANDREA CHAN, ANNIE LUK, AND JACK QUARTER

UNIVERSITY OF TORONTO PRESS
Toronto Buffalo London

ISBN 978-1-4875-0671-1 (cloth)   ISBN 978-1-4875-3471-4 (EPUB)
ISBN 978-1-4875-2450-0 (paper)   ISBN 978-1-4875-3470-7 (PDF)

Library and Archives Canada Cataloguing in Publication

Title: Selling social : procurement, purchasing, and social enterprises /
    edited by Jennifer Sumner, Andrea Chan, Annie Luk, and Jack Quarter.
Names: Sumner, Jennifer, 1949– editor. | Chan, Andrea, 1979– editor. |
    Luk, Annie, editor. | Quarter, Jack, editor.
Description: Includes bibliographical references and index.
Identifiers: Canadiana (print) 20220424640 | Canadiana (ebook) 20220424691 |
    ISBN 9781487506711 (cloth) | ISBN 9781487524500 (paper) |
    ISBN 9781487534714 (EPUB) | ISBN 9781487534707 (PDF)
Subjects: LCSH: Government purchasing – Social aspects – Canada. |
    LCSH: Government purchasing – Environmental aspects – Canada. |
    LCSH: Nonprofit organizations – Canada. | LCSH: Social entrepreneurship –
    Canada.
Classification: LCC JF1525.P85 S45 2023 | DDC 352.5/30971 – dc23

We wish to acknowledge the land on which the University of Toronto
Press operates. This land is the traditional territory of the Wendat, the
Anishnaabeg, the Haudenosaunee, the Métis, and the Mississaugas of the
Credit First Nation.

University of Toronto Press acknowledges the financial support of the
Government of Canada, the Canada Council for the Arts, and the Ontario
Arts Council, an agency of the Government of Ontario, for its publishing
activities.

Canada Council   Conseil des Arts
for the Arts   du Canada

ONTARIO ARTS COUNCIL
CONSEIL DES ARTS DE L'ONTARIO
an Ontario government agency
un organisme du gouvernement de l'Ontario

Funded by the   Financé par le
Government   gouvernement
of Canada   du Canada

Canada

Contents

Part 3: The Importance of Parent Organizations

Part 4: The Dilemma of Selling Social Value

Part 5: Balancing Multiple Bottom Lines

Acknowledgments

We would like to thank all the organizations and people who participated in this research project. Your generous sharing of experience, insight, and stories has made this book possible and helped us significantly in our work. We lack sufficient space to recognize all of the contributors but wish to single out the organizations, including their staff and customers, who graciously agreed to serve as cases in our book:

- BUILD (Winnipeg, Manitoba)
- Calgary Progressive Lifestyles Foundation (Calgary, Alberta)
- Challenge Disability Resource Group (Whitehorse, Yukon)
- Diversity Food Services (Winnipeg, Manitoba)
- EMBERS (Vancouver, British Columbia)
- EthniCity Catering (Calgary, Alberta)
- Ever Green Recycling (St. John's, Newfoundland & Labrador)
- Groupe PART (Montreal, Quebec)
- Harbourview Training Centre (Souris, Prince Edward Island)
- Horizon Achievement Centre (Sydney, Nova Scotia)
- ImagineAbility (Winnipeg, Manitoba)
- Let's Work Atlantic (pseudonym; Atlantic Canada)
- LOFT Kitchen (Toronto, Ontario)
- Rainbow's End Community Development Corporation (Hamilton, Ontario)
- SARCAN (Saskatchewan)
- SHIP – Services and Housing In the Province (Mississauga, Ontario)
- Social Crust Cafe & Catering (Vancouver, British Columbia)
- Stone Hearth Bakery (Halifax, Nova Scotia)
- Wachiay Studios (Courtenay, British Columbia)

This book draws on research supported by the Social Sciences and Humanities Research Council. We are grateful for the financial support we received throughout this three-year research project.

Jennifer DiDomenico, editor of business and economics at the University of Toronto Press, has been an invaluable support from the beginning in helping us see through this project, always available and always generous with her time and thoughtful suggestions. We would also like to thank other staff at the University of Toronto Press who have assisted us.

We recognize the personal support of our families and friends while we completed this work and are grateful for their enduring patience.

We dedicate this book to the tens of thousands of organizations and individuals who work tirelessly in bringing social benefits to their communities and to the memory of Jack Quarter, the original principal investigator of this research project, who passed away in February 2019.

Andrea Chan, Annie Luk, and Jennifer Sumner
Toronto, Canada

SELLING SOCIAL

Introduction: Selling Social

ANDREA CHAN, SHELLEY LEPP, ANNIE LUK,
JACK QUARTER, AND JENNIFER SUMNER

In February 2010, all eyes were on Canada as the Vancouver Olympic Games captured the hearts and imagination of spectators from around the globe. As world-class performances filled television screens and victors mounted podiums, the stories emerging in the media weren't all focused on the athletes standing atop the podium – some were focused on the podiums themselves. As Gordon Campbell, premier of British Columbia, said at the time:

> Built from wood donated by communities, First Nations, businesses and individuals across the province, each one of these podiums has a story to tell about the people and places that make up British Columbia and about the forest industry that is the heart of so much of our culture and history. We hope all the athletes feel this connection and are inspired by this close connection to the people of British Columbia when they step up to receive their medals on these incredible platforms. (Office of the Premier, Ministry of Forests and Range, British Columbia, 2010)

The statement above was issued by the Office of the Premier of British Columbia and the Ministry of Forests and Range as a joint news release days before the opening ceremonies of the 2010 Olympic Games. The release went on to detail how the podiums were assembled by the Canadian hardware retailer, RONA, which set up a fabrication shop specifically for the occasion – a shop established as a community-based training centre equipping new Canadians and at-risk youth with invaluable carpentry skills (Office of the Premier, Ministry of Forests and Range, British Columbia, 2010). The initiative was premised on the notion that governments have an opportunity to include social value or benefits when making purchasing decisions. In this instance, not only did the government end up with the podiums they required, but a group of individuals who might have faced marginalization also benefited from carpentry training for their futures.

Although the Vancouver Olympic Games took place more than a decade ago, it marked a turning point where procurement for social value or benefits became more publicly visible. International sporting events like the Olympic Games are notorious for the infrastructure investments and financial strains imposed upon the host city (Short, 2018). Before every modern Olympic Games, news stories highlight delays in venue construction, overspending, and emerging local tensions. Rarely does any form of financial, environmental, or community impact go unscrutinized. From large construction projects like athletes' villages, media facilities, and sporting arenas to small initiatives like the merchandise, accreditation badges, and the influx of food required – every decision matters.

While the International Olympic Committee officially encouraged and supported environmental and social responsibility in host cities during the 1994 Centennial Olympic Congress, the Vancouver Organizing Committee for the 2010 Olympic and Paralympic Games (VANOC) were the first to explicitly include social considerations in their purchasing and procurement strategy as well as notions of sustainability into the Games' management structure (Ponsford, 2011). The VANOC was one of the early high-profile organizations ready to embrace social procurement on a large scale. Among the Games' priorities were considerations of social, environmental, and economic accountability; Indigenous participation and collaboration; and a rethinking of accessibility and inclusivity to ensure that inner-city residents and local businesses would benefit from the economic opportunities created by the Games (VANOC, 2010). Apart from the podium construction, other examples of VANOC's efforts included training and employing marginalized women to assemble the floral bouquets awarded to athletes (Mickleburgh, 2010) and requirements for contractors working the construction of the athletes' village to provide employment to low-income residents of the Downtown Eastside (LePage, 2014).

Critics noted that the social impact of the Games was limited because VANOC did not have a framework in place early enough and contracts awarded to social enterprises through the tendering process were relatively small in both number and dollar value (Revington et al., 2015). However, the Vancouver Olympics Games undoubtedly raised the profile of the social enterprise sector as a whole and established an important precedent for social procurement in Canada. VANOC's inclusion of social benefits also became a model for future Olympic Games such as the 2012 Games in London (UK), Sochi (Russia) in 2014, and Rio de Janeiro (Brazil) in 2016, as well as Toronto's Pan Am Games in 2015. Each of these organizing committees looked beyond the traditional economic bottom line to consider the environmental, social, and cultural implications of their purchasing choices.

The Rise of Social Procurement and Social Purchasing

The story of the Vancouver Olympics outlines a larger trend coalescing in the late 2000s. While the purchasing considerations of individuals, businesses, and governments were (and still are) typically focused on quality, cost, and risk mitigation, the range of criteria was beginning to expand. The 1970s brought a new consideration for the environment. By the 1990s, mounting awareness of social needs created significant pressure for corporations and government to account for the social impact of their purchasing habits. These trends represented a shift from the conventional financial accounting for just an economic bottom line to an increased accountability for environmental and social impacts (Mook, 2007). Policies around Corporate Social Responsibility (CSR) emerged and social enterprises were included as possible suppliers – together forming the foundations for social procurement and social purchasing (LePage, 2014). In particular, when buying from social enterprises that offer training/work opportunities to individuals traditionally marginalized (work integration social enterprises, or WISEs), the buying decisions contribute not only revenue to support the social enterprises' missions, but also positive work experience for those struggling to find work in the job market at large.

Since the 2010s, all levels of governments in Canada (municipal, provincial, and federal) have gradually initiated adoption of social procurement as a policy tool to further their social agendas. Social enterprises of various shapes and sizes across the country have served as partners in the execution of those agendas. What remains to be examined is the experiences of the social enterprises in social procurement and social purchasing – what we call *selling social*.

Specifically, we distinguish between buying with and without social value/benefit and why the consideration of social value/benefit is important as people make buying decisions. Further, we differentiate social procurement from social purchasing with the former occurring at a much broader scale and higher value, and thus leading to more social value/benefit. One of the emerging trends with buying social is the idea of buying local. We see buying local as a subset of social procurement and social purchasing (depending on the scale and value), based on the understanding that benefits to local businesses are a social value/benefit. However, the social value/benefit that really interests us in this book goes far beyond benefiting local businesses and communities. We mostly emphasize the social value/benefits going to those who have been traditionally marginalized, such as people with disabilities or youth living in precarious circumstances.

It is within this broad context that we conceived our research project. In the beginning, our goal was to examine the prevalence and impact of social procurement from the perspectives of social enterprises in Canada today. We hoped our contributions would bridge the divides between policy and practice in social procurement by encouraging partnerships as well as advancing and sharing knowledge across sectors and academic disciplines. Specifically, we sought to understand the impact government procurement policies might be having on social enterprises that sell goods and services while also providing social benefits to their communities. We also wanted to learn more about who among the social enterprises might be benefiting from social procurement and how they were experiencing these benefits and tackling the obstacles. We believed that the experiences from those organizations would be invaluable for paving the road for the future. These questions formed the basis of our research – the findings of which are the subject of this book.

About This Book

Selling Social: Procurement, Purchasing, and Social Enterprises presents the findings of a three-year (2017–20), pan-Canadian research project detailing experiences with social procurement and social purchasing from the perspective of WISEs selling goods and services to organizational purchasers (governments, businesses, and non-profit organizations). At the onset of our research project, we conceptualized social procurement as "the use of purchasing power to create social value. In the case of public sector purchasing, social procurement involves the utilization of procurement strategies to support social policy objectives" (Barraket & Weissman, 2009, p. 3).

We conducted our research using mixed methods. We began with a review of social procurement policies at various levels of government across Canada. We then completed a pan-Canadian survey in late 2017, which included 129 social enterprise respondents. As we examined the survey results, we were surprised to discover that the survey respondents reported very little social procurement by governments, businesses, or non-profit organizations through a formalized purchasing process. However, many still reported these organizations as their regular or intermittent customers, so we surmised that many of the social enterprises were beneficiaries of social purchasing.

This unexpected revelation from the survey results caused us to shift the project in two ways. First, we modified our working definition of social procurement as specific to social enterprises as sellers/suppliers and offer the following instead: social procurement refers to all higher-value purchases from social enterprises by organizations (corporate, government, or non-profits), typically involving formal contracts that may or may not be secured through competitive tendering and that include a social, cultural, or environmental intention. We also expanded the research scope to include social purchasing, which we considered a more informal, often spontaneous form of exchange. Second, our initial intention was to examine how social procurement worked from both the seller and the buyer perspectives. In the end, however, the low number of social enterprises participating in social procurement led us to examine both social procurement and social purchasing from the perspective of the social enterprises and the challenges they face in selling social benefits as part of their work.

Based on our survey findings, we selected a diverse group of social enterprises as cases to gain a deeper understanding of their experiences with social procurement and social purchasing. We used semi-structured interviews with these social enterprises and also some of their customers to elaborate the survey results. We supplemented our interviews with publicly available information as part of our data collection. The series of qualitative cases, as they are featured in this book, were completed between June 2018 and October 2019.

As we present the findings from our research project in this book, we were guided by the following research questions:

1. How do social enterprises understand social procurement and social purchasing?
2. To what extent are social enterprises benefiting from social procurement and social purchasing?
3. What are the characteristics of social enterprises that are most likely to attract social procurement and social purchasing?
4. What are the obstacles for social enterprises to benefit from social procurement and social purchasing?
5. How do social enterprises approach social procurement and social purchasing?

We envision two principal audiences who are interested in these questions. The first audience is the academic circle, including students and scholars engaged with the social economy who seek to further their understanding of how social enterprises are situated in the growing trend of social procurement and social purchasing, based on real-life examples. We aim to extend the understanding of social enterprises beyond their social and economic outcomes and into their engagement with social procurement and social purchasing. Our interest is driven by the potential for social procurement and social purchasing to contribute to the sustainability of social enterprises, which in turn could amplify the social, economic, cultural, and environmental values these organizations create. Many of these values reflect the 2030 Sustainable Development Goals (SDGs), which represent a global attempt to "shift the world onto a sustainable and resilient path" (UN, n.d., p. 5). In fact, the United Nations Inter-Agency Task Force on Social and Solidarity Economy (2014, p. iv) "believes that the SSE [social and solidarity economy] holds considerable promise for addressing the economic, social and environmental objectives and integrated approaches inherent in the concept of sustainable development."

The second audience includes policymakers and practitioners wrestling with how to make social procurement and social purchasing work. For those drafting policies to facilitate and encourage social procurement and social purchasing, this book offers insights from the perspective of social enterprises by showcasing their successes and their challenges. For those working in social enterprises who are wondering how to approach social procurement and social purchasing, the findings presented in this book provide a broad view of the experiences in the field and also some tried-and-tested lessons from their peers.

This book follows the chronology of our research journey – with all the twists and turns we faced along the way. Part 1 includes three introductory chapters; each subsequent part of the book presents cases pertaining to one of the themes arising from the research. While most cases touch on all the themes to varying degrees, we selected those that provided the most salient examples of four emergent themes. An overview of the book is as follows:

Part 1: Overview of Non-profit Social Enterprises, Social Procurement and Social Purchasing

Chapter 1 provides a literature review on the concepts of social enterprise, social procurement, and social purchasing. Chapter 2 offers a scan of social procurement policies by governments in Canada, highlighting examples from the federal, provincial/territorial, and municipal levels. Chapter 3 presents the results of our 2017 pan-Canadian survey of social enterprises and their experiences in social procurement.

Part 2: Securing Large Contracts through Relationship Building

Chapters 4–7 look at the importance of relationship building when entering into large contracts with governments. The cases in part 2 demonstrate how social enterprises, aided by a range of policy measures and also champions for social procurement, have been able to secure large contracts through long-term efforts to build and maintain relationships with their purchasers.

Part 3: The Importance of Parent Organizations

Chapters 8–12 highlight the importance of support from parent non-profit organizations. The cases under this theme have been reliant on parent organizations to secure sales or contracts. The support could be in the form of purchasing from the social enterprise or connecting the social enterprise to other customers. Some also depend on their parent organizations for in-kind and/or financial support.

Part 4: The Dilemma of Selling Social Value

Chapters 13–17 look at the dilemma of selling social value. The cases in this theme struggle with whether or not to talk about the social value they create in their goods and services. While social value is core to these social enterprises, many cannot or would not market it as value-add or part of their value chain. We could infer this to mean that many of their purchasers have yet to incorporate social value into their supply chain. Ultimately, price and quality still trump social impact for purchasers in these cases.

Part 5: Balancing Multiple Bottom Lines

Chapters 18–22 offer insight into how social enterprises balance multiple bottom lines. The cases under this theme discuss how difficult it has been to balance the programming with the selling aspects of their work. Sometimes these dual aspects of operations conflict with each other, and many decisions require a compromise to either social impact or economic success.

We conclude the book by looking into the future to offer suggestions to practitioners, scholars, and policymakers on where to go from here. This chapter includes a series of purchaser profiles based on the cases in this book to provide some concrete next steps.

REFERENCES

Barraket, J., & Weissman, J. (2009). *Social procurement and its implications for social enterprise: A literature review.* Working Paper No. CPNS 48. The Australian Centre for Philanthropy and Nonprofit Studies. https://eprints .qut.edu.au/29060/1/Barraket_and_Weissmann_2009_Working_Paper _No_48_Final.pdf

LePage, D. (2014). *Exploring social procurement.* Accelerating Social Impact CCC, Ltd. https://ccednet-rcdec.ca/sites/ccednet-rcdec.ca/files/ccednet /exploring-social-procurement_asi-ccc-report.pdf

Mickleburgh, R. (2010, January 16). Olympic flower power helps troubled women bloom. *The Globe and Mail.* https://www.theglobeandmail.com /news/national/olympic-flower-power-helps-troubled-women-bloom /article1320311/

Mook, L. (2007). *Social and environmental accounting: The expanded value added statement* (Publication No. NR39955) [Doctoral dissertation, University of Toronto]. ProQuest Dissertations Publishing.

Office of the Premier, Ministry of Forests and Range, British Columbia. (2010, February 2). *2010 podiums put B.C. wood in the world spotlight* [Press release]. https://archive.news.gov.bc.ca/releases/news_releases_2009-2013 /2010PREM0022-000117.htm

Ponsford, I.F. (2011). Actualizing environmental sustainability at Vancouver 2010 venues. *International Journal of Event and Festival Management, 2*(2), 184–96. https://doi.org/10.1108/17582951111136595

Revington, C., Hoogendam, R., & Holeton, A. (2015). *The social procurement intermediary: The state of the art and its development within the GTHA.* Learning Enrichment Foundation. https://ccednet-rcdec.ca/en/toolbox/social -procurement-intermediary-state-art-and-its

Short, J.R. (2018). *Hosting the Olympic Games: The real costs for cities.* Routledge, Taylor & Francis Group.

UN. (n.d.). *Transforming our world: The 2030 agenda for sustainable development.* United Nations. https://sustainabledevelopment.un.org/content/documents

United Nations Inter-Agency Task Force on Social and Solidarity Economy. (2014). *Social and solidarity economy and the challenge of sustainable development.* https://knowledgehub.unsse.org/wp-content/uploads/2020/11/2014

-EN-Social-and-Solidarity-Economy-and-the-Challenge-of-Sustainable
-Development-UNTFSSE-Position-Paper.pdf
Vancouver Organizing Committee for the 2010 Olympic and Paralympic
Winter Games (VANOC). (2010). *Sustainability report 2009–2010*. https://
stillmed.olympic.org/Documents/Games_Vancouver_2010/VANOC
_Sustainability_Report-EN.pdf

PART 1

Overview of Non-profit Social Enterprises, Social Procurement, and Social Purchasing

Social enterprises are organizations operating in the market that have a social mission. Some maintain that social enterprises represent a shift in the economy from one that has a pure profit orientation to one that includes some social consideration. Others argue that social enterprises are the latest turn in the neoliberal economy where governments offload responsibility for the public to the private and non-profit sectors (Ganz et al., 2018; Spicer et al., 2019). Both sides, however, would agree that the impact of social enterprises goes well beyond the traditional bottom line. This is particularly true of non-profit social enterprises, which reinvest their profits into their social mission rather than paying them out to shareholders. One type of non-profit social enterprise – Work Integration Social Enterprises (WISEs) – aims to integrate marginalized social groups into the mainstream workforce.

While WISEs that employ or train members of marginalized social groups have often relied on support from their parent organizations, government funding, charitable foundations, and social purchasing at the community level, increasing policy interest in social procurement offers a new revenue opportunity for social enterprises. The experiences of WISEs engaging in both social procurement and social purchasing have not been studied until now. To set the context for such a study, the first section of this book provides an overview of social enterprises, social procurement, and social purchasing.

Chapter 1 presents a literature review providing depth and breadth to these central concepts. It describes the changing marketplace before focusing on social enterprises, particularly WISEs. It also delves into how existing research literature defines two forms of buying social: social purchasing and social procurement.

Chapter 2 explores the policies around buying for social value on behalf of governments in Canada. In particular, it focuses on different policy perspectives that underlie the various initiatives as well as a range of approaches that governments use to include social benefits in their purchasing decisions.

Chapter 3 presents the nuts and bolts of the survey research underpinning the case studies in this book. It outlines the survey design and methodology, describes the participants, and presents our findings. These findings set the stage for the cases at the heart of this book and allow for a novel examination of social enterprises, social procurement, and social purchasing.

Guiding Questions:

1. How does the literature prepare us for understanding the findings of the survey?
2. Why is it difficult for governments to include social value in their procurement policies?
3. Describe the differences between social procurement and social purchasing.
4. How are the perspectives different between buying social and selling social?

REFERENCES

Ganz, M., Kay, T., & Spicer, J. (2018). Viewpoint: Social enterprise is not social change. *Stanford Social Innovation Review,* Spring, 59–60. https://keough .nd.edu/wp-content/uploads/2015/12/SSIR-Spring_2018_social _enterpise_is_not_social_change.pdf

Spicer, J., Kay, T., & Ganz, M. (2019). Social entrepreneurship as field encroachment: How a neoliberal social movement constructed a new field. *Socio-Economic Review,* 17(1), 195–227. https://doi.org/10.1093/ser/wz014

1 Literature Review

ANDREA CHAN, SHELLEY LEPP, ANNIE LUK,
JACK QUARTER, AND JENNIFER SUMNER

A Changing Marketplace

The need for businesses and governments to acquire goods and services through a formalized process has existed for millennia. While the procurement process was historically much simpler and less heavily regulated, it has always had both positive and negative social impact. Ancient cities built on the backs of slaves with materials extracted and acquired through a wide range of channels are part of procurement history around the globe (Basheka, 2013).

The relevance of procurement began to grow in the late 1800s with the emergence of materialmen as a formal role in business operation (Usifoh, 2018). The publication of procurement principles in the early 1900s and the obvious challenges of acquiring goods and maintaining production during and in the aftermath of the Second World War highlighted the social significance of procurement throughout the supply chain (Usifoh, 2018). Despite the recognition of social value in the supply chain, purchasing considerations were still heavily focused on quality, cost and mitigating risk (LePage, 2014).

The suggestion that institutionalized purchasing power could be used to achieve a broader agenda only emerged in the 1970s with an increased pressure for governments and corporate entities to consider how their decisions impacted the environment. The utilization of procurement to create *social* value is a relatively new phenomenon that has gained traction globally since the 1990s (LePage, 2014). Increasingly, business corporations have been under pressure from activist groups to demonstrate social responsibility. For example, activists spearheaded a Nike boycott to push for humanizing working conditions at factories in economically poorer countries that produce goods for wealthier nations (Doorey, 2011; Rothenberg-Aalami, 2004).

On the side of the purchaser, governments and businesses are becoming more conscious about how they source their goods and services. Purchasing decisions are no longer only about price and quality but also about the social good that purchases could generate. The trend of including social value in purchasing decisions has evolved to formalized practices in various aspects of operations within a business, known as corporate social responsibility (CSR). Examples of CSR include the following:

- the development of socially responsible or impact investing (Bugg-Levine, 2011) and the creation of large mutual funds that rank corporations on environmental, social, and governance (ESG) factors (Quarter et al., 2008; Social Investment Organization, 2007)
- innovations in accounting such as the social return on investment and the field of social accounting more broadly (Mook, 2013; Mook, Maiorano, et al., 2015; Mook et al., 2007)

On the supply side of the equation, new entrepreneurial forms of business that incorporate social benefits as they sell their goods and services have emerged – *social enterprises*. There has been a growth of firms with a blended purpose, such as the community contribution company in British Columbia and the community interest company in the UK (Spear & Bidet, 2005). Both contain features of for-profit businesses and non-profit social agencies. Support for social entrepreneurship also comes from wealthy foundations such as the Schwab Foundation for Social Entrepreneurship and the Skoll Foundation (Dees, 2001; Martin & Osberg, 2007, 2015).

This chapter begins with an overview of social enterprises, specifically those that include social benefits in their goods and services through training and employment opportunities for individuals facing marginalization. We also review how social procurement and social purchasing have been conceptualized in research literature.

What It Means to Be a Social Enterprise

A social enterprise is a commercial entity with a social mission. Social enterprises can be either profit-oriented businesses or non-profit organizations and are often referred to as having a *double-plus bottom line* – delivering financial, environmental, social, cultural, and possibly other value to stakeholders. The assets and profits of these organizations are dedicated not only to achieving business objectives, but also to addressing social problems. Examples of social enterprises can be found around the world, including community interest companies in Britain (Spear & Bidet, 2005), similar entities in Nova Scotia and British Columbia (both legislated in 2012), benefit corporations in the US, low-profit limited liability companies (Mook, Quarter, et al., 2015), and social businesses (Yunus, 2007).

Social enterprises have gained both positive and negative attention for their efforts to address the growing social problems of a global economy (Bacchiega & Borzaga, 2001; Dart, 2004; Ganz et al., 2018; Spicer et al., 2019). Premised on a reduced role for government to address social issues, this model can be considered either part of the neoliberal agenda or a vision of social transformation. There is undoubtedly potential for a socially conscious procurement process to play a role in poverty reduction, community development, social inclusion, and employment training (LePage, 2014). However, critics point out that the proliferation of social enterprises is a reflection of governments and big businesses increasingly offloading or privatizing social issues and not addressing the root causes of such issues, which stem from growing income disparity (Spicer et al., 2019). This book does not aim to defend or promote social enterprises but rather examine how they operate within an evolving economy and in relationship to the emerging social procurement and social purchasing trends. Specifically, we focus on non-profit social enterprises and their place within these trends.

Non-profit Social Enterprises

The Social Enterprise Council of Canada (2016), one of the partners in this research, defines non-profit social enterprises as "community-based businesses that sell goods or services in the market place to achieve a social, cultural and/or environmental purpose; they reinvest their profits to maximize their social mission." As can be seen, the emphasis is on using profits for maximizing social mission rather than for private gain (e.g., dividends paid to shareholders).

Non-profit social enterprises can be subdivided into two categories: (1) those that function with autonomy in the marketplace and in some cases support a parent non-profit organization; and (2) those that are not autonomous and are supported by a parent non-profit, government programs, foundations, or corporations. Often the social enterprises in the latter group serve members of specific marginalized social groups, usually people with disabilities.

An example of the first category is ReStore of Habitat for Humanity, which generates income in order to make it possible for Habitat to build houses for the working poor. ReStore differs from most conventional businesses because the goods sold at ReStore are donated and those who work there are predominantly volunteers. In this respect, ReStore is similar to the Thrift Shop model pioneered by the Salvation Army and used by other agencies (Quarter et al., 2018).

In contrast, the second category of social enterprise sells a product or service from which the organization earns revenues, but they are also supported externally, typically through funding from governments and foundations (Chan et al., 2017; Elson & Hall, 2012; Quarter et al., 2015). A primary reason for the need for ongoing support is that the main focus of these social enterprises is to employ or train members of marginalized social groups (e.g., people with serious disabilities or members of minority groups with a history of oppression). In cases where the disabilities are severe, the participants tend to work part-time to supplement their disability pensions. The parent organizations of these social enterprises often provide space and management/administrative support such as bookkeeping and payroll. Therefore, this form of social enterprise could be viewed as a hybrid arrangement with characteristics both of a business and a social welfare organization. The most common label for this hybrid model is Work Integration Social Enterprises (WISEs), a label adopted widely in Europe, where many categories of WISE initiatives are found such as social enterprises providing employment subsidized by the public (Nyssens, 2014).

Work Integration Social Enterprises (WISEs)

WISEs aim to integrate marginalized social groups into the mainstream workforce – even if only as part-time players. In the US, WISEs provide employment opportunities for disadvantaged workers in primarily low-skill, low-wage jobs, and subsidies are needed for their long-term sustainability (Cooney, 2011). An early example is Minnesota Diversified Industries (MDI), established in the 1960s to provide training and employment opportunities for individuals with disabilities by securing contracts from governments (MDI, n.d.; Warner & Mandiberg, 2006).

Since then, WISEs have spread internationally, including across Canada, where they have become part of a growing movement designed to assist marginalized social groups to have productive work roles that enhance their income and sense of worth (Borzaga & Loss, 2006; Nelson et al., 2008; Parmenter, 2011; Wolfensberger, 2000). In Canada, the degree of external assistance for WISEs varies. For those employing people with serious disabilities, external assistance can be extensive (Akingbola, 2015; Mook, Maiorano, et al., 2015; Owen et al., 2015; Quarter et al., 2015). Governments and foundations have generally taken interest in non-profits developing enterprises to provide employment opportunities to people on the social margins. Non-profit organizations establish these enterprises not only in response to government funding priorities but also because of a growing body of research about the positive impact of WISEs on their clients (e.g., Carini et al., 2012; Cohen et al., 2008; Cooney, 2011; Farmer et al., 2016; Ferguson, 2013; Jackson et al., 2009; Krupa et al., 2003; Lysaght & Krupa, 2011; Mook, Maiorano, et al., 2015; Quarter et al., 2015; Roy et al., 2014; Tan, 2009; Vieta et al., 2015; Warner & Mandiberg, 2006). While the economic impact in terms of jobs and earnings may be modest, research, as cited above, shows that the participants strengthen their skills (human capital), social networks (social capital), and their psychological well-being. The importance of these gains should not be underestimated.

Research on WISEs around the globe has offered a wide range of insights as researchers probe everything from organizational practices to the impact on the program participants who are often people with serious disabilities. Social enterprises, particularly WISEs, create significant social value as the organizations actively work with individuals from marginalized communities through training and employment. In our research study and in this book, all the social enterprises belong to the WISE category even though we interchangeably use the terms WISEs and social enterprises. The WISEs run programs that bring social benefits to their communities, but this is only half of the equation. These social enterprises rely on their customers to make their purchases at least in part because of the social value.

Buying Social: Social Purchasing and Social Procurement

While social enterprises try to sell their goods and services to fulfil their social mandate, customers who buy from social enterprises may be motivated by a range of reasons from economic to social, cultural, or environmental. Customers may include individuals making personal purchases as well as those who buy on behalf of the organizations for which they work. We refer to this latter group as *organizational purchasers* because the purchases are made on behalf of organizations, such as governments, private businesses, and non-profit organizations. The purchases made by these organizational purchasers can be categorized as social procurement or social purchasing depending on the transaction value and the degree of formality in the decision-making process; social procurement generally involves higher value and more formality than social purchasing.

Social Purchasing

There is a lengthy history of individuals making purchases based on social criteria such as wanting to support an organization whose mission they identify with. One of the best examples is Girl Guide cookies, which have been on sale in Canada since 1927; many of those who buy Girl Guide cookies are primarily motivated by their desire to support the organization more than a desire for sweets (Girl Guides of Canada, 2016). Organizations can also engage in social purchasing by deciding to purchase certain goods or services from a social enterprise because they want to support its social mission. For example, our research centre at the University of Toronto – the Centre for Learning, Social Economy, and Work (CLSEW) – regularly purchases catering from Common Ground Co-Operative, which supports people with developmental disabilities through training and employment.

Unlike social procurement, social purchasing is more informal, discretionary, and possibly spontaneous. While social procurement often involves bids on tenders with criteria that are governed by formal government or corporate policies and a formal contractual agreement, social purchasing does not necessarily require any contract or even formal agreement. Many social-purchasing decisions tend to be one-off, but some like the CLSEW example above are recurring. For social enterprises, social purchases could involve a decision by individual customers and organizational purchasers (i.e., governments, businesses, and non-profits) to support a social enterprise's sales because these customers wish to support their social missions. Although these purchases are in some ways analogous to a philanthropic contribution or donation because of the intent to support an organization's social mission, such purchases do not usually qualify as such because they are ultimately a business transaction – i.e., an exchange of goods or services for cash. What distinguishes a social purchase from other forms of purchasing is that the item or service could have been acquired elsewhere using criteria that consumers normally apply (e.g., price, quality, convenience) with the exception of the mission-based considerations that at least in part determine the purchase from a social enterprise. Despite this, we are not suggesting that all purchases from social enterprises are necessarily mission based. Nonetheless, to varying degrees, all purchases from social enterprises result in the realization of an added social value.

Social Procurement

There are two key concepts in social procurement: social and procurement. The latter – *procurement* – often refers to policies and processes in which governments, private businesses or corporations, and non-profit organizations make purchases that are of significant value or importance to these institutions. In this case, they often rely on procurement policies to guide such decisions, using criteria including competition process, price, quality, timeliness, etc. The simplest example of a procurement policy could be the requirement to obtain at least three price quotes when buying anything over a certain amount, say $1,000. Procurement policies and processes (discussed further in chapter 2) can become increasingly complex, depending on the nature of the goods or services being purchased. For example, the procurement process for the design and construction of a new light rail line in a municipality or the development of a capital campaign for a non-profit organization would involve complex decisions on requirements, budgeting, approvals, etc. Many of the procurement policies and processes are in place to improve the transparency of using public funds and to leverage competition for better pricing or quality of goods and services from suppliers.

The former concept – *social* – adds a new dimension in that it builds social benefits into procurement. As such, *social procurement* can be defined as "the use of purchasing power to create social value. In the case of public sector purchasing, social procurement involves the utilization of procurement strategies to support social policy objectives" (Barraket & Weissman, 2009, p. 3). Recent studies on social procurement in public construction projects have found that country and contract size predict inclusion of the widest range of social criteria, including employment of people facing exclusion (Montalbán-Domingo et al., 2019), and that the rise of social procurement has created new roles and responsibilities within the construction sector to manage employment-related contract requirements (Troje & Gluch, 2020).

More generally, social procurement involves modifying the supply chain, so it includes criteria such as quality and price as well as social value (LePage, 2014). The underlying idea is that social procurement policies should open the door for WISEs to bid and be successful on tenders and that social procurement could become one of the ways to support WISEs in their social missions. As a result, social procurement is an increasingly significant option in the context of market-based approaches to workforce integration for marginalized social groups.

The concept of leveraging public purchasing to achieve social value dates back before the terminology of social procurement (Barraket et al., 2016; Gardin, 2006; McCrudden, 2004, 2006). Procurement by governments is typically labelled as public procurement; in the context of recent research it is described as social procurement when the criteria include policies that are based on enhancing social benefits or value. Governments in Canada have a long history of linking funding to social goals: a classic example is programs after the Second World War to reduce regional inequalities through such means as funding for small to medium-sized enterprises (SMEs) in economically impoverished areas (Beaumier, 1998; Quarter et al., 2018). In the 1980s, the federal government introduced legislation – the Employment Equity Act and the Federal Contractors Program – to encourage businesses selling to the federal government to meet basic equity standards pertaining to women, members of visible minorities, Indigenous people, and people with disabilities. Despite concerns about whether the legislation is meeting its intended goals (Grundy & Smith, 2010; Harish et al., 2010), it serves as evidence of social procurement policies by the federal government.

Business corporations are also involved in social procurement and other forms of support for WISEs. However, while anecdotal examples of corporate social procurement are available, there is little research on how widespread it is or to what extent it is targeted to WISEs. Social procurement is believed to be a way for business corporations, as well as government agencies and non-profits, to help WISEs improve the lives of those they train or employ. Social procurement within the corporate sector has been theorized as part of the broader CSR phenomenon (Barraket et al., 2016). Like governments, businesses could also demonstrate their social commitments through social procurement, e.g., supplier diversity programs that engage minority-owned enterprises. Although some research exists on supplier diversity initiatives (Canadian Centre for Diversity and Inclusion, 2016; Shah & Ram, 2006), research on social procurement targeted to WISEs remains scant.

For non-profit organizations, social procurement typically involves incorporating environmental benefits for long-term sustainability (Pacheco-Blanco & Bastante-Ceca, 2016; Young et al., 2015). Universities and hospitals are among the largest and the highest profile non-profit organizations facing mounting pressure to consider their purchasing as well as investing with a social lens (Klein, 2015; Yona & Lenferna, 2016). One of the most common ways universities and hospitals engage in social procurement is through their food purchases. The shift to local, organic, and nutritious meals reflects more than fashionable changes in dietary preferences. This shift signals a broader and deeper transformation in how universities and hospitals see their relationships with the local sellers and suppliers who make up the community (Bohunicky et al., 2019; Klein, 2015). Part of this transformation includes procuring from small businesses as well as partnering with social enterprises instead of relying on large contracts with multinational corporations that have dominated in the foodservices on university and hospital campuses for years (Bohunicky et al., 2019; Klein, 2015; Stahlbrand, 2019).

Despite this change in procurement practices, price remains a dominant factor when it comes to purchasing decisions, leaving social value as a secondary consideration (Young et al., 2015).

Selling Social: The Leap from Policy to Practice

For social enterprises, the barriers to accessing social procurement opportunities can be viewed as extensions of barriers to conventional (economic or non-social) procurement. Lack of familiarity with the procurement process, capacity to bid, knowledge of procurement opportunities, and understanding of ways to measure and demonstrate social value have been noted in the literature as obstacles for social enterprises in supplying to public procurement (Barraket & Weissman, 2009; Muñoz, 2009).

Pointing to research that has shown similarities between SMEs and social enterprises, Muñoz (2009) notes that burden on human resources, difficulty navigating e-procurement, and lack of confidence are some procurement challenges faced by SMEs. The assumption is that such barriers may also be applicable to social enterprises. Orser (2009) reports findings by the Canadian Federation of Independent Businesses (CFIB) that the size of enterprise as measured by the number of employees varies with likelihood of selling to government, and that SMEs appear more likely to learn of public procurement opportunities via business associations than by monitoring MERX, an official public tendering website (www.merx.com). The relevance of social capital in procurement processes has been examined more generally. Social capital can be engendered through long-term supply chain relationships with the public sector, but this type of partnership approach can have positive outcomes (e.g., improved resource and information sharing, cooperation, reduced transaction costs) as well as negative outcomes (e.g., reduced transparency and opportunism) (Erridge & Greer, 2002). Suggestions from the public sector to social enterprises have included greater professionalization ("more businesslike") and the forming of consortiums between social enterprises in order to improve the chance of successfully bidding on tender (Muñoz, 2009).

Despite the challenges noted above, social procurement is believed to be a way for government agencies, business corporations, and nonprofits to help WISEs assist those they serve. While the prevalence of procurement policies and social enterprises both continue to rise across Canada, there has been little research into their interaction. The objective of our three-year, pan-Canadian research project was to shed light on the relationship between policy and practice, and offer valuable insight for organizational purchasers, policymakers, and social enterprises attempting to engage in social procurement and social purchasing. Our findings in the survey of social enterprises in Canada revealed that although approximately 60 per cent of the respondents have submitted bids to at least one type of organizational purchaser, the percentage of those with the bidding experience drops considerably when looking at each individual type of organizational purchaser. This suggests that while WISEs are at least somewhat active in social procurement in the broadest sense, they appear to engage in social procurement on a limited basis as shown in the much lower participation rate when looking at individual types of organizational purchasers. Following up on our survey finding, which revealed this low engagement in a formalized bidding process with the individual types of organizational purchasers, we completed a series of cases taking a close look at how the WISEs were engaged in social procurement and social purchasing. Our results suggest that the WISEs in Canada are often successfully securing contracts – just through different channels, usually long-term relationship building and champions. As a result of the findings, we extended the definition of *social procurement* from the research literature we have reviewed earlier in this chapter to include all higher-value purchases from WISEs by organizations, typically involving formal contracts that may or may not be secured through competitive tendering.

In addition to this enhanced definition of social procurement, we also delineated the two sides of buying and selling social for this research project. For organizational purchasers, social procurement and social purchasing can be characterized as attempts by organizations purchasing goods and services to modify their supply chain to include social value (LePage, 2014). For example, the province of Saskatchewan contracts SARCAN to run a portion of recycling for businesses and residents in the province. The fact that SARCAN offers training and employment opportunities for individuals with disabilities to work in the recycling business adds social value to the province's overall waste management service. By this definition, social procurement is conceptualized primarily from the side of the *purchaser*.

From the perspective of the WISEs as the *sellers* of goods and services, we can conceptualize social procurement and social purchasing as channels through which the WISEs could add social value in their *value chain*. The concept of added social value is related to the analysis of competitive advantages where sellers attempt to stand out in the marketplace by offering something that is of value to the customers, rare, inimitable, and an integral part of their organizational capabilities

(Barney, 1995). Our study investigates the activities the WISEs undertake to create and communicate their value, in particular their social, environmental, and cultural value, to those purchasing or procuring various goods and services.

REFERENCES

Akingbola, K. (2015). When the business is people: The impact of A-Way Express courier. In J. Quarter, S. Ryan & A. Chan (Eds.), *Social purpose enterprises: Case studies for social change* (pp. 52–74). University of Toronto Press.

Bacchiega, A., & Borzaga, C. (2001). Social enterprises as incentive structures: An economic analysis. In C. Borzaga & J. Defourny (Eds.), *The emergence of social enterprises* (pp. 273–95). Routledge.

Barney, J.B. (1995). Looking inside for competitive advantage. *The Academy of Management Executive, 9*(4), 49–61. http://doi.org/10.5465/AME .1995.9512032192

Barraket, J., Keast, R., & Furneaux, C. (2016). *Social procurement and new public governance.* Routledge.

Barraket, J. & Weissman, J. (2009). *Social Procurement and its implications for social enterprise: A literature review* (Working Paper No. CPNS 48). The Australian Centre for Philanthropy and Nonprofit Studies. https://eprints.qut.edu .au/29060/1/Barraket_and_Weissmann_2009_Working_Paper_No_48 _Final.pdf

Basheka, B.C. (2013). The science of public procurement and administration. In G.L. Albano, K.F. Snider & K.V. Thai (Eds.), *International public procurement conference, book 5* (pp. 289–330). IPPC.

Beaumier, G. (1998). *Regional development in Canada.* Government of Canada, Economics Division.

Bohunicky, M., Desmarais, A.A., & Entz, M. (2019). Self-operated vs. corporate contract: A study of food procurement at two universities in Manitoba. *Canadian Food Studies, 6*(1), 43–74. https://doi.org/10.15353/cfs-rcea.v6i1.280

Borzaga, C., & Loss, M. (2006) Profiles and trajectories of participants in European work integration social enterprises. In M. Nyssens (Ed.), *Social enterprise: At the crossroads of market, public policies and civil society* (pp. 169–94). Routledge.

Bugg-Levine, A. (2011). *Impact investing: Transforming how we make money while making a difference.* John Wiley & Sons.

Canadian Centre for Diversity and Inclusion. (2016). *Supplier diversity in Canada: Research and analysis of the next step in diversity and inclusion for forward-looking organizations.* https://ccdi.ca/media/1066/ccdi-report -supplier-diversity-in-canada-updated-4072016.pdf

Carini, C., Costa, E., Carpita, M., & Andreaus, M. (2012). *The Italian social cooperatives in 2008: A portrait using descriptive and principal component analysis* (Euricse Working Paper, N.035/12). Fondazione Euricse.

Chan, A., Ryan, S., & Quarter, J. (2017). Supported social enterprise: A modified social welfare organization. *Nonprofit and Voluntary Sector Quarterly, 46*(2), 261–79. https://doi.org/10.1177/0899764016655620

Cohen, M., Goldberg, M., Istvanffy, N., Stainton, T., Wasik, A., & Woods, K. (2008). *Removing barriers to work: Flexible employment options for people with disabilities in BC*. Canadian Centre for Policy Alternatives.

Cooney, K. (2011). The business of job creation: An examination of the social enterprise approach to workforce development. *Journal of Poverty 15*(1), 88–107. https://doi.org/10.1080/10875549.2011.539505

Dart, R. (2004). Being "business-like" in a nonprofit organization: A grounded and inductive typology. *Nonprofit and Voluntary Sector Quarterly, 33*(2), 290–310. https://doi.org/10.1177/0899764004263522

Dees, J.G. (2001). *The meaning of social entrepreneurship*. Center for the Advancement of Social Entrepreneurship at Duke University's Fuqua School of Business.

Doorey, D.J. (2011). The transparent supply chain: From resistance to implementation at Nike and Levi-Strauss. *Journal of Business Ethics, 103*(4), 587–603. https://doi.org/10.1007/s10551-011-0882-1

Elson, P., & Hall, P. (2012). Canadian social enterprises: Taking stock. *Social Enterprise Journal, 8*(3), 216–36. https://doi.org/10.1108/17508611211280764

Erridge, A., & Greer, J. (2002). Partnerships and public procurement: Building social capital through supply relations. *Public Administration, 80*(3), 503–22. https://doi.org/10.1111/1467-9299.00315

Farmer, J., De Cotta, T., McKinnon, K., Barraket, J., Muñoz, S.A., Douglas, H., & Roy, M.J. (2016). Social enterprise and wellbeing in community life. *Social Enterprise and Wellbeing, 12*(2), 235–54. https://doi.org/10.1108/SEJ-05-2016-0017

Ferguson, K.M. (2013). Using the social enterprise intervention (SEI) and individual placement and support (IPS) models to improve employment and clinical outcomes of homeless youth with mental illness. *Occupational Social Work: Current Perspectives, 11*(5), 473–95. https://doi.org/10.1080/15332985.2013.764960. Medline:24294127

Ganz, M., Kay, T., & Spicer, J. (2018). Viewpoint: Social enterprise is not social change. *Stanford Social Innovation Review,* Spring, 59–60. https://doi.org/10.48558/z8f0-3080

Gardin, L. (2006). A variety of resource mixes inside social enterprises. In M. Nyssens (Ed.), *Social enterprise: At the crossroads of market, public policies, and civil society* (pp. 111–36). Routledge.

Girl Guides of Canada. (2016). Cookie History. https://www.girlguides.ca/WEB/GGC/Cookies/Cookie_History/GGC/Cookies/Cookie_History.aspx

Grundy, J., & Smith, M. (2010). Evidence and equity: Struggles over federal employment equity policy in Canada, 1984–95. *Canadian Public Administration, 54*(3), 335–57. https://doi.org/10.1111/j.1754-7121.2011.00179.x

Harish J., Lawler, J., Bai, B., & Lee, E. (2010). Effectiveness of Canada's employment equity legislation for women (1997–2004): Implications for policy makers. *Relations Industrielles/Industrial Relations, 65*(2), 304–29. https://doi.org/10.7202/044304ar

Jackson, Y., Kelland, J., Cosco, T.D., McNeil, D.C., & Reddon, J.R. (2009). Nonvocational outcomes of vocational rehabilitation: Reduction in health services utilization. *Work, 33*(4), 381–7. https://doi.org/10.3233/WOR-2009-0886. Medline:19923660

Klein, K. (2015). Values-based food procurement in hospitals: The role of health care group purchasing organizations. *Agriculture and Human Values, 32*(4), 635–48. https://doi.org/10.1007/s10460-015-9586-y

Krupa, T., Lagarde, M., & Carmichael, K. (2003). Transforming sheltered workshops into affirmative businesses: An evaluation of outcomes. *Psychiatric Rehabilitation Journal, 26*(4), 359–67. https://doi.org/10.2975/26.2003.359.367. Medline:12739906

LePage, D. (2014). *Exploring social procurement.* Accelerating Social Impact CCC, Ltd. https://ccednet-rcdec.ca/sites/ccednet-rcdec.ca/files/ccednet/exploring-social-procurement_asi-ccc-report.pdf

Lysaght, R. & Krupa, T (2011). *Social business: Advancing the viability of a model for economic and occupational justice for people with disabilities.* Project Final Report, Phase 1. https://ccednet-rcdec.ca/sites/ccednet-rcdec.ca/files/ccednet/_Social_Business__Disablity_Study_-_Report_1.pdf

Martin, R., & Osberg, S. (2007). Social entrepreneurship: The case for definition. *Stanford Social Innovation Review,* Spring. http://www.ssireview.org/articles/entry/social_entrepreneurship_the_case_for_definition/

Martin, R., & Osberg, S. (2015). *Getting beyond better: How social entrepreneurship works.* Harvard University Review Press.

McCrudden, C. (2004). Using public procurement to achieve social outcomes. *Natural Resources Forum, 28*(4), 257–67. https://doi.org/10.1111/j.1477-8947.2004.00099.x. https://ccednet-rcdec.ca/sites/ccednet-rcdec.ca/files/ccednet/pdfs/2004-mccrudden-public_procurement.pdf

McCrudden, C. (2006). *Corporate social responsibility and public procurement* (Working Paper No 9/2006). University of Oxford Faculty of Law Legal Studies Research Paper Series. http://www.csringreece.gr/files/research/CSR-1289990795.pdf

Minnesota Diversified Industries (MDI). (n.d.). *Our history.* https://www.mdi.org/history/

Montalbán-Domingo, L., García-Segur, T., & Sanz, M.A., & Pellicer, E. (2019). Social sustainability in delivery and procurement of public construction contracts. *Journal of Management in Engineering, 35*(2), 1–11. https://doi.org/10.1061/(ASCE)ME.1943-5479.0000674

Mook, L. (Ed.). (2013). *Accounting for social value.* University of Toronto Press.

Mook, L., Maiorano, J., Ryan, S., Armstrong, A., & Quarter, J. (2015). Turning social return on investment on its head: The stakeholder impact statement. *Nonprofit Management & Leadership, 26*(2), 229–46. https://doi.org/10.1002/nml.21184

Mook, L., Quarter, J., Armstrong, A., & Whitman, J.R. (2015). *Understanding the social economy of the United States.* University of Toronto Press.

Mook, L., Quarter, J., & Richmond, B.J. (2007). *What counts: Social accounting for nonprofits and cooperatives.* Sigel Press.

Muñoz, S. (2009). Social enterprise and public sector voices on procurement. *Social Enterprise Journal, 5*(1), 69–82. https://doi.org/10.1108/17508610910956417

Nelson, G., Janzen, R., Trainor, J., & Ochocka, J. (2008). Putting values into practice: Public policy and the future of mental health consumer-run organizations. *American Journal of Community Psychology, 42*(1–2), 192–201. https://doi.org/10.1007/s10464-008-9191-y. Medline:18594963

Nyssens, M. (2014). European work integration social enterprises: Between social innovation and isomorphism. In J. Defourny, L. Hulgård, & V. Pestoff (Eds.), *Social enterprise and the third sector: Changing European landscapes in a comparative perspective* (pp. 211–29). Routledge.

Orser, B. (2009). *Procurement strategies to support women entrepreneurs.* Retrieved from https://www.researchgate.net/publication/274699418_Procurement_Strategies_to_Support_Women_Entrepreneurs

Owen, F., Readhead, A., Bishop, C., Hope, J., & Campbell, J. (2015). Common ground co-operative: Supporting employment options. In J. Quarter, S. Ryan, & A. Chan (Eds.), *Social purpose enterprises: Case studies for social change* (pp. 27–51). University of Toronto Press.

Pacheco-Blanco, B., & Bastante-Ceca, M.J. (2016). Green public procurement as an initiative for sustainable consumption: An exploratory study of Spanish public universities. *Journal of Cleaner Production, 133*(1), 648–56. https://doi.org/10.1016/j.jclepro.2016.05.056

Parmenter, T.R. (2011). Promoting training and employment opportunities for people with intellectual disabilities: International experience. *DigitalCommons@ILR.* https://core.ac.uk/download/19957664.pdf

Quarter, J., Carmichael, I., & Ryan, S. (Eds.). (2008). *Pensions at work: Socially responsible investment of union-based pension funds.* University of Toronto Press.

Quarter, J., Mook, L., & Armstrong, A. (2018). *Understanding the social economy: A Canadian perspective* (2nd ed.). University of Toronto Press.

Quarter, J., Ryan, S., & Chan, A. (Eds.). (2015). *Social purpose enterprises: Case studies for social change.* University of Toronto Press.

Rothenberg-Aalami, J. (2004). Coming full circle? Forging missing links along Nike's integrated production networks. *Global Networks, 4*(4), 335–54. https://doi.org/10.1111/j.1471-0374.2004.00097.x

Roy, M.J., Donaldson, C., Baker, R., & Kerr, S. (2014). The potential of social enterprise to enhance health and well-being: A model and systematic review. *Social Science & Medicine, 123,* 182–93. https://doi.org/10.1016/j.socscimed.2014.07.031

Shah, M., & Ram, M. (2006). Supplier diversity and minority business enterprise development: Case study experience of three US multinationals. *Supply Chain Management: An International Journal, 11*(1), 75–81. https://doi.org/10.1108/13598540610642493

Social Enterprise Council of Canada (SECC). (2016). About the SECC. http://secouncil.ca

Social Investment Organization (SIO). (2007). *Canadian socially responsible investment review 2006: A comprehensive survey of socially responsible investment in Canada.* https://web.archive.org/web/20070621204909/http://www.socialinvestment.ca/documents/SRIReview.pdf

Spear, R., & Bidet, E. (2005). Social enterprise for work integration in 12 European countries: A descriptive analysis. *Annals of Public and Cooperative Economics 76*(2), 195–231. https://doi.org/10.1111/j.1370-4788.2005.00276.x

Spicer, J., Kay, T., & Ganz, M. (2019). Social entrepreneurship as field encroachment: How a neoliberal social movement constructed a new field. *Socio-Economic Review, 17*(1), 195–227. https://doi.org/10.1093/ser/mwz014

Stahlbrand, L. (2019). Disruptive innovation and operationalization in local and sustainable food systems: Examining the University of Toronto-Local Food Plus partnership. *Canadian Food Studies, 6*(1), 120–39. https://doi.org/10.15353/cfs-rcea.v6i1.269

Tan, B.L. (2009). Hybrid transitional-supported employment using social enterprise: A retrospective study. *Psychiatric Rehabilitation Journal, 33*(1), 53–5. https://doi.org/10.2975/33.1.2009.53.55. Medline:19592381

Troje, D., & Gluch, P. (2020). Populating the social realm: New roles arising from social procurement. *Construction Management and Economics, 38*(1), 55–70. https://doi.org/10.1080/01446193.2019.1597273

Usifoh, D. (2018). *The evolution of procurement.* Gateway Procurement. https://www.gatewayprocurement.co.uk/insights/the-evolution-of-procurement/

Vieta, M., Schatz, N., & Kasparian, G. (2015). Social return on investment for Good Foot Delivery. *Nonprofit Management & Leadership, 26*(1), 1–16. https://doi.org/10.1002/nml.21186

Warner, R. & Mandiberg, J. (2006). An update on affirmative businesses or social firms for people with mental illness. *Psychiatric Services, 57,* 1488–92. https://doi.org/10.1176/ps.2006.57.10.1488. Medline:17035570

Wolfensberger, W. (2000). A brief overview of social role valorization. *Mental Retardation, 38*(2), 105–23. https://doi.org/10.1352/0047-6765(2000) 038<0105:ABOOSR>2.0.CO;2. Medline:10804701

Yona, L., & Lenferna, A. (2016). The fossil fuel divestment movement within universities. In G. Sosa-Nunez & E. Atkins (Eds.), *Environment, climate change and international relations* (pp. 190–205). E-International Relations Publishing.

Young, S., Nagpal, S., & Adams, C.A. (2015). Sustainable procurement in Australian and UK universities. *Public Management Review, 18*(7), 993–1016. https://doi.org/10.1080/14719037.2015.1051575

Yunus, M. (2007). *Creating a world without poverty: Social business and the future of capitalism.* Public Affairs.

2 Procurement and Purchasing Policies for Social Value by Governments in Canada

RACHEL LAFOREST AND ANNIE LUK

Introduction

Historically, procurement decisions by organizational purchasers, and more specifically governments, have primarily been based on choosing suppliers with the lowest prices and the technical capacity to deliver goods or services. Although price remains a critical factor in purchasing decisions, governments in Canada have gradually started leveraging their purchasing power to advance their social policy agendas. The potential for social procurement and social purchasing by governments in Canada is staggering when you consider the federal government alone is "one of the largest public buyers of goods and services in Canada, purchasing approximately $22 billion worth every year on behalf of federal departments and agencies" (Public Works and Government Services Canada [PWGSC], 2019). In addition, other levels of government – i.e., provincial/territorial and municipal – are also major buyers in their jurisdictions. For example, each year the Government of British Columbia purchases approximately $7 billion worth of goods and services (BC Ministry of Citizens' Services, 2020).

The use of procurement strategies to increase the likelihood of achieving social policy goals is a process that McCrudden (2004, p. 257) refers to as "linkage," connecting a social agenda with other processes already in place. The policy objective that governments want to achieve in buying social is to promote social benefits through the procurement process. Barraket and Weissman (2009) specify four different circumstances of social procurement:

1. Making purchases from a supplier who represents characteristics that a government agency or department wants to encourage – e.g., youth training and employment

2. Inserting social benefits or public-interest clauses into tendering agreements or what is labelled as social tendering – e.g., a certain percentage of materials used must be sourced locally within a specific radius

3. Negotiating social value clauses into contracts with a supplier – e.g., suppliers are required to comply with specific environmental protection protocols

4. Creating policy frameworks that set aside a proportion of purchases for enterprises with a strong social mission – e.g., a certain percentage of contracts within an organization or a specific project must be awarded to social enterprises

Although social procurement policies are a recent phenomenon in Canada, different levels of government have linked aspects of procurement to social purpose for a long time – albeit not necessarily under the label of social procurement. One of the earliest federal programs to leverage government purchasing power for social impact is the *Procurement Strategy for Aboriginal Business* (PSAB). Created in 1996, PSAB leverages procurement to create employment opportunities for Indigenous communities. The information available from Indigenous and Northern Affairs Canada (2015) describes the strategy as a policy that "supports Aboriginal business capacity development on behalf of the government of Canada." More recently, BC Hydro – a provincial Crown corporation in British Columbia – adopted the *Indigenous Contract and Procurement Policy* giving priority to Indigenous vendors (BC Hydro, n.d.). The Ontario Government announced a social enterprise development policy in 2016, which includes a phrase that explicitly supports "Developing a Social Enterprise Procurement Action Plan to increase the Ontario Government's procurement from social enterprises" (Ontario Ministry of Economic Development, Job Creation and Trade, 2016). At the municipal level, the City of Toronto adopted a social procurement program in May 2016 providing support to "diverse suppliers, including social purpose enterprises, who experience inequitable barriers to accessing City competitive procurement processes" (City of Toronto, 2016, p. 3). These examples not only represent a diverse set of approaches to leveraging government purchasing power to achieve social good, but they also highlight the wide range of terminology used by policymakers. The lack of consistent terminology, even among practitioners, reflects the experimentation still taking place within the field as well as competing or even conflicting policy agendas (Keast et al., 2012).

While the policies and programs on social procurement and social purchasing represent attempts at creating more diversified supply chains and bringing social benefits to a broad range of communities, implementing them is not without challenges. Although the 2010 Vancouver Olympic Games established an important example for engaging social enterprises through social procurement, contracts awarded were comparatively few and small (Revington et al., 2015). Similarly, the 2015 Pan Am Games were lauded for specifying social enterprises as recognized diversity suppliers, but criticisms pointed to the delay in granting such recognitions, leaving only a few contracts to be awarded to social enterprises and requiring significant efforts from multiple stakeholders to connect social enterprises with procurement opportunities (Revington et al., 2015).

In this chapter, we discuss the different policy perspectives that undergird some of the social procurement policies and programs currently in place in Canada. It is important to understand these underlying perspectives because the policies and programs that governments design are often reflections of their ideologies. Next, we present an overview of the different approaches the three levels of government in Canada use to create social benefits for those who are marginalized in society. We also discuss some of the challenges in policy implementation. The information presented in this chapter is drawn from a document review of select policies and programs on procurement – more specifically social procurement currently in place across Canada at all three levels of government. The review is not intended to be exhaustive; instead, we want to paint a broad picture of how governments in Canada are approaching social procurement. Our methodology consists of a scan of government policy documents related to procuring and purchasing for achieving social impacts as well as interviews with eight key informants representing government agencies at all levels and stakeholders in the private and social economy sectors. We rely on key informant interviews to elaborate on the information contained in the document review and to understand the various dynamics in implementation. We hope this chapter enhances your overall understanding of how social procurement has evolved as a policy tool in Canada. In addition to providing a policy context for the book, this chapter helps frame our understanding of how government policies might, in turn, impact the social enterprises that employ and train marginalized people.

Policy Perspectives for Governments to Buy Social

Behind the promotion of social procurement policies at the government level are two dominant policy perspectives: social investment and new public governance (Barraket et al., 2016; Jenson, 2015). Although not mutually exclusive, these two policy perspectives represent different ways to view the role of government policies in achieving social agendas.

A focus on *social investment* began to emerge in the early 2000s (Jenson, 2015; Jenson & Saint-Martin, 2003). The social investment perspective is based "on the claim that social policy spending – usually termed 'investments' – can be a contribution, rather than a cost or burden, to economic growth, especially if that growth is 'inclusive'" (Jenson, 2015, p. 108). The social investment perspective recognizes the problems stemming from multigenerational challenges related to social inequalities and promotes the use of social investment to prevent these cycles of inequality (Jenson & Saint-Martin, 2003). In the context of these inequalities, government policies on childcare, education, lifelong learning, and active labour market are seen as investments towards improving inclusive participation in the labour market (Jenson & Saint-Martin, 2003). Opportunities for training and skill improvement created through social procurement can help people facing inequalities join the labour force and have access to good jobs, making social procurement an effective policy tool for increasing labour participation (Jenson, 2015; Jenson & Saint-Martin, 2003). Research shows that employment generated through procurement can be used to support local or minority-owned businesses (Loader, 2013; Walker & Preuss, 2008). According to McCrudden (2004), social procurement has been used by governments in Canada in order to bring about more equality in the procurement process by mitigating challenges resulting from discrimination and by imposing employment requirements for promoting equity, specifically for Indigenous communities.

Early iterations of social procurement policies based in the social investment perspective were focused on directly setting aside procurement opportunities for Indigenous communities or directly negotiating contracts with Indigenous businesses (McCrudden, 2004). More recently, governments have expanded the use of social procurement to support other communities that are traditionally marginalized. These policies and programs such as the *BC Social Impact Procurement Guidelines* (Government of BC, n.d.) and the City of Toronto's *Social Procurement Program* (City of Toronto, 2016) now often include, but are not limited to, people who are marginalized by poverty, unemployment, re-entry from incarceration, and addictions; women; racial minorities; persons with disabilities; newcomers; and LGBTQ+ persons. The goal of the policies and programs is to diversify the suppliers to include businesses and organizations traditionally excluded from government procurement opportunities. Supply diversity is a well-established process used by large business corporations especially in the US with a focus on buying from businesses owned by minority groups (Adobor & McMullen, 2007). This idea builds on the assumption that businesses owned by those traditionally excluded from the procurement process, such as women and Indigenous people, are more likely to hire from within their own communities thereby creating more employment and economic opportunities for those communities (Canadian Centre for Diversity and Inclusion, 2016). From this perspective, the use of social procurement constitutes an attempt to use existing procurement needs within governments to advance inclusive economic growth.

Alongside the social investment perspective, there is a second philosophy of social procurement that sees it as a fast-emerging tool of *new public governance* (Barraket et al., 2016; Furheaux & Barraket, 2014). New public governance (Laforest, 2011; Osborne, 2018) refers to a process of governing that is no longer done exclusively or primarily by governments. From this perspective, organizations in the public, private, and voluntary sectors share responsibility and work collaboratively on complex social, political, and economic issues. As Osborne (2018) notes, new public governance requires a shared value approach, where all actors in the system work towards the same goal. Governments need to create shared value systems and governance processes that "facilitate the generation of implementable agreements among wide-ranging stakeholders who may disagree on what course of actions will produce maximum public value" (Bao et al., 2013, p. 447). Through the new public governance perspective, Barraket et al. (2016, p. 2) view social procurement as a mechanism "of aligning routine actions and processes with the creation of positive social impacts." Social procurement becomes a tool to encourage purchasers to consider the added social value when issuing their tender requests, and it incentivizes suppliers to include social benefits in their bids, leading to the creation of shared value projects. The economic aspect is important, as one government official interviewed for this book noted, "In a slow-growth economy, you can't leave any value on the table." For example, in 2007, when the City of Toronto started the *Regent Park Social Development Plan* to revitalize and redevelop the public housing complex and the surrounding neighbourhood in downtown Toronto, the city included an employment plan where local residents would receive training and employment to work on the project. At the completion of the Regent Park Revitalization project, the city reported that 582 jobs were created in construction, retail, hospitality, and administration and 348 local residents participated in training programs (City of Toronto, 2019).

As governments embrace new public governance by creating shared value projects, they push to promote diversity in the supply chain, support suppliers that provide employment opportunities to those who are marginalized, create workforce development opportunities, enable local economic development, and develop technical guidance for others in the private sector and the social economy to pursue social procurement. All these examples illustrate that there are overlapping discourses and approaches to implementing social procurement in Canada with some focusing on labour market activation and others on social value creation. Although there is growing consensus around the language of social procurement, the ways that governments use social procurement vary.

Approaches to Leveraging Government Purchases for Social Benefits

In Canada, governments have used procurement policies to create social benefits, including economic opportunities for Indigenous communities and environmental goals. In leveraging procurement to support social benefits, governments demonstrate leadership through their own procurement policies to influence organizations in the private sector and the social economy to embed non-economic values across their supply chains for goods and services.

In recent years, the approach to social procurement by different levels of government in Canada has shifted from ad hoc projects to a system-based design. One of the key informants stated that "money that is going out the door for capital projects, for operations, professional services, we need to be thinking about how it can do double, triple duty: on environmental, social, and economic sides." This shift has given rise to policies and programs specifically designed to promote social procurement as well as the retooling of existing procurement programs to provide better linkages with policies at other levels of government. The review of select procurement policies and programs in this chapter reveals four broad approaches used by governments in Canada to pursue social benefits by leveraging their own procurement.

Buying from Businesses and Organizations Owned or
Operated by Marginalized Groups

The first approach, perhaps one of the longest standing, is to set aside procurement opportunities specifically for businesses and organizations that are owned or operated by individuals from marginalized groups. This is akin to affirmative action policies in the past that ensured a portion of the government procurement opportunities would be allocated to those who have historically been excluded from such opportunities, e.g., women, Indigenous people, people with disabilities, etc. This approach is also known as supplier diversity, meaning it represents governments' attempts to diversify the suppliers they would use instead of rewarding the same ones that have always been successful (Adobor & McMullen, 2007).

The federal government's *Procurement Strategy for Aboriginal Business* (PSAB), which was established in 1996, is an example of this approach. Using mandatory and voluntary set asides as well as other methods, the PSAB is designed to assist Indigenous businesses to compete for and win federal contracts. In 2014, when the then Aboriginal Affairs and Northern Development Canada (AANDC) evaluated the PSAB, the department expressed "concern that the approach generally favours larger and more established firms over new and smaller businesses and entrepreneurs" (AANDC, 2014, p. ii). This is a finding first identified in a 2007 evaluation and appears to have remained unresolved (Mah, 2014). The 2014 report also highlights the need to provide "direct and regional training to support newer and smaller Aboriginal firms to navigate the increasingly complex and competitive procurement environment" (AANDC, 2014, p. 35). Despite the policy having been in place for almost twenty-five years, the benefits of the PSAB to Indigenous businesses remain unclear. Mah (2014) reviewed the value of contracts awarded through the PSAB from 1996 to 2006 and found that the value of work through the PSAB as a percentage of the federal government's overall procurement had actually declined after peaking in 1998, suggesting the policy has not necessarily worked consistently and reliably for Indigenous businesses. In addition, Mah (2014) also warned that while procurement policies for social benefits have the potential to support communities and businesses that are marginalized, over-reliance on such policies could make the gains made by these communities and businesses short-lived, suggesting the need for broader support.

In August 2019, the federal government launched a one-year pilot project specifically for social procurement. The goal of the pilot is to "increase the number of under-represented suppliers bidding on, and winning, federal government temporary help services contracts in the National Capital Region" (Public Services and Procurement Canada [PSPC], 2020). The definition for qualified suppliers includes businesses that are at least 51 per cent owned by under-represented groups or Indigenous Peoples. The pilot project is to be evaluated after one year and may be further expanded to other types of government contracting. It could also set the stage for further social procurement at the federal level since social procurement was specifically mentioned in the mandate letter, dated December 2019, for the minister of Public Services and Procurement (Office of the Prime Minister, 2019).

Buying from Social Enterprises

The second approach is a variation of the first with a focus on social enterprise. While the first approach generates social benefits by directing economic opportunities towards those who are marginalized (assuming they would in turn employ others from the same group), the second approach sees social benefits through social enterprises with missions to create social impact, such as employing, training, or programming for those who are marginalized. This is particularly the case when the social enterprises belong to the subset of Work Integration Social Enterprises (WISEs) that are featured in this book. This second approach is a more recent policy development because social enterprises themselves are a more recent phenomenon.

To date, provinces and territories have engaged social enterprises in their procurement to varying degrees. To illustrate the broad range of scope and approaches in their attempt to include more social enterprises in their procurement processes, we use three provinces – Manitoba, Québec, and Nova Scotia – as examples. The development of policies and programs for social procurement in these three provinces in part reflects the long-standing history of these provincial governments nurturing and supporting the social enterprises in their jurisdictions (Bouchard et al., 2015; Elson et al., 2015; Lionais, 2015). The Province of Manitoba, in conjunction with the Canadian Community Economic Development Network, launched the Manitoba Social Enterprise Strategy in 2015 (Government of Manitoba & the Canadian Community Economic Development Network, 2015). One of the components in the strategy is designed to increase the number of procurement opportunities that the Government of Manitoba can offer social enterprises, such as doubling the current amount Manitoba Housing spends on maintenance and capital contracts with social enterprises. Building on the success seen in the case of Manitoba Housing (which has worked with BUILD, one of the cases featured in this book), the Manitoba Social Enterprise Strategy includes a recommendation to mandate provincial "departments and Crown corporations to partner with social enterprises to create business plans for other targeted opportunities, such as child and youth care workers, or northern healthy food" (Government of Manitoba & the Canadian Community Economic Development Network, 2015, p. 17).

Also in 2015, the Government of Québec (2015) released its five-year *Social Economy Action Plan*. The plan had the objective to strengthen the overall social economy sector in the province. Specifically, it included a new interdepartmental working group to develop and integrate procurement criteria focused on social benefits into tenders issued by the province. The government would also develop an awareness campaign to promote social procurement across departments, public agencies, and municipalities. As the plan stands to conclude in 2020, it is unclear at this time what may be next for social procurement policies in Québec. Finally, the Government of Nova Scotia (2017) launched a policy framework – *Advancing Social Enterprise in Nova Scotia* – to "create a thriving, sustainable social enterprise sector" (p. 1). The policy recognizes the barriers facing social enterprises in their growth and sustainability as well as the social benefits they generate. One of the pillars in the framework is focused on increasing market opportunities for social enterprises by creating a "strategic procurement planning process to identify procurement opportunities … that have been identified by the social enterprise sector in Nova Scotia" (Government of Nova Scotia, 2017, p. 9).

Buying with a Social Purpose

The third approach shifts the policy focus directly on creating the social benefits governments seek in the individual procurement opportunities, such as specific environmental standards and employment and training opportunities for people who have traditionally been unable to access them. This approach creates social benefits through government procurement in two ways. On the one hand, it allows governments to directly specify the kind of social impacts they want to generate. For example, the government could specify that the paper products it purchases must meet specific environmental standards. On the other hand, this approach also broadens the types of businesses or organizations that governments can buy from to create social benefits because it enables them to generate social benefits through all types of businesses and organizations, and not only social enterprises or businesses owned or operated by those who are marginalized. In this sense, the governments connect somewhat indirectly with the organizations that are actually generating the social benefits (Barraket et al., 2016). For example, since construction companies are generally not in the habit of hiring and training at-risk youth to work on their projects, governments could specify that a certain percentage of the labour working on these projects be set aside for at-risk youth. Using this approach, governments would be able to direct their procurement dollars to benefit at-risk youth without being limited to only dealing with businesses that fit a specific profile.

In 2006, the federal government implemented the *Policy on Green Procurement* which "requires that the procurement of goods and services actively promote environmental stewardship" (Government of Canada, 2018). Together with the establishment of the Office of Greening Government Procurement in 2005 (Attwater, 2014), the policy is intended to "lever the purchasing power of the federal government to achieve economies of scale in the acquisition of environmentally preferable goods and services, thereby reducing the cost for government and strengthening greener markets and industries" (Government of Canada, 2018). Despite the broad coverage of the policy on every aspect of operation within the federal government, the policy does not have any specific goal in terms of the amount of purchased goods and services or any specific environmental criteria for goods and services; such goal setting is left up to the individual departments to decide (Attwater, 2014). While the policy attempts to set a broad framework to expand procurement considerations beyond the economic ones, it also specifies that "green procurement is set within the context of achieving value for money ... [including] the consideration of many factors such as cost, performance, availability, quality and environmental performance" (Government of Canada, 2018). Specifically, the environmental criteria remain non-mandatory for procurement decisions, thus reducing the weight of environmental considerations when compared against economic factors such as price (Attwater, 2014).

The overriding factor of price or value for money is similarly found in other social procurement policies and programs, indicating that social benefits remain secondary to economic considerations for most governments. For example, the *BC Procurement Strategy* specifies that social impact criteria should only be included when appropriate. Even when social impact is a criterion, the strategy indicates that it cannot be a mandatory criterion and can account for no more than 10 per cent of the total points for evaluating bids (BC Ministry of Citizens' Services, 2020). The circuitous journey of a private member bill – first as Bill C-227 in 2016 and then as Bill C-344 in 2017 – to require the inclusion of community benefits in federal infrastructure spending also highlights this point. From the initial instigation of Bill C-227 in February 2016 to the second reading of a new version of the same bill, Bill C-344, in the Senate in May 2019, the twists and turns this simple amendment has navigated during the legislative process shows the challenge of making a broad change to legislation regarding government procurement. Even though leveraging government procurement for social impact does have broad support, the overall preference within the government is that such requirements be voluntary and remain subordinate to economic considerations (Bill C-227, 2016; Bill C-344, 2018; Canada/Senate of Canada, 2019). At the writing of this chapter, the bill appears to be in limbo, facing an uncertain future because the second reading in the Senate did not reach any decision on whether the bill should proceed to a committee.

On the provincial/territorial level, governments have enacted legislation to leverage their infrastructure spending to create social value. Ontario, for example, adopted the Infrastructure for Jobs and Prosperity Act in 2015 based on the principle of community benefits. The act (2015, p. 3) states that

> Infrastructure planning and investment should promote community benefits, being the supplementary social and economic benefits arising from an infrastructure project that are intended to improve the well-being of a community affected by the project, such as local job creation and training opportunities (including for apprentices, within the meaning of section 9), improvement of public space within the community, and any specific benefits identified by the community.

In April 2014, the Toronto Community Benefits Network, a coalition of communities impacted by the construction of the Eglinton Crosstown Light Rail Transit, signed the Community Benefits Framework with Metrolinx (the Ontario provincial agency in charge of the infrastructure project). The framework provides for employment, training, apprenticeship, and social procurement opportunities for local residents and businesses. As the first community benefits program for Metrolinx, the project also serves as a test case for application across future transit projects in Ontario (Metrolinx, 2014).

At the local level, a group of like-minded officials including those from rural and remote areas in British Columbia came together to form the British Columbia Social Procurement Initiative (BCSPI). The BCSPI serves as a learning and resource hub that provides support to local governments and First Nations to develop and implement a common approach to social procurement. The BCSPI offers training for elected officials and procurement staff, as well as suppliers and contractors, and as of 2022, thirty-two local government and organization members are part of the initiative (BCSPI, n.d.).

Buying with the Help of Intermediaries

While the three approaches described so far are not necessarily mutually exclusive and could be use jointly, they do represent distinct approaches to social procurement (Barraket et al., 2016). The fourth approach – the use of intermediaries – is complementary to the other three (Barraket, 2019). Intermediaries reflect the governments' recognition that the connection between governments on the demand side and social benefits on the supply side is not nearly as robust as the conventional commercial contracting relationships (Dragicevic & Ditta, 2016). As such, intermediaries provide support to initiate and maintain such connection, especially on the supply side where the businesses and organizations may be less familiar with government procurement processes (Dragicevic & Ditta, 2016). Intermediaries can serve a range of functions in social procurement, as Barraket's (2019) research on intermediaries in Australia indicates. With participants from both the sellers' and the buyers' sides, Barraket (2019) identifies five functions that intermediaries could serve: (1) developing and nurturing linkages between sellers and buyers; (2) supporting those involved in social procurement through training; (3) capacity building; (4) building awareness and providing policy advice to governments; and (5) enhancing credibility around buying for social value.

In Canada, many of these intermediaries are organizations from the social economy sector itself. For example, Buy Social (www .buysocialcanada.com) actively supports organizations on both the selling and the buying side of social procurement through consulting and training services. Social enterprises could also be certified by Buy Social as a way to objectively demonstrate the social value they generate. Another example is the Canadian Community Economic Development Network (https://ccednet-rcdec.ca); established in 1999, it is a grassroots organization with a broad mandate to promote "inclusion, diversity, and equity." CCEDNet has been working with governments (such as Manitoba) and social enterprises in encouraging social procurement through initiatives such as the Social Enterprise Ecosystem Project and in creating a standardized approach to demonstrate social benefits.

Challenges in Implementation

As reflected in this chapter so far, approaches to leveraging government purchases for social benefits require a change in organizational culture to channel spending in ways that are more deliberate and strategic. Despite various discussions on the potential benefits of social procurement policies, there is scant research on the implementation aspect and how procurement specialists are adjusting their practice (Petersen & Kadefors, 2016). Some of the challenges in implementation are related to the procurement process, such as specifying selection criteria, reporting requirements, and balancing against economic considerations. Regardless of the approach governments may choose to buy for social benefits, they need to spell out reporting requirements for suppliers. This is challenging because very little information is available on how to measure and verify the social impact the suppliers are expected to deliver. With very little operational information available, many government officials need to figure out implementation through trial and error.

As we have seen in the review of policies above, the balance between economic and social interests in procurement is often difficult to strike. Governments are reluctant to concede on economic considerations or value for money to pursue social benefits despite acknowledging they could potentially leverage considerable social benefits from their contracting activities (e.g., requiring that social value be a desirable but not mandatory criterion or limiting the points assigned for social benefits). The overall impact of social procurement policies is likely to be limited as long as governments continue to consider social benefits only as secondary and not always required. However, any broad and meaningful changes to the way procurement criteria are set up will need to go beyond the procurement departments. Such changes would need extensive management support to overcome internal resistance. As we see in some of the cases featured in this book (e.g., BUILD and SARCAN), champions who are unreservedly committed to leveraging procurement for social benefits are needed to translate these policies into a meaningful change of practices. The lack of such champions connecting policy to practice leads to inconsistencies in the application of the policy as we see in other cases in this book which work mostly with sporadic procurement opportunities (e.g., Horizon Achievement Centre).

This points to one of the underlying factors for the limited and inconsistent implementation of social procurement in governments: buying for social benefits requires cultural or institutional changes that are often not possible for procurement specialists to carry out alone (Petersen & Kadefors, 2016). In addition to an overhaul of how government procurement is conducted, another example of where broad changes are required is the need to coordinate with trade agreements. The implementation of social procurement requires an understanding of the regulations surrounding trade requirements. As Dragicevic and Ditta argue (2016, p. 17), "community benefits and social procurement policies operate within a highly complex legal environment, defined by domestic public procurement and business discrimination laws as well as international trade treaties." This legal environment can create confusion, particularly at the municipal and provincial levels, in terms of obligations. Specific clarifications for social procurement within the context of trade agreements can be beneficial for ensuring compliance while pursuing social benefits through procurement (Ludlow, 2016).

Conclusion

This review of Canadian procurement and purchasing policies for social value provides a broad picture of how governments make social procurement a reality in the four circumstances described by Barraket and Weissman (2009). As more governments turn their attention to their ability to leverage procurement for social benefits, they are also becoming aware that culture plays a fundamental part in the shift toward meeting these social objectives. At present, governments still struggle with the balance between economic considerations and social value as they manage their day-to-day procurement processes or supply chains. As they build internal capacity and shift organizational culture, governments may be able to increase social value in their procurement processes.

REFERENCES

Aboriginal Affairs and Northern Development Canada (AANDC). (2014). *Final Report – Evaluation of the Procurement Strategy for Aboriginal Businesses* (Project Number: 1570-7/13057). https://www.rcaanc-cirnac.gc.ca /DAM/DAM-CIRNAC-RCAANC/DAM-AEV/STAGING/texte-text /ev_psab_1446467643497_eng.pdf

Adobor, H., & McMullen, R. (2007). Supplier diversity and supply chain management: A strategic approach. *Business Horizon, 50*(3), 219–29. https:// doi.org/10.1016/j.bushor.2006.10.003

Attwater, D. (2014). Promoting sustainable development with Canadian public procurement. *Public Contract Law Journal, 44*(1), 79–111. www.jstor .org/stable/44742587

Bao, G., Wang, X., Larsen, G.L., & Morgan, D.F. (2013). Beyond new public governance: A value-based global framework for performance management, governance, and leadership. *Administration & Society, 45*(4), 443–67. https://doi.org/10.1177/0095399712464952

Barraket, J. (2019). The role of intermediaries in social innovation: The case of social procurement in Australia. *Journal of Social Entrepreneurship, 11*(2), 1–21. https://doi.org/10.1080/19420676.2019.1624272

Barraket, J., Keast, R., & Furneaux, C. (2016). *Social procurement and new public governance.* Routledge.

Barraket, J. & Weissman, J. 2009. *Social procurement and its implications for social enterprise: A literature review* (Working Paper No. CPNS 48). The Australian Centre for Philanthropy and Nonprofit Studies. https://eprints.qut.edu .au/29060/1/Barraket_and_Weissmann_2009_Working_Paper_No_48 _Final.pdf

BC Hydro. (n.d.). Indigenous contract and procurement policy at BC Hydro. https://www.bchydro.com/content/dam/BCHydro/customer-portal /documents/corporate/community/Indigenous-Procurement-Policy.pdf

BC Ministry of Citizens' Services. (2020). British Columbia Procurement Strategy Update 2020. https://news.gov.bc.ca/files/Procurement -Strategy-2020.pdf

Bill C-227: An Act to Amend the Department of Public Works and Government Services Act (Community Benefit). Second Reading 5 December 2016, 42nd Parliament, First Session. https://www.parl.ca/DocumentViewer/en/42-1 /bill/C-227/second-reading

Bill C-344: An Act to Amend the Department of Public Works and Government Services Act (Community Benefit). Third Reading 13 June 2018, 42nd Parliament, First Session. https://www.parl.ca/DocumentViewer/en/42-1 /bill/C-344/third-reading

Bouchard, M.J., Filho, P.C., & Zerdani T. (2015). Social enterprise in Québec: Understanding their "institutional footprint." *Canadian Journal of Nonprofit and Social Economy Research, 6*(1), 42–62. https://doi.org/10.22230 /cjnser.2015v6n1a198

Canada. Senate of Canada. (2019). Chamber Sitting: 284 on 7 May 2019, 42nd Parliament, First Session. https://sencanada.ca/en/content/sen/chamber/421 /debates/284db_2019-05-07-e?language=e

Canadian Centre for Diversity and Inclusion. (2016). *Supplier diversity in Canada: Research and analysis of the next step in diversity and inclusion for forward-looking organizations.* https://ccdi.ca/media/1066/ccdi-report -supplier-diversity-in-canada-updated-4072016.pdf

City of Toronto. (2016). *City of Toronto social procurement program.* https://www .toronto.ca/wp-content/uploads/2017/09/9607-backgroundfile-91818.pdf

City of Toronto. (2019). *Supplementary report – Resourcing the Regent Park social development plan: Update on investments, employment and training.* https:// www.toronto.ca/legdocs/mmis/2019/cc/bgrd/backgroundfile-139392.pdf

British Columbia Social Procurement Initiative (BCSPI). (n.d.). What is social procurement? https://bcspi.ca/what-is-social-procurement/

Dragicevic, N., & Ditta, S. (2016). *Community benefits and social procurement policies: A jurisdictional review*. Mowat Centre and Atkinson Foundation. https://ccednet-rcdec.ca/sites/ccednet-rcdec.ca/files/mowat_-_community _benefits_and_social_procurement_policies_a_jurisdictional_review.pdf

Elson, P.R., Hall, P., Leeson-Klym, S., Penner, D., & Andres, J. (2015). Social enterprises in the Canadian west. *Canadian Journal of Nonprofit and Social Economy Research*, *6*(1), 83–103. https://anserj.ca/index.php/cjnser/article /view/194

Furheaux C., & Barraket, J. (2014). Purchasing social good(s): A definition and a typology of social procurement. *Public Money & Management*, *34*(4), 265–72. https://doi.org/10.1080/09540962.2014.920199

Government of British Columbia. (n.d.). *Social impact procurement guidance for BC procurement resources*. https://www2.gov.bc.ca/gov/content/bc -procurement-resources/policy-and-strategies/strategies-and-initiatives /social-purchasing

Government of Canada. (2018, June 13). *Policy on green procurement*. https:// www.tbs-sct.gc.ca/pol/doc-eng.aspx?id=32573

Government of Manitoba & the Canadian Community Economic Development Network. (2015). *Manitoba social enterprise strategy: A strategy for creating jobs through social enterprise*. Government of Manitoba. https:// www.gov.mb.ca/housing/pubs/mb_social_enterprise_strategy_2015.pdf

Government of Nova Scotia. (2017). *Advancing social enterprise in Nova Scotia*. Government of Nova Scotia. https://beta.novascotia.ca/sites/default /files/documents/1-700/advancing-social-enterprise-nova-scotia-en.pdf

Government of Québec. (2015). *L'Économie sociale: Des valeurs qui nous enrichissent (plan d'action gouvernemental en économie sociale, 2015–2020)*. Government of Québec. https://ccednet-rcdec.ca/sites/ccednet-rcdec.ca /files/ccednet/pdfs/plan_action_economie_sociale_2015-2020.pdf

Indigenous and Northern Affairs Canada. (2015, April 9). *PSAB: Bringing meaning to procurement*. Procurement Strategy for Aboriginal Business (PSAB). https://www.sac-isc.gc.ca/eng/1354798736570/1610985991318

Infrastructure for Jobs and Prosperity Act, Statutes of Ontario. (2015, c. 15). https://www.ontario.ca/laws/statute/15i15

Jenson, J. (2015). The "social" in inclusive growth: The social investment perspective. In R. Hasmath (Ed.), *Inclusive growth, development and welfare policy: A critical assessment* (pp. 120–35). Routledge.

Jenson, J., & Saint-Martin, D. (2003). New routes to social cohesion? Citizenship and the social investment state. *Canadian Journal of Sociology*, *28*(1), 77–99. https://doi.org/10.2307/3341876

Keast, R.L., Furneaux, C.W., & Barraket, J. (2012, April 11–13). *Juggling competing public values: Resolving conflicting agendas in social procurement in Queensland*. 16th Annual Conference of the International Research Society for Public Management (IRSPM XVI): Contradictions in public management managing in volatile times, Rome, Italy. IRSPM. https://researchportal.scu .edu.au/esploro/outputs/conferencePaper/Juggling-competing-public -values--resolving/991012821009702368?institution=61SCU_INST

Laforest, R. (2011). *Voluntary sector organizations and the state: Building new relations*. UBC Press.

Lionais, D. (2015). Social enterprises in Atlantic Canada. *Canadian Journal of Nonprofit and Social Economy Research*, *6*(1), 25–41. https://doi.org/10.22230 /cjnser.2015v6n1a200

Loader, K. (2013). Is public procurement a successful small business support policy? A review of the evidence. *Environment and Planning C: Government and Policy*, *31*(1), 39–55. https://doi.org/10.1068/c1213b

Ludlow, A. (2016). Social procurement: Policy and practice. *European Labour Law Journal*, *7*(3), 479–97. https://doi.org/10.1177%2F201395251600700310

Mah, E. (2014). An evaluation of Canada's procurement policies for Aboriginal businesses. *Manitoba Policy Perspectives*, *1*(1), 65–81. https://umanitoba.ca /centres/mipr/media/5._PSAB_Mah.pdf

McCrudden, C. (2004). Using public procurement to achieve social outcomes. *Natural Resources Forum*, *28*(4), 257–67. https://ccednet-rcdec.ca/sites/ccednet -rcdec.ca/files/ccednet/pdfs/2004-mccrudden-public_procurement.pdf

Metrolinx. (2014). *Metrolinx community benefits framework*. http://www .thecrosstown.ca/sites/default/files/metrolinx_community_benefits _framework_0.pdf

Office of the Prime Minister. (2019). *The minister of public services and procurement mandate letter*. https://pm.gc.ca/en/mandate-letters/2019/12/13/minister -public-services-and-procurement-mandate-letter

Ontario Ministry of Economic Development, Job Creation and Trade. (2016, June 21). *Ontario launches new social enterprise strategy*. https://news.ontario .ca/medg/en/2016/06/ontario-launches-new-social-enterprise-strategy .html

Osborne, S.P. (2018). From public service-dominant logic to public service logic: Are public service organizations capable of co-production and value co-creation? *Public Management Review*, *20*(2), 225–31. https://doi.org /10.1080/14719037.2017.1350461

Petersen, D., & Kadefors, A. (2016, September 5–7). Social procurement and employment requirements in construction. In P.W. Chan and C.J. Neilson (Eds.), *Proceedings of the 32nd Annual ARCOM Conference, Manchester, UK*. Association of Researchers in Construction Management, Volume 2, 997–1006. http://www .arcom.ac.uk/-docs/proceedings/1783e99fa10b4c8f3efffe28bfc7c0a6.pdf

Public Services and Procurement Canada (PSPC). (2020, January 2). *Temporary help services social procurement pilot*. https://www.tpsgc-pwgsc.gc.ca/app -acq/ma-bb/ppasst-thsspp-eng.html

Public Works and Government Services Canada (PWGSC). (2019, May 23). *The procurement process.* https://buyandsell.gc.ca/for-businesses/selling-to-the -government-of-canada/the-procurement-process

Revington, C., Hoogendam, R., & Holeton, A. (2015). *The social procurement intermediary: The state of the art and its development within the GTHA.* Learning Enrichment Foundation. https://ccednet-rcdec.ca/en/toolbox/social -procurement-intermediary-state-art-and-its

Walker, H., & Preuss, L. (2008). Fostering sustainability through sourcing from small businesses: Public sector perspectives. *Journal of Cleaner Production, 16*(15), 1600–9. https://doi.org/10.1016/j.jclepro.2008.04.014

3 A Pan-Canadian Survey of Social Enterprises

ANDREA CHAN, ANNIE LUK, SHELLEY LEPP,
LAURIE MOOK, MARTY DONKERVOORT,
RACHEL LAFOREST, GORDON M. DJONG,
ARIELLE VETRO, AND JACK QUARTER

After much discussion, our research team was keen to examine the extent to which work integration social enterprises (WISEs)[1] in Canada responded to tenders issued by public, private, and non-profit organizations, especially given the recent implementation of social-procurement policies in the public sphere. Our initial intention was to gain insight into the practice of social procurement from the perspective of both sellers and buyers. In November 2017, we embarked upon a nationwide survey of social enterprises, which was supplemented with semi-structured interviews to elaborate the survey results with further qualitative findings. We hoped the survey would give us an understanding of the engagement level of social enterprises in social procurement. We planned to use this as a point of contrast with a similar survey of the customers of social enterprises afterwards. Our expectation was that we would see a robust level of social enterprises participating in social procurement, implying a robust number of customers pursuing social procurement. Imagine our surprise when we found a low level of engagement and success in bidding.

In this chapter, we outline the methodology and provide some background about the social enterprises that participated in our study. We then review the key findings from the survey and the follow-up interviews before discussing how these findings guided the selection of cases for a more in-depth understanding of social procurement and social purchasing in Canada. The findings from this first stage of

---

1 In this chapter and elsewhere in the book, we use WISE and social enterprise interchangeably since all the survey participants and cases are WISEs.

research provide a snapshot of the social enterprises' experience with (social) procurement and social purchasing and are also instrumental for guiding the project into the next stage of examining the experiences of a select group of social enterprises.

Survey Design and Methodology

The pan-Canadian survey was designed using mixed methods, starting with an online survey questionnaire followed by semi-structured phone interviews to explore survey responses in more depth (Creswell & Plano Clark, 2007). The mixed-method approach within the survey used the quantitative-qualitative sequence that leveraged "methodological eclecticism" to investigate the prevalence of social procurement among social enterprises and the decision to submit bids or not (Morse, 2015; Teddie & Tashakkori, 2015, p. 10). In the survey design, we distinguished procurement from purchasing by suggesting the former involves more formality and "higher order decisions" (Barraket et al., 2016, p. 1). As such, we specifically asked the survey participants about their experiences of responding to and working with procurement strategies, policies, and processes. Since individual customers rarely, if ever, institute any strategies, policies, and processes in their purchasing decisions, our focus for social procurement in the survey was on organizational purchasers – i.e., government agencies, private businesses, and non-profit organizations such as universities, hospitals, and community organizations.

Our initial list of organizations to be invited to the survey was drawn from the sampling frame of the Canadian National Social Enterprise Sector Survey or SESS (Elson & Hall, 2012), which our team screened to identify organizations that met the criteria of a WISE. In addition, we conducted online research and reviewed sectoral reports and websites of non-profit organizations to augment the SESS sampling frame. As a result, we added social enterprises including several from Quebec, which was not surveyed by the SESS. Through this approach, we identified a list of 349 WISEs as potential participants for the survey. We sent survey invitations to the organizations via email and then followed up with phone calls and emails. Ultimately, 129 WISEs (a response rate of 37 per cent) completed the survey and formed our survey sample.

Following the preliminary analysis of our quantitative data from the survey, we conducted follow-up interviews with twelve survey respondents to explore in greater depth some of the patterns revealed in the survey responses. We purposively sampled for WISEs that represented varied experiences with procurement bidding (i.e., having submitted bids or not and having been successful in bids or not). In addition, we included both large and small social enterprises as determined by revenue. We were also interested in the possible differences between social enterprises that indicated they were promoting their social value in their sales and marketing, and those that did not.

The twelve social enterprises that we interviewed as part of the survey included four that had never bid on procurement contracts. Among the eight with experience in bidding for procurement, six had been successful while the other two had not. Three of the successful six indicated they emphasize their social mission in their marketing, whereas the other three did not. The two organizations that had not been successful in their social procurement bids noted that they were promoting their social mission in their marketing.

Survey Participants

This section provides an overview of where the survey participants are located across Canada; who their customers are; whether they have parent organizations and, if so, what their relationship is; and how big or small they are.

Geographic Representation

The provincial breakdown of the WISEs that participated in the survey is presented in table 3.1. The social enterprises in our survey illustrate a reasonable representation from across Canada, except for Quebec, which is under-represented in our sample likely due to the fact that the survey was only available in English, and most of the organizations in the province operate in French. The large majority of the survey respondents are based in Ontario, the most populous province in Canada. Interestingly, two of the smallest provinces by population – Prince Edward Island and Newfoundland & Labrador – have the highest response rates.

Customers

Approximately 67 per cent of the WISEs in the survey indicate having regular individual customers. Nearly 60 per cent of the survey respondents report organizational purchasers as regular customers. Among those with organizational purchasers, 58 per cent of the WISEs in the survey report that private businesses purchase from them regularly whereas only 32 per cent of the social enterprises have governments as their regular customers and 40 per cent of the WISEs say non-profit organizations buy from them regularly. The responses suggest that if we look at these purchases

Table 3.1. Distribution of Responses and Response Rate by Province/Territory

Location	% of Total Distribution	Response Rate (%)
British Columbia	14.7	38.0
Alberta	3.1	28.6
Saskatchewan	5.4	21.2
Manitoba	9.3	34.3
Ontario	36.4	41.4
Quebec	1.6	25.0
New Brunswick	5.4	38.9
Nova Scotia	16.3	40.5
Prince Edward Island	3.1	66.7
Newfoundland & Labrador	1.6	50.0
Yukon, Northwest Territories, and Nunavut[2]	3.1	23.5
Total	100.0	37.0

from the supply-chain perspective, many of the WISEs in the survey are still very much operating at a business-to-consumer retail level rather than a business-to-business level. Individual customers engage only in social purchasing while organizational purchasers engage in both social procurement and social purchasing, depending on the specific transactions. Since our research project initially had the objective to investigate the connection between the discussion on social procurement at the policy level and the actual experiences by the WISEs, it is the organizational purchasers and how the WISEs engage with them in social procurement and social purchasing that we were most interested in. Procurement in terms of both volume of sales and resulting revenue have the greatest potential not only to promote the financial sustainability and growth of social enterprises but also to bolster the value they generate in the community.

Support from Parent Organizations

Despite nearly half of survey respondents being incorporated, almost 80 per cent of the WISEs in the survey have parent organizations. The support the survey respondents receive from parent organizations may include management, space, and monetary assistance. Only 6 per cent

---

2 The three territories are grouped together because of the small number of survey respondents from each of the territories.

of the social enterprises with parent organizations consider themselves as an independent social enterprise without much influence or oversight from the parent organization. Although support from their parent organizations and the degree to which WISEs are attached to their parents are not noted in the literature as a factor in social enterprises' procurement activities, we hypothesized that those with a strong attachment could be more likely to engage in social procurement because of the opportunity to leverage the resources of their parents. We made this inference based on our understanding of the complexity of identifying, understanding, and responding to procurement opportunities as well as the resources and know-how required in navigating these opportunities.

Organizational Size

The WISEs in our survey are relatively small, with 41 per cent of them having revenue under $250,000. Nearly half in this subgroup have revenues exceeding $100,000 but less than $250,000. However, we should also note that 25 per cent of the WISEs in the survey report at least $1 million in revenue, with a handful of them making $5 million or more. Similarly, 68 per cent of the WISEs have at least one but fewer than ten full-time employees. Apart from their board members, these social enterprises do not rely heavily on volunteers, with 73 per cent saying that volunteers in total contribute less than ten hours per week to their services. These responses on revenue and employees are consistent with the finding that most WISEs in the survey have parent organizations and are dependent on these parents. We could surmise that many of the WISEs that are dependent on their parents operate to some degree as programs or divisions within their parent organizations. The small number of employees is also consistent with the response that many of the WISEs rely on their parents for administrative and human-resources support.

Findings

While we did not hypothesize a specific level of participation in social procurement at the outset of our study, we were surprised to discover a lower-than-expected level of engagement. Nearly 40 per cent of the WISEs report never having submitted procurement bids to any organizational purchasers. Further, less than 40 per cent of the bids submitted are for tenders with social criteria as part of the evaluation process. Put another way, less than a quarter of all the

WISEs surveyed have tried to secure contracts through formal social procurement.

A number of scenarios may account for this result. For example, despite the growing discussion on the policy level among organizational purchasers, WISEs have not been able to participate in social procurement. A possible reason for this is the lack of expertise in accessing opportunities or developing proposals as suggested in the research reviewed (Muñoz, 2009; Revington et al., 2015). However, this may be only a partial explanation, as our data suggest WISEs have moderate success with procurement in general. Another potential explanation is that despite growing discussion on the policy level among organizational purchasers, actual procurement opportunities that include social value have yet to materialize broadly. The small proportion of WISEs with experience submitting bids using social criteria points to this explanation. It is also possible that social procurement may be occurring without the formalized higher-order decision-making we initially envisioned as social procurement. Most likely, the reality is a combination of all the above.

Our second surprise was that despite moderate engagement and success in formal bidding, many respondents report that their organizational purchasers also buy from them regularly or intermittently. Again, a number of likely scenarios could explain these findings. It is possible that organizational purchasers are sometimes making one-off purchasing decisions (similar to individual customers), and thus they engage in social purchasing more than social procurement. It could also be that social procurement may not occur strictly through the bidding process (as we asked in the survey questions), and there may be other ways for organizational purchasers to create opportunities for social procurement. It is also possible that the WISEs who participated in the survey have a different understanding of what constitutes social procurement than that which can be found in research literature.

A third interesting finding from the survey is related to the importance of social mission to customers. We asked social enterprises to rate their understanding of the importance of their social mission to their organizational purchasers. The survey results indicate that overall, WISEs believe that their organizational purchasers place a high degree of importance on social mission when making purchasing considerations. The social enterprises in the survey understand their social value to be more important to non-profit purchasers than to governments and businesses.

Engagement and Success of WISEs in (Social) Procurement

In the survey, we asked the WISEs about their experiences of submitting social procurement bids, on their own or in collaboration with other social enterprises, to any of three different types of organizational purchasers: governments, businesses, and non-profit organizations. Almost 40 per cent report that they have submitted procurement bids to governments. The proportions are slightly lower for bids to businesses (36 per cent) and other non-profit organizations (33 per cent). Although 38 per cent of the WISEs indicate that they have never submitted bids to any of these organizational purchasers, almost half of all the WISEs in the survey have won contracts with organizational purchasers through the process of bidding.

However, when we turn our focus to *social* procurement, only 40 per cent of the WISEs that have submitted bids report having been asked to specify social criteria as part of their submission. Strictly speaking, the bids that do not include social criteria should be considered conventional rather than social-procurement bids, because the purchasers have not identified in the tenders their interest in creating social, cultural, and/or environmental value or their use of social, cultural, and/or environmental criteria to evaluate potential vendors. Nonetheless, our research is interested in sales through procurement more broadly as well, since the organizational capacity required to prepare procurement bids presumably overlaps with those needed for social-procurement bids. We can infer that organizational purchasers are not yet actively asking for social value in their purchases, and thus social value is not yet broadly incorporated into the supply chain by organizational purchasers. Because of this, the social enterprises in our survey have not had the opportunity to leverage their social value more widely as a differentiator in the marketplace. Regardless of purchasing or procuring intent, we acknowledge that all sales facilitate social enterprises' ability to create social, environmental, and cultural value in addition to economic value in the community.

The absence of social value being broadly included as procurement and purchasing criteria by organizational purchasers means the social value generated by social enterprises remains secondary or even a non-factor when compared to the primary purchasing considerations such as price and quality. This is supported by survey findings where WISEs consistently rank price and quality higher than social value because of their understanding of success determinants in acquiring business. Despite the limited emphasis on social benefit in *formal* procurement tendering encountered by those surveyed, we continued our analysis

Table 3.2. Proportion of Social Enterprises (SEs) Bidding on Procurement Contracts by Purchaser Groups

	Purchaser Groups			
	Governments	Businesses	Non-profits	All 3 Combined
% of SEs having bid for *any* procurement contracts	40	36	33	62
% of SEs having bid for *social* procurement contracts	10	9	11	23
% of SEs having won *any* procurement contracts	27	25	25	49

into factors that may influence the likelihood that social enterprises would bid on procurement contracts.

FACTORS INFLUENCING CONTRACT BIDDING

Considering that there was moderate engagement and success in securing contracts through procurement (just not *social* procurement), we were curious to understand the possible factors leading some WISEs to engage with procurement opportunities. We conducted logistic regressions to identify potential characteristics of the WISEs that would be more likely to submit bids to organizational purchasers. The predictor variables we selected clustered into five areas of organizational characteristics:

1. Parental attachment – whether the WISE has deeper attachment to its parent and the number of different types of parental support the WISE receives
2. Marketing capability – whether the social enterprise has marketing staff and the self-evaluated marketing capability
3. Bidding capability – whether the WISE has at least one person with the expertise in preparing bids, the self-evaluated capability in preparing bids, and the self-evaluated capability in demonstrating social values[3]
4. Total revenue[4]
5. Human resources capacity – the number of full-time staff, part-time staff, volunteers, and weekly volunteer hours

---

3 Self-rating on capacity from 1 to 10: 1 for no capacity at all to 10 for great capacity.
4 Total revenue by categories: Less than $30,000; $30,000 to $99,999; $100,000 to $249,999; $250,000 to $499,999; $500,000 to $999,999; $1,000,000 to $2,499,999; $2,500,000 to $4,999,999; and $5,000,000 and up.

The selection of these areas was based on existing literature alongside our own understanding of social enterprises through our collective research experience in the field. Parental attachment and support are not noted in the literature as factors in social enterprises' procurement activities. However, we hypothesized that organizations with strong attachment to their parents would be more likely to bid for contracts because they could leverage the resources of their parents. Variables related to marketing capability were included as proxies for social enterprises operating in a more businesslike manner: marketing orientation, professionalization, and corporatization (Maier et al., 2016). Capacity to prepare bids and demonstrate social value were both noted challenges to securing procurement contracts for social enterprises (Barraket & Weissman, 2009; Muñoz, 2009). Total revenue and human resources were measured for the size of organization, which was noted to influence engagement with procurement by small to medium-sized enterprises (SMEs) (Orser, 2009).

The results from our logistic regression analysis show that only two of the five areas of organizational characteristics are statistically significant predictors. The two variables significantly associated with bids to governments are the WISE's self-evaluated capacity on bidding and total revenue. The odds of social enterprises submitting bids to governments would increase by 36 per cent for every unit increase in the way they self-evaluate their bidding capacity ($OR = 1.36$, $p < .0001$). Likewise, the odds for bids to governments would increase by 48 per cent ($OR = 1.48$, $p = .029$) for every jump in the total revenue bracket. The higher a social enterprise rates its capacity to prepare bids and the higher its total revenue, the more likely it is to submit a government bid.

Repeating the analysis with bids on contracts for non-profit organizations as the outcome variable, we found similar results, with self-evaluated bidding capacity and total revenue again predicting likelihood for social enterprises to bid.[5] In contrast, when we conducted the analysis a third time with bids on contracts with private businesses as the outcome variable, we found no statistically significant predictors. In other words, none of the predictor variables we looked at could explain whether a social enterprise would submit bids to businesses.

---

5 The odds of social enterprises submitting bids to non-profit organizations increase by 19 per cent for every increase in their self-evaluated bidding capacity (OR = 1.19, p = .030), controlling for other variables. The odds of bidding to non-profit organizations increase by 50 per cent for every increase in the total revenue categories (OR = 1.50, p = .024), controlling for all else in the model.

We also asked social enterprises to rate their own understanding of the importance of their social mission to their organizational purchasers. On a 10-point scale with 10 indicating extreme importance to an organizational purchasing group (i.e., high value associated with social mission), social enterprises perceived their social mission to be most important to non-profit purchasers (mean rating of 8.2), followed by government purchasers (mean rating of 7.3) and private-business purchasers (mean rating of 6.3). On whether this perceived importance of social mission is tied to the social enterprises' likelihood to bid, we found only one statistically significant result. The social enterprises that have submitted bids for government contracts also say that they perceive their social mission to be significantly more important to government purchasers than those that are non-bidders, $t(108.80) = -3.62$, $p < .0001$.[6] There is no significant difference between bidders and non-bidders in the way they perceive the importance of their social mission, regarding non-profit or private-business purchasers.

OTHER POSSIBLE FACILITATORS AND CHALLENGES FOR SOCIAL PROCUREMENT

We were surprised by the survey results showing that only 23 per cent of the respondents have submitted *social* procurement bids (although around 60 per cent have experience with procurement bidding more broadly), especially considering that social procurement has garnered substantive policy interest for some time. We used qualitative interviews to gain a better understanding of why those who have submitted bids have chosen to do so when many of their peers have not. The interviews added to the research literature, which has so far generally focused on the challenges facing social enterprises preparing bids and fulfilling contracts, by investigating the approaches to securing procurement contracts as well as the rationale behind whether to bid on (social) procurement tenders or not (Barraket & Weissman, 2009; Muñoz, 2009).

Since the total number of respondents with experience submitting social procurement bids is small, we do not distinguish between social and conventional procurement bids or between different types of organizational purchasers. Experiences varied, with some interviewees

---

6 Three independent sample *t*-tests were conducted on the scores of perceived importance of social mission, one for each of the three respective purchasing groups (e.g., government, businesses, and non-profit organizations). The comparison groups for each t-test were social enterprises that (1) bid on tenders, and (2) did not bid on tenders put out by the purchasing group under consideration.

saying they would wait passively for organizational purchasers to invite submissions while others, especially those without major funders and thus with more pressure to be financially sustainable, take a more proactive approach. WISEs proactively looking for opportunities from both private and public sectors report doing so because bidding is their only means of survival. One interviewee mentions that his organization began actively bidding on government projects after building close relationships with other non-profits and social enterprises (one of which is a major social enterprise in North America), which previously introduced them to the concept. But in general, WISEs appear to be more reactive than proactive in their engagement with the bidding process. One interviewee reports that "[Years ago] someone from the government might have told us that they needed certain products or services, therefore inviting us to bid, as we're a qualified bidder I guess. From there, we would start looking at their tender list once again and see if that's something we can or cannot do and then trying hard to get on their 'preferred' list." Although revenue serves as the primary motivation for pursuing bid opportunities, another reason articulated by an interviewee is "the pride of producing something of value that we can sell, and skill-building of course."

Overall, follow-up discussions through interviews confirm the survey findings and align with the challenges identified in research literature – confirming that size and capacity have considerable impact on whether social enterprises choose to submit bids or not. One interviewee mentions that "the government ... [has] a very robust and time-consuming process of bidding that is not easy ... But again, having the resources, time, capacity, staff to participate in a proper bid, is a full-time thing to do," highlighting that capacity remains a major issue. Many of the social enterprises in this study are small, suggesting that they lack the necessary resources to submit bids. These WISEs often do not have the budget to hire dedicated staff, and their current staff are already overburdened, further limiting their ability to take on additional projects.

Depending on the nature of the projects, some interviewees identify space and modes of transportation as limitations in being able to fulfil the demands of large projects. One interviewee selling baked goods in a rural area points out that it would be difficult to transport products to the nearest urban centre where most organizational purchasers are located. Another interviewee talks about their inability to deliver large orders on short notice, saying this is not possible for the clients or program participants that they employ (i.e., people with disabilities). Yet another interviewee argues that the bureaucracy associated with submitting bids to the governments is too complex. She feels the social enterprise where she works lacks the confidence to compete with larger organizations that may be generating a financial surplus. A weak financial position, in her mind, could be interpreted by purchasers as not being properly managed to generate a surplus, and as such, the social enterprise might not be trusted with additional projects. In sum, rural locations, complicated bureaucracy, lack of confidence, and lack of organizational capacity are obstacles to submitting social procurement bids.

We also asked WISEs whether they believe the inclusion of social mission as part of their bids or proposals (i.e., highlighting the potential social value they could realize as the chosen contractor) could improve success in securing procurement contracts. Many interviewees include their social mandates in their promotional tools (e.g., websites and advertisements) and proposal bids when and if they have submitted. One states that "we have always included our social mandate in our proposals, but the way we talk about it will depend on our understanding of the values of whom we are bidding for," echoing other interviewees who claim their social mandates as an important part of their identity. The mandates can serve as an edge in promotion and proposal bids, since the social mandates demonstrate how the WISEs can add value by employing individuals from marginalized groups. Although most interviewees see their social mission as an important element of their value chain that should be central to their marketing and sales, some do not feel the same. One interviewee points out that every potential customer has different needs and requirements, and that discussing the social mandate may not always be the best approach. As a result, this WISE only speaks of its social mandate if doing so would be beneficial.

Purchasing by Organizations Outside of Competitive Procurement

Survey findings reveal that beyond procurement contracts, WISEs are selling to governments, businesses, and non-profit organizations outside of any procurement framework. For all three organizational purchaser groups, substantively more WISEs report having them as regular, non-procurement customers than procurement purchasers.

We infer that government agencies, businesses, and non-profit organizations may be engaged in a form of social purchasing, given how central a WISE's social mission can be to their sales and marketing. These purchases are distinct from procurement as we initially defined it in that they may be smaller in value and executed with less systematic deliberation, as a way for organizations to support WISEs through less formalized and more business-to-consumer type purchases. However,

Table 3.3. Social Enterprises (SEs) by Purchaser Groups, by Purchasing Types

	Purchaser Groups		
	Governments	Businesses	Non-profits
% of SEs with group as regular or intermittent purchaser	66	90	91
% of SEs with group as procurement purchaser	27	25	25

there is also the possibility that these purchases include higher-value transactions formalized by contractual agreements, but these contracts are not secured through competitive bidding. Some of the survey participants hint at the importance of relationship-building with (potential) purchasers during interviews, and a few talk about their substantive and formalized service contracts with governments and non-profit organizations while having no experience with bidding on tenders.

Discussion

The results of our study reveal that, contrary to expectations, a surprisingly small percentage of respondents have submitted social procurement bids, whether to governments, businesses, or non-profit organizations. Only two factors predict whether a WISE would bid: the level of revenue and the organization's own evaluation of its capacity to prepare bids. Revenue is typically correlated with the number of employees, and perhaps unsurprisingly the WISEs with higher revenue inevitably have more staff and thus a greater capacity to organize bids. This finding is consistent with those from previous research on SMEs and social enterprises, which found that size and understanding of the tendering process influence engagement with procurement (Barraket & Weissman, 2009; Muñoz, 2009). Our inability to pinpoint consistent organizational characteristics among the successful WISEs may be attributable to the low proportion of respondents experiencing success with bids within each of the three purchaser groups, which is one impediment in our analysis. We were also surprised by these survey results, given the publicity of recent policies designed to facilitate bids from social enterprises (as discussed in chapter 2). These results point to a multitude of possibilities for additional research: for example, what is the capacity threshold that a social enterprise needs to reach before bidding?

The supplemental survey interviews affirm the findings of the quantitative data. Small WISEs (in terms of revenue) do not have the capacity to bid. The WISEs see bureaucracy as a hindrance, suggesting that staff who are skilled at running WISE programs are not necessarily comfortable or adept at understanding and navigating a complicated bidding process. Organizations that have proceeded with bids may have specifically pursued such skills and resources to support their ability to bid.

Although the WISEs in our study have some features of a business, they are different in significant ways and operated as "modified social welfare organizations" (Chan et al., 2017). With few exceptions, these WISEs rely on the support of parent organizations (typically social-service agencies) and on government funding – much like social-welfare organizations. Indeed, it may be cynical speculation, but a critique of social enterprises as being part of broader neoliberal policymaking is that government is primarily interested in WISEs as a means of reducing its necessary social-welfare contributions (Spicer et al., 2019). However, they do earn a portion of their revenues from the sale of goods and services. Although 47 per cent of the social enterprises in the survey report having more than 75 per cent of their revenue from selling goods or services, 41 per cent of these organizations have less than $250,000 in total revenue. This finding suggests that sales revenue is still only earned in small amounts. The post-survey interviews point out that a relatively small per cent of our sample would fit the business end of the continuum and a larger portion would be at the social-service end since many allude to the challenge of providing social benefits for their clients while trying to run a business.

Is it realistic to think that social procurement can bridge the funding gap, leading to financial stability? Our study suggests that small WISEs, those more akin to social-service agencies, lack the capacity to bid and possibly to deliver the goods if they are successful. These opportunities are best availed by larger social enterprises that are more professionalized. Even if the small WISEs could bid as a group (Muñoz, 2009; Revington et al., 2015), they would require, at minimum, sharing a common service, a willingness to cooperate, and some capacity to coordinate such efforts.

Another unexpected but compelling finding is that overall, a sizeable portion of WISEs' sales are attributed to government, business, and non-profit purchasers. Some of the sales are likely smaller, casual purchases that we categorized as *social purchasing* and differentiated from *social procurement* at the outset of our study. However, our post-survey interviews suggest that there is a portion of sales that falls between social purchasing and social procurement as we initially conceived it. Specifically, we see relatively large service contracts generating substantive revenue for WISEs but not as a result of any competitive tendering process. In some cases, these arrangements hint at some form of partnership between the purchasers and the delivery of social programs, which is distinct from the traditional purchaser-supplier relationships.

Based on what we have learned from the survey results, we moved to the second phase of our study with a realization that we should pay greater attention to other formal and informal supplier arrangements with organizational purchasers. Exploration of these alternative supplier/purchasing arrangements is one of the central features of the cases that follow in this book.

REFERENCES

Barraket, J., Keast, R., & Furneaux, C. (2016). *Social procurement and new public governance*. Routledge.

Barraket, J. & Weissman, J. (2009). *Social procurement and its implications for social enterprise: A literature review* (Working Paper No. CPNS 48). The Australian Centre for Philanthropy and Nonprofit Studies. https://eprints .qut.edu.au/29060/1/Barraket_and_Weissmann_2009_Working_Paper _No_48_Final.pdf

Chan, A., Ryan, S., & Quarter, J. (2017). Supported social enterprise: A modified social welfare organization. *Nonprofit and Voluntary Sector Quarterly, 46*(2), 261–79. https://doi.org/10.1177/0899764016655620

Creswell, J.W., & Plano Clark, V.L. (2007). *Designing and conducting mixed methods research*. Sage Publications.

Elson, P., & Hall, P. (2012). Canadian social enterprises: Taking stock. *Social Enterprise Journal, 8*(3), 216–36. https://doi.org/10.1108/17508611211280764

Maier, F., Meyer, M., & Steinbereithner, M. (2016). Nonprofit organizations becoming business-like: A systematic review. *Nonprofit and Voluntary Sector Quarterly, 45*(1), 64–86. https://doi.org/10.1177/0899764014561796

Morse, J. (2015). Procedures and practice of mixed method design: Maintaining control, rigor, and complexity. In A. Tashakkori & C. Teddie (Eds.), *SAGE handbook of mixed methods in social & behavioral research* (pp. 339–52). SAGE Publications.

Muñoz, S. (2009). Social enterprise and public sector voices on procurement. *Social Enterprise Journal, 5*(1), 69–82. https://doi.org/10.1108/17508610910956417

Orser, B. (2009). *Procurement strategies to support women entrepreneurs*. https:// www.researchgate.net/publication/274699418_Procurement_Strategies_to _Support_Women_Entrepreneurs

Revington, C., Hoogendam, R., & Holeton, A. (2015). *The social procurement intermediary: The state of the art and its development within the GTHA*. Learning Enrichment Foundation. Retrieved from https://ccednet-rcdec.ca/en /toolbox/social-procurement-intermediary-state-art-and-its

Spicer, J., Kay, T., & Ganz, M. (2019). Social entrepreneurship as field encroachment: How a neoliberal social movement constructed a new field. *Socio-Economic Review, 17*(1), 195–227. https://doi.org/10.1093/ser/mwz014

Teddie, C., & Tashakkori, A. (2015). Overview of contemporary issues in mixed methods research. In A. Tashakkori & C. Teddie (Eds.), *SAGE handbook of mixed methods in social & behavioral research* (pp. 1–42). SAGE Publications.

PART 2

Securing Large Contracts through Relationship Building

As social procurement gains traction in an increasing number of policy jurisdictions, it would be logical for social enterprise supporters to advocate for the sector's share of new trading opportunities (Buy Social Canada, 2018; Revington et al., 2015). With Canadian governments procuring around $200 billion worth of goods and services annually (Government of Canada, 2020), even directing a small fraction of such purchases towards social enterprises could significantly enhance the social and environmental benefits created by the sector.

When we think about procurement and purchasing by governments, we typically envision a process of competitive tendering, especially where the goods and services to be bought represent a higher dollar value (for example, the construction of a new highway or the contract for computer support services). As such, the discussion in research literature regarding social enterprises' engagement with procurement opportunities has often focused on capacity building for the sector to win public-service contracts. To that end, researchers, practitioners, policy actors, and other interested parties have offered a variety of recommendations (Buy Social Canada, 2018; Lupick, 2017; Muñoz, 2009; Revington et al., 2015). Their suggestions have included establishing intermediaries or matchmakers specifically for social procurement who would certify social enterprises and connect them with procurement opportunities. Intermediaries could improve social enterprises' overall business capacity including competency around identifying potential opportunities, preparing bids, supporting social enterprises in creating consortia, and facilitating subcontracting – particularly as part of broader community benefit agreements. For organizational purchasers interested in buying social, recommendations have included simplifying the overall procurement process, reserving a portion of tenders specifically for social enterprises, hosting "meet the buyer" events, and dividing up large contracts into smaller ones to accommodate the capacity of social enterprises.

While any of the above might help foster a more hospitable environment for social enterprises to engage in competitive tendering, implicit in the recommendations is the importance of investing in long-term relationship building with potential organizational purchasers who may be interested in buying social. The four cases in part 2 clearly illustrate the importance of relationship building and demonstrate that this message should be more explicitly underscored.

- BUILD Inc. (Building Urban Industries for Local Development) (Winnipeg, Manitoba)
- SARCAN Recycling (Across Saskatchewan)
- Ever Green Recycling (St. John's, Newfoundland and Labrador)
- EMBERS Staffing Solutions (ESS) (Vancouver, British Columbia)

These social enterprises are some of the largest featured in this book, all with annual revenue in the millions or even tens of millions. Their ability to take on larger contracts reinforces their efforts to build capacity and generate social benefits in the community through their employment and training programs. The revenue coming from the relative stability and security of larger-scale or ongoing contracts allows these social enterprises to create virtuous cycles of social and economic value creation. While these enterprises have benefited from a variety of policy- or purchaser-side measures, such measures only reveal half the success story of these social enterprises. For example, BUILD Inc. is a construction social enterprise in Winnipeg whose single largest purchaser is Manitoba Housing, the provincial body responsible for housing policy and programs. Manitoba Housing already has a strong commitment to social procurement and an established intermediary – The Social Enterprise Initiative – to work with social enterprise suppliers. BUILD's success is built on the organization's longstanding relationship with Manitoba Housing and Manitoba Hydro, which preceded the formalization of social procurement policies at the provincial level. The multiple crossovers of key social procurement champions between BUILD and the province (including Manitoba Housing) at the management level over time also strengthened the ability of these key individuals to continually advocate for and solidify the relationships between BUILD and various provincial bodies.

Similarly, SARCAN Recycling is a social enterprise whose primary revenue comes from its service contract with the Saskatchewan government. SARCAN was established in 1998 by its parent non-profit organization to initiate a partnership with the province to implement a new recycling program for non-refillable beverage containers. This procurement relationship was instigated, and is still championed, by both SARCAN's parent organization and the province, both of which understand the potential of the partnership to address two key policy areas: environmental sustainability and the removal of employment barriers for people living with disabilities.

Located in Vancouver's Downtown Eastside (a neighbourhood struggling with marginalization due to a myriad of social challenges), EMBERS Staffing Solutions (ESS) is a temporary staffing agency whose parent organization is a community economic development organization. Staffing primarily for the construction industry, ESS has benefited from municipal and provincial social-procurement programs including community-benefit agreements that require the hiring of local residents and groups facing severe employment barriers and social exclusion. In essence, ESS functions as the labour provider in agreements between the organizational purchasers interested in hiring those who are marginalized and private-sector contractors constructing infrastructure projects for governments. The case shows that arrangements such as community-benefit agreements have contributed significantly to ESS's financial and social bottom line, and these benefits would not have materialized if ESS had not spent years fostering its relationship with developers and contractors.

Lastly, Ever Green Recycling, another recycling social enterprise, operates in St. John's, Newfoundland and Labrador. Although Ever Green has won service contracts through procurement tendering, as the case explains, it "largely attributes its successful acquisition of contracts to relationship building."

The cases in part 2 all illustrate the importance of relationship building. Although the social enterprises all possess the technical competencies required to prepare procurement bids and to service large contracts, those contracts would not have been secured without champions on both the supplier and purchaser sides. In order to leverage these competencies and cultivate such champions, it is essential for social enterprises to invest in relationship building with relevant public- and private-sector stakeholders.

Guiding Questions:

1. What impact do organizational size and the goods and services the social enterprises offer have upon social procurement?
2. How is relationship building connected to social value?

3. What is the role of a champion in relationship building?
4. How is relationship building for WISEs different with public- and private-sector partners?
5. What does relationship building mean for social enterprises that are smaller than those featured in these cases?

REFERENCES

Buy Social Canada. (2018). *A guide to social procurement*. https://buy-social -canada.cdn.prismic.io/buy-social-canada%2F47fa7b64-c5f0-4661-9a00 -93a936f38dd0_bsc_socialprocurement_screen-opt.pdf

Government of Canada. (2020, January 15). *2018 Canadian collaborative procurement initiative newsletter*. https://web.archive.org/web/20191127122447/https:// www.tpsgc-pwgsc.gc.ca/app-acq/app-collaborat-procur/annuelle-update -2018-eng.html

Lupick, T. (2017). *Social procurement: State of practice*. https://sustain.ubc.ca /sites/default/files/2017-41_%20Social%20Procurement%20State%20of%20 Practice_Lupick.pdf

Muñoz, S. (2009). Social enterprise and public sector voices on procurement. *Social Enterprise Journal, 5*(1), 69–82. https://doi.org/10.1108/17508610910956417

Revington, C., Hoogendam, R., & Holeton, A. (2015). *The social procurement intermediary: The state of the art and its development within the GTHA*. Learning Enrichment Foundation. https://ccednet-rcdec.ca/en/toolbox/social -procurement-intermediary-state-art-and-its

4 BUILD Inc.

MARTY DONKERVOORT AND ART LADD

Introduction

It takes time, perseverance, and leadership to develop a successful relationship between a social enterprise and an organizational purchaser. Winnipeg's BUILD Inc., a work integrated social enterprise in the construction sector, has developed relationships with government, non-profit organizations, and private-sector businesses resulting in large contracts totalling nearly $15 million in total revenue since its establishment in 2006. The annual earned revenue has increased from $86,000 in 2006 to approximately $1.25 million in the fiscal year ending in 2018 for a compounded annual growth rate of 28 per cent. Backed by a series of champions, BUILD has been a trailblazer in developing social procurement relationships with government, which account for approximately 93 per cent of all BUILD's earned revenue since its creation in 2006. BUILD's success has been recognized with numerous awards including ScotiaBank's EcoLiving Green Employer (2011), Apprenticeship Manitoba's Employer of the Year (2013), Winnipeg Chamber of Commerce's Spirit of Winnipeg Award (2015 and 2020), and Manitoba Chambers of Commerce's Business Award (Finalist 2018).

Mission

BUILD – which stands for Building Urban Industries for Local Development – is a non-share capital (or non-profit) corporation without charitable status, whose mission is to empower people facing multiple barriers to employment by providing training and employment opportunities. These barriers can include criminal records, low levels of formal education, little or no work experience, and the lack of official identification such as a driver's licence or bank account. Some of

BUILD's trainees have experience with the child welfare system, either having aged out of care themselves or having their children in custody of the system. For BUILD's participants, one of the most serious barriers to employment stems from systemic racism towards Indigenous Peoples and the intergenerational impacts of colonization and residential schools.

Almost all of BUILD's trainees are Indigenous, indicative of how that population disproportionally experience barriers to employment. BUILD works with its trainees to overcome these barriers through a six-month (or 910 hours) training program covering both classroom and on-the-job learning. Participants in the program earn a wage and are provided with a wide range of skills training. The training includes technical skills, such as safety certifications and the use of different tools in the construction trades. Essential skills such as numeracy and literacy tutoring are provided, particularly trades math, where trainees master their skills with tape measures, fractions, and arithmetic. The BUILD program also embeds interpersonal skills and life skills including nutrition, money management, healthy relationships, maintaining stable housing, and managing mental health and addictions, among other topics. Supported by skills instructors, academic tutors, and a case coordinator, trainees spend two months in the classroom and the workshop learning these different skills, preparing them for many challenges they will encounter in work and life. After completing two months of intensive training, trainees are ready to join BUILD's construction crews on job sites. Over the next four months, trainees work under BUILD's skilled tradespeople, who lead them through different jobs and scopes of work, mentoring them along the way. BUILD recruits twenty to twenty-four new trainees every two months to replace the trainees who complete the initial two-month in-house training sessions and continue on to BUILD's construction sites.

The BUILD model is different from a conventional work practicum, which typically involves engaging a learner on small discreet projects. At BUILD, trainees are part of the crew and learn the entire scope of work, on actual worksites, for real clients, with deadlines and quality assurance mechanisms. The learning opportunities are immense, as trainees become engaged with on-the-job problem-solving while working with their mentors who often have experienced similar life circumstances or are BUILD graduates themselves. Individual crews are small, providing a desirable instructor-to-trainee ratio. Typically BUILD uses a three- or four-person crew, with a crew lead, a lead hand, and one or two trainees. If a trainee requires extra guidance on any aspect of the work, the crew lead is able to work one-on-one with the trainee while the lead hand keeps the job site moving towards completion.

As the trainees move through the six-month program, they set goals with the Training Department at BUILD, planning for future education or employment aspirations. The trainees develop their résumés, write cover letters, and do mock job interviews, all of which help them transition towards the end of their time at BUILD. To date, approximately one thousand people have completed BUILD's training program. As trainees near the end of their six-month term at BUILD, they begin looking for work. Typically, they look for work in the open market, through many of BUILD's social-enterprise partners, or through employers who subcontract work to BUILD. The last option listed is becoming increasingly successful for trainees. When private-sector construction companies subcontract work to BUILD, trainees have the opportunity to showcase their attendance, work ethic, and willingness to learn directly to the foreman.

History

In the fall of 2005, going into the winter of 2006, Manitoba experienced a 17.1 per cent spike in the price of primary natural gas, the main source of heating in the province (The Manitoba Public Utilities Board, n.d.). This was a significant increase affecting all Manitobans; however, those already in poverty were hit hardest. In Winnipeg's inner city, where poverty was concentrated, the old and poorly insulated housing stock combined with the jump in heating prices made for a perfect storm of human misery. People living in poverty in Winnipeg's inner city were faced with even more impossible circumstances, unable to afford to heat the home in winter, pay rent, and still feed the family.

Lawrence Poirier, Executive Director of Kinew Housing, saw these impacts first-hand with his tenants and in the surrounding community. He and other members of the Indigenous community, as well as community activists including Tom Simms, executive director at Community Education Development Association, looked at possible solutions to address the cascading issues of poverty and high utility costs.

They were familiar with the success of Inner City Renovation, a Winnipeg-based social enterprise focusing on construction that had laid the groundwork for the role of social enterprises in the construction sector (Donkervoort, 2013). They were also familiar with the role played by Neechi Foods Co-op Ltd., a social enterprise that in 1990 started up a grocery store in Winnipeg's North End to provide sustainable, meaningful jobs for individuals from the local Indigenous community and to offer a healthy selection of food at affordable prices.

Around the same time, Shaun Loney, director of Energy Policy in the provincial government's Department of Science, Technology, Energy, and Mines had been working with his team to develop policy addressing the same issue. Their work led to the introduction of Bill 11 in 2006, which required Manitoba Hydro to set aside a percentage of its profits from export sales to establish a fund for the reduction of energy consumption through retrofitting in low-income communities.

In the spirit of entrepreneurialism, these individuals conceived an innovative way to address the crisis. Together, they created a contractor enterprise to insulate these inner-city homes and hire the people who lived there to do the work. In July 2006, Building Urban Industries for Local Development (BUILD) was incorporated as a non-profit social enterprise and began changing the employment and energy-consumption landscape in Winnipeg's inner city.

BUILD's first board of directors included several members from Winnipeg's Indigenous community, including Jerry Woods (chair of the Manitoba Human Rights Commission) and Lawrence Poirier (executive director of Kinew Housing). Knowing that private-sector general contractors were reluctant to work in their neighbourhoods mainly due to safety concerns and low profit margins, they created BUILD to complete the insulation work others were unwilling to do.

In the beginning, BUILD's staff consisted of two community-housing workers, a social-support staffer, a carpenter, and a small number of trainees. They operated out of a two-room shared office space in the same building as Kinew Housing at 424 Logan Avenue, in Winnipeg's inner city.

Around the same time, a number of public and private partners including the province, Manitoba Hydro (a provincial crown corporation), Winnipeg Partnership Agreement (a federal-provincial-municipal funding agreement), and Winnipeg Foundation (a community foundation) funded the Centennial Project[1] to address a variety of inner-city issues, such as energy-saving initiatives. The pilot program from the Centennial Project involved energy-saving retrofits in 120 Centennial neighbourhood homes. BUILD was hired by individual homeowners

---

1 In 1967, as Canada marked its centennial of confederation, the federal government funded a multitude of construction projects across the country, including housing projects in Winnipeg, which by 2005 were in serious need of repair and retrofit (Sanderson, 2016).

to complete the insulation retrofits on a number of these homes. Homeowners were then compensated by the Centennial Project partners.

Another facet of the Centennial Project, the Centennial Fencing Project, saw the City of Winnipeg compensate property owners to repair and build fences on residential properties. BUILD was hired by individual homeowners to do the work. Kinew Housing also took advantage of this city-funded initiative and hired BUILD to install fencing for their residential housing units. The Centennial Project led the way for BUILD's future relationships with Manitoba Housing and Manitoba Hydro.

Between 2006 and 2008, BUILD retrofitted two hundred homes in the inner city. Most of their early projects were installing water-saving devices like shower heads and aerators, as well as insulating basements and attics. The work was made possible by Manitoba Hydro's Lower Income Energy Efficiency Program (LIEEP), a precursor to the Power Smart Affordable Energy Program (AEP). Labour in those early days was subsidized primarily by grants from government. Most of this initial energy-saving-related work was completed in residences operated by Manitoba Housing.

In BUILD's early years, the organization was managed by the volunteer board along with a project manager who provided leadership to the construction crews. There was no executive director, and the enterprise struggled to find its feet. By 2008, a major development occurred that would significantly change BUILD's future. Shaun Loney, who had been working with the Manitoba Government, was hired as BUILD's first executive director. Making the argument that government is the financial beneficiary of the work done by non-profit organizations like BUILD, Loney negotiated a successful secondment from the province to BUILD. This hiring proved to be an important milestone in BUILD's history and significantly propelled the organization forward. Based on the experience gained from the Centennial Project, BUILD shifted its focus to enter into similar work with other community-renewal corporations in the city. BUILD's training program component became more robust, providing numeracy tutoring and a wide range of health and safety trades training. In addition to the training enhancements, BUILD also secured a wide variety of new work and formed new partnerships.

Shortly after Loney started as executive director, BUILD played a critical role in the establishment of Manitoba Green Retrofit (MGR), another social enterprise in the construction sector. Since BUILD's existing funding agreements prevented it from pursuing work in the private sector, BUILD created MGR as a new non-profit social enterprise that would not be dependent on government funding and thus not restricted by funding agreements. One of BUILD's senior managers became MGR's general manager; MGR also hired some of BUILD's training program graduates. Since the establishment of MGR in 2011, the funding-related restrictions posed by government have changed and both enterprises have since been able to pursue contracts in the private sector while receiving government funding.

Not long afterwards, BUILD formed a partnership with MGR and Pollock's Hardware, a consumer co-op, to jointly purchase an old warehouse in the north end of Winnipeg. BUILD was hired by the newly constituted partnership to renovate the space for a new social enterprise centre that was to act as a hub for a number of social enterprises and community non-profit organizations. At the same time, BUILD worked with Pollock's Hardware to purchase low-flush toilets and other building products – a good example of a social enterprise leveraging its purchase power to support another social-economy organization. This relationship was mutually beneficial until the demand for toilets decreased and Pollock's was unable to sustain its wholesale operations.

Key Customers

Even after the completion of the Centennial Project, BUILD continued its fruitful relationship with Manitoba Hydro and developed new purchasing relationships with Manitoba Housing as well as private-sector enterprises such as Transcona Roofing Ltd. and community non-profit organizations like Kanata Housing Corp. Each of these relationships is presented in this section.

Manitoba Housing

Manitoba Housing is a division of the province's Department of Families, responsible for a wide range of subsidized housing throughout the province. It partners with other government agencies, community organizations, and non-profit groups to provide housing to individuals and families who are not able to find affordable, adequate, or suitable housing in the private market. By embracing a service-oriented approach, Manitoba Housing is working toward more positive relationships with its tenants, community residents, and stakeholders.

Manitoba Housing was keen to work in partnership with social enterprises to reduce both poverty and energy consumption. As the largest landlord in the province, Manitoba Housing was interested in reducing energy consumption since many utility bills were paid through social assistance programs, ultimately funded by taxpayers.

BUILD's relationship with Manitoba Housing started in 2006 and remained at the time of writing. In those thirteen years, Manitoba Housing purchased more than $12 million in services. In the beginning, the volume of purchasing was slow, totalling less than $3,000 in the first two years. However, it increased steadily thereafter, peaking at more than $2.5 million in 2013. Since then, the amount Manitoba Housing spent with BUILD has declined to just over $800,000 in 2018. Two factors contributed to the gradual increase to 2013. The first was the purchase and installation of low-flush toilets. Once this initiative came to an end, purchasing levels dropped by more than a million dollars over the next year. By 2014, most of the purchasing was related to apartment turnovers.

The second factor took place in 2009, shortly after then minister of Housing Kerri Irvin-Ross had taken significant interest in pursuing opportunities for social enterprises and started directing Manitoba Housing to pursue opportunities with social enterprises. By 2011, BUILD's revenue from Manitoba Housing purchases more than doubled from 2010; and by 2013, it doubled again to $2.5 million. BUILD's success took champions at both BUILD and Manitoba Housing to consummate the procurement relationship. Historical contract values between BUILD and Manitoba Housing are documented as a supplement at the end of this case.

After some initial growing pains related to quality, pricing, and delivery times, BUILD now enjoys an "easy and beneficial" relationship with Manitoba Housing, according to Michael Burrows, director of Social Enterprise Initiative at Manitoba Housing. In consultation with BUILD and other social enterprises in the construction sector, Manitoba Housing works with a standard price cost book for the various components involved in the repair of rental housing units between renters. This has streamlined the relationship with social enterprises as the contract for each unit is based on an agreed-upon price, which, in turn, is based on the components documented in a scope of work prepared by Manitoba Housing. The introduction of this standard price cost book eliminated the tendering for social enterprises. At the time of writing, Manitoba Housing issued purchase orders for one to five units at a time to BUILD based on the predetermined contractual price. The average cost for a standard suite turnover is between $3,000 and $5,000, and completion is expected within thirty days. Units requiring more substantial work can cost as much as $30,000, with a longer completion date.

Based on discussions and negotiations in 2013, the Manitoba government announced its Manitoba Social Enterprise Strategy Framework in 2014. The framework made a commitment for Manitoba Housing to double its then current annual investment in social procurement to $10 million. It also created an intermediary at Manitoba Housing, called the Social Enterprise Initiative, to work directly with social enterprises. The use of an intermediary insulated social procurement from the organization's other procurement operations. As part of this new initiative, BUILD and Manitoba Housing signed their first Memorandum of Understanding (MOU), which specified their relationship. The MOU was renewed in 2015 and 2017. The MOU signed on 29 May 2017 established a mutually beneficial relationship for repair, maintenance, and minor renovation projects of Manitoba Housing's residential stock in the City of Winnipeg. One of the missions of the MOU states that "Together the parties enter into this MOU to improve the condition of [Manitoba Housing's] stock and create local training and economic opportunities." As such, Manitoba Housing is committed to compensating BUILD for each project according to agreed-upon contract pricing up to a maximum of $100,000 per project and up to a maximum value of $3 million over two years.

In 2015, BUILD's then executive director, Annetta Armstrong, was seconded to Manitoba Housing to assist with developing its social procurement policy. She also helped resolve some of the difficulties in the procurement relationship between Manitoba Housing and other social enterprises. In addition to BUILD and MGR (operating as Purpose Construction), Manitoba Housing started procurement relationships with two other Winnipeg-based social enterprises and one Brandon-based social enterprise in the construction sector: Genesis Property Services, North End Community Renewal Corporation (NECRC), and Brandon Energy Efficiency Program. Manitoba Housing is responsible for approximately $4 to 5 million of annual social procurement with the five social enterprises in Manitoba mentioned above. This amount represents approximately 50 per cent of its $10 million budget for unit turnover renovations and approximately 5 per cent of Manitoba Housing's annual budget. Purchase orders are issued monthly to each of the social enterprises based on their location and capacity.

Manitoba Housing is extremely satisfied with its procurement relationship with BUILD as well as the other social enterprises. It is pleased that some of BUILD's employees are tenants in Manitoba Housing units and that BUILD is part of removing long-term barriers to employment for residents in inner-city, low-income neighbourhoods.

Manitoba Hydro

Manitoba Hydro is the electric power and natural gas utility in the province of Manitoba, Canada. Founded in 1961, it is a provincial Crown corporation, governed by the Manitoba Hydro-Electric Board and the Manitoba Hydro Act. Manitoba Hydro started its relationship with BUILD in 2006, its first year of operation. In those early years, Manitoba Hydro's purchases exceeded those of Manitoba Housing. In the first year (fiscal year ending in 2007) BUILD earned more than $83,000 from Manitoba Hydro. Revenue from Manitoba Hydro increased annually until 2011–13 when there was little or no revenue. It picked up again in 2015 and has continued to grow to more than $265,000 in fiscal year end 2018. Since BUILD's start-up, Manitoba Hydro has purchased services totalling nearly $2 million.

From the outset in 2006, the relationship was different from that with Manitoba Housing. The relationship started with a pilot project in Winnipeg's Centennial neighbourhood where BUILD completed energy retrofits for two hundred houses. Upon completion of this project, Manitoba Hydro developed a partnership with NECRC to promote energy efficiency upgrades in the local community. Once a homeowner's application to the Power Smart Program was approved, they could choose a service provider. BUILD was well known in the community and recommended by NECRC. Once picked by a homeowner, BUILD would complete the work and invoice Manitoba Hydro. Over the years, pricing the work varied between a predetermined fixed price and a negotiated price. In this way, although Manitoba Hydro pays the invoices, the purchasing decision is actually made by the individual homeowner or housing organization.

Through this relationship, BUILD was completing work for Manitoba Hydro's Lower Income Energy Efficiency Program (LIEEP), which later developed into the PowerSmart Affordable Energy Program (AEP) to increase energy efficiency by better insulating basements and attics (Loney, 2012). The Manitoba Hydro energy saving programs also provided homeowners with free water-saving shower heads and aerators, which were installed by BUILD while also installing low-flush toilets. The relationship with Manitoba Hydro resulted in lower utility bills for inner city residents, created employment for inner-city residents, and provided BUILD with a revenue stream.

Manitoba Hydro developed relationships with other social enterprises including Manitoba Green Retrofit (MGR, now Purpose Construction). This relationship saw Manitoba Hydro pay the upfront costs of the energy retrofits on homeowner properties to MGR and recover their costs by charging homeowners a repayment over time on their utility bills. Energy savings resulting from the energy retrofits enabled homeowners to repay the upfront costs to Manitoba Hydro and once repaid, homeowners were able to enjoy the savings from reduced utility costs.

The Manitoba government is restructuring some its departments and it is anticipated that the Affordable Energy Programs previously administered by Manitoba Hydro will move to a newly created Crown corporation called Efficiency Manitoba.

Transcona Roofing Ltd.

Based in Winnipeg, Transcona Roofing Ltd. is a for-profit business specialized in the installation of new roofing and architectural cladding as well as the service and maintenance of roofing for industrial, commercial, and residential customers. Transcona Roofing employs more than one hundred workers in peak season. Trancona's relationship with BUILD began in 2017, when Art Ladd, BUILD's executive director at the time, approached Transcona. After a few trial projects, Transcona was impressed and developed a purchasing relationship with BUILD. In fact, Transcona was so impressed with BUILD's employees that it started hiring graduates from the BUILD training program. This turned out to be a very successful strategy for Transcona since the company was able to test them out and then hire them if there was a mutual interest. It was a solution for Transcona's chronic labour shortages and the high labour turnover rate in the industry, which had consequently led to high costs for training. Since 2017, Transcona has hired eleven BUILD graduates. Richard Marchetti, president of Transcona says, "We have had a better-than-expected experience with BUILD graduates than with our own labour practices resulting in a higher success rate and workers with better work ethic and ultimately reduced training costs due to their work experience in the BUILD program." Transcona employees start at $17.50 per hour ($36,400 annual income), which is increased to $25 per hour ($52,000 annual income) after approximately two thousand hours with the company. Employees also get a health benefit package after six months of employment and are able to participate in the company's pension program.

The relationship with Transcona has been very beneficial to BUILD because it not only provides work and income for BUILD (approximately $100,000 in 2017–2019) but it also offers excellent employment opportunities to trainees graduating from BUILD's training program.

Marchetti commented, "The relationship with BUILD to secure labour on a one-off basis has worked out very well to fill the peak demands at Transcona Roofing."

Kanata Housing Corporation

Kanata Housing Corporation is an Indigenous non-profit community housing organization that provides non-profit rental housing specifically for families of the Indigenous community. It has eighty-six rental units in its housing portfolio in Winnipeg. BUILD started working with Kanata in May 2014, providing insulation services for energy efficiency upgrades. By 2016, the relationship expanded to include renovation services for unit turnovers similar to the service BUILD provides to Manitoba Housing. BUILD's earned revenue from Kanata in 2018 was approximately $113,000, and the total earned revenue with Kanata since 2014 is $285,000.

The relationship with Kanata is slightly different from that with Manitoba Housing. Kanata provides a scope of work for the unit, and BUILD submits a quote. Price is not the only consideration. Kanata is interested in working with BUILD because of BUILD's social mission. Similar to Manitoba Housing, some of Kanata's renters are BUILD employees, which Kanata sees as a positive reason to support BUILD. The relationship with BUILD is described as "very good and positive" by Gord Meiklejohn, Kanata's general manager.

Summary: Lessons Learned

The success experienced by BUILD in social procurement offers invaluable lessons and important insights into the challenges and opportunities facing social enterprises trying to develop procurement/purchasing relationships.

1. Relationship building with governments takes time and patience. BUILD spent many years cultivating a successful procurement relationship with Manitoba Housing. Still, after thirteen years of a successful procurement relationship with BUILD, Manitoba Housing remains the only Manitoba government department with a social procurement policy and only one of the few provincial and federal departments with social procurement experience. Although there are some examples of successful procurement relationships with municipal governments across Canada, BUILD has still not

been able to establish a formal social procurement relationship with the City of Winnipeg. On 13 July 2022, after years of relationship building, Winnipeg city council adopted the introduction of a sustainable procurement action plan.

2. Champions who believe in the social mission at both the social enterprise and the organizational purchaser are critical. Early champions at BUILD included Lawrence Poirier (Kinew Housing) and Jerry Woods (chair of the Manitoba Human Rights Commission), both of whom are BUILD's founding board members, as well as Shaun Loney, BUILD's first executive director and Annetta Armstrong, who seconded to Manitoba Housing when she was BUILD's executive director. Each of the organizational purchasers also had champions who supported relationships with social enterprises. Of particular interest is Shaun Loney's role while still in government. His connections and influence were critical to BUILD's early development.

3. Social enterprises as a sector need critical mass to develop procurement relationships with governments. The fact that there are four social enterprises in Manitoba that can provide construction services has contributed to Manitoba Housing's social procurement strategy. If Manitoba only had one or two small social enterprises, it would be much more difficult to establish procurement relationships with the government. For governments to develop social procurement policies and maintain procurement relationships with social enterprises, there need to be enough social enterprises to work with the governments.

4. Policies at government procurement departments contribute to the development of relationships with social enterprises. Since champions move on and departmental staff change, social enterprises need to rely on policies so that social procurement is not dependent on one or two individuals. Manitoba Housing has developed social procurement policies and has entered into MOUs with BUILD as well as other social enterprises as suppliers, providing stability to both suppliers and organizational purchasers.

5. Diversifying and expanding the customer base is difficult for social enterprises. BUILD has been heavily dependent on two organizational purchasers – i.e., Manitoba Housing and Manitoba Hydro, who together have accounted for 93 per cent of all BUILD's earned revenue since the beginning. Part of the reason is that BUILD provides significant training to its employees, which limits the type of construction projects it can take on. The work for Manitoba Housing

and Manitoba Hydro is repetitive in nature and thus fits well with BUILD's training program. Organizational purchasers need to understand how best to package contracts that would fit well with social enterprises.

6. Price is an important factor in the purchasing decision. The importance of price, however, varies between social procurement and social purchasing. Price may be less important to governments if they assess a net benefit resulting from reduced social costs such as policing, incarceration, housing, and medical services.

7. Most non-profit social enterprises providing local employment and training require grant funding in order to balance their budgets. Earned revenue alone is not sufficient to sustain them. This is true for BUILD, as the organization has received grants from various levels of government. Grant funding can be justified by Social Return on Investment (SROI) associated with social enterprises. In BUILD's case, every dollar spent by Manitoba Housing generated a return of $2.23 (Simpact Strategy Group, 2016).

REFERENCES

Donkervoort, M. (2013). *Inner city renovation: How a social enterprise changes lives and communities*. Fernwood Publishing.

Loney, S. (2012). *BUILD prosperity: Energizing Manitoba's local economy*. BUILD Inc.

The Manitoba Public Utilities Board (n.d.). *Primary gas – Quarterly rates*. http://www.pubmanitoba.ca/v1/regulated-utilities/natural-gas/rates/s_supply.html

Sanderson, B. (2016, June 29). 50 years on, centennial buildings still important symbols. *CBC News*. https://www.cbc.ca/news/canada/centennial-buildings-50th-anniversary-1.3654283

Simpact Strategy Group. (2016). *The social return on investment of four social enterprises in Manitoba*. https://ccednet-rcdec.ca/sites/ccednet-rcdec.ca/files/mbh_final_report_draft_jan_19v2.pdf

OTHER SOURCES

Interviews with BUILD, Manitoba Housing, Manitoba Hydro, Transcona Roofing Ltd., and Kanata Housing Corporation.

BUILD, https://buildinc.ca/

SUPPLEMENTAL INFORMATION

Revenue by Customer (2007–18): Build

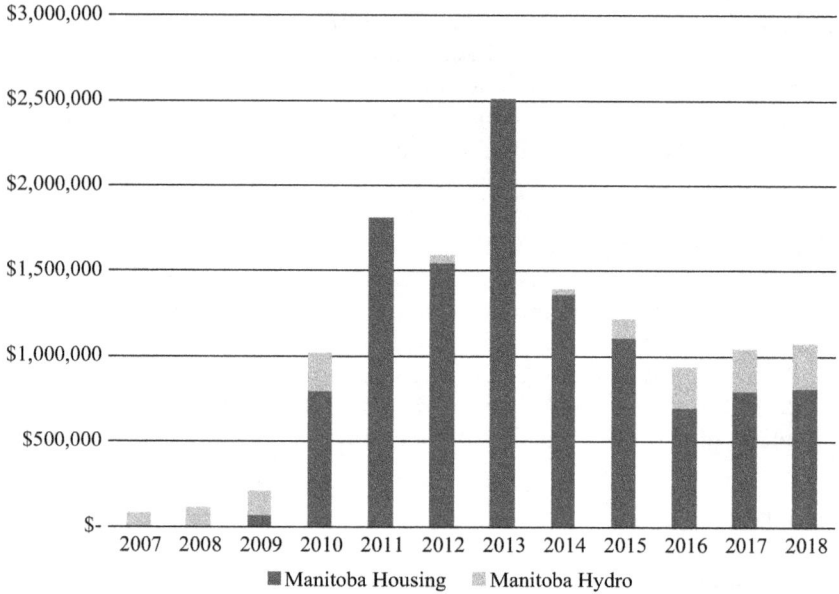

■ Manitoba Housing   ▨ Manitoba Hydro

5 SARCAN Recycling: A Division of SARC

ANDREA CHAN

Introduction

"Crushing it since 1988": SARCAN is a recycling social enterprise with a mandate to provide employment opportunities for people living with disabilities across the province of Saskatchewan (SARCAN, 2018). Since its inception, SARCAN has maintained a special relationship with the Saskatchewan government; it holds an exclusive contract with the province to administer its recycling program of ready-to-serve, non-refillable beverage containers. SARCAN operates with a hybrid workforce, where in 2018 66 per cent of its more than seven hundred employees identified with disability or had been in social assistance programs prior to joining the social enterprise. With an annual revenue of almost $38 million in 2017/2018, SARCAN is an anomaly among social enterprises across Canada, for both its size of operation as well as its long-standing procurement arrangement with a government that has generated tremendous economic, social, and environmental value in the community. Similar to another case in this collection – BUILD – SARCAN is of a significant size and its primary source of revenue is through service contracts with the government. This case presents an overview of SARCAN's origin story and its current operations (including its employment program and environmental impact) and a discussion on the challenges of bidding for procurement in more recent years. The case also explores the implications of having government revenue (albeit through contracts, not grants) as the primary revenue source for any social enterprise.

Parent Organization

SARCAN is a social enterprise of SARC, a charitable non-profit organization with ninety-plus member agencies that provide assistance to people experiencing disability. The member agencies of SARC are direct service providers in the community, offering a range of assistance including housing, vocational, volunteer, and recreational programs. SARC as the umbrella organization supports its members through sectoral advocacy, networking opportunities, organizational development, and consultancy in areas including human resources, labour relations, and facility planning. Furthermore, SARC administers pension and benefits plans for SARCAN and its other member organizations in the community. As the parent organization, SARC also contributes personnel, space, and financial support towards SARCAN's operation.

A Win-Win Opportunity

In Saskatchewan in the mid-1980s, litter and debris (including discarded bottles in ditches and alongside highways) had become a public nuisance. With increased sales and production of beverages in non-refillable containers, the province had to formulate a plan in anticipation of the waste increase. The province decided upon a strategy that would address two concerns with one policy, modelling their efforts on similar affirmative business models found in other jurisdictions. A recycling depot operated by agencies that provide employment and job training to marginalized people would address two issues: the Ministry of Social Services' need to support individuals facing barriers to employment and the strain felt by the Ministry of the Environment's under-equipped recycling system.

SARC's expansive network of member agencies was a vital advantage for creating a province-wide recycling system; in 1988, SARCAN was awarded the provincial contract to create and administer a recycling operation for aluminum cans. The Ministry of the Environment would retain exclusive rights to determine locations for the depots based on population and geography, the types of beverage containers collected, and the amount of the refundable deposit fee on containers paid at the point of purchase. With its member agencies and the Ministry of Social Services, SARC mapped out depot locations with members that indicated an interest in being a part of the business; where there were geographic gaps in coverage, SARC would directly operate the depots through its newly developed social enterprise, SARCAN.

Operations

SARCAN was launched in 1988 with thirty-two drop-off depots across the province, offering five cents for every aluminum can dropped off for deposit return. Over the years, the contract with the province expanded to include all ready-to-serve beverage containers as part of its deposit-return program. SARCAN itself has also grown to include other streams of services at its depots, including the collection of refillable beer bottles, leftover household paint, and end-of-life electronics through negotiated contracts with paint and electronics manufacturers and retailers.

Currently present in sixty-five communities, SARCAN directly operates thirty of its seventy-two depots. The other forty-two depots are run by SARC's member agencies through a franchise arrangement, in which SARCAN covers the expenses incurred by each depot (e.g., wages and rent). SARCAN oversees the collection and operation of the entire social enterprise and provides management services to all depots (i.e., its own as well as all the franchises). SARCAN is also in charge of the logistics of transporting and processing all collected material at its two plants in Regina and Saskatoon, getting the processed material to the end market for recycled material, and ensuring compliance of all contract requirements with the Ministry of the Environment.

Financial Position

In fiscal year ending 2018, SARCAN's revenue from its legislated program (i.e., handling of beverage containers that are legislated by the Ministry of the Environment) totalled $37 million. In addition, revenue from its non-legislated program (i.e., handling of used paint and electronics) accounted for just over $1 million. The net income (revenue less expenditure) from SARCAN's combined recycling programs was approximately $3 million for the same year.

SARCAN's primary revenue source is through activities under contract with the Ministry of the Environment. For the fiscal year 2013–14, the majority of SARCAN's total revenue came from the legislated program (73 per cent), with salvage sales accounting for 25.5 per cent, and other revenue for the remaining 1.5 per cent. The Ministry of the Environment funds the program primarily through the non-refundable environmental handling charge.

Environmental Impact

In its 2017–18 Annual Report, SARCAN boasts an overall annual return rate of approximately 85 per cent for all non-refillable beverage containers sold in the province and 7.5 billion containers recycled in total since the beginning of operations in 1998. Since 2011, SARCAN has collected forty-nine million pounds of materials thus diverting them from landfill. Each year, its recycling programs result in greenhouse gas emissions savings (57,137 metric tonnes) and energy conservation (887,319 BTU) that according to SARCAN's reporting, are the equivalent to taking more than 12,000 cars off the road and powering more than 8,000 homes, respectively.

Supported Employment

In order to provide meaningful employment to people living with disabilities, SARCAN provides competitive wages and adheres to a supported-employment model that tailors wraparound support to suit individual employees. For most employees, this involves a person-centred approach focused on helping the individuals succeed in their work through training, skill development, coaching, and mentoring. For some employees, they are best accommodated with a job coach their entire time at work. For others, they meet with their support person once a month as a check-in to ensure well-being at work. Supervisory staff members also receive training that would allow them to best support their team (e.g., communication in accessible language, sign language where a team member has hearing impairment).

People-Focused Marketing

Compared to some of the social enterprises that participated in the survey discussed in chapter 3, SARCAN has a sophisticated marketing program reflective of the size and complexity of its operations. Although it is the exclusive provider of deposit return on non-refillable beverage containers in the province, SARCAN's annual return rate of 85 per cent means the remaining 15 per cent represents opportunity for new customers. As part of its annual market survey, SARCAN solicits feedback and perception of the organization's three pillars: social responsibility, environmental sustainability, and community building. Consistently, survey respondents indicate that social responsibility and employment opportunities through SARCAN are the primary motivations for their support of the depots above other considerations (e.g., deposit-return fees). Based on its own research, SARCAN's social mandate continues to be a central feature in all its marketing. Furthermore, it has made a conscious decision to not use stock photos of actors but actual photos of employees in all of its advertising and annual reports. The manager at SARCAN points out that

> We try and show the diversity of our organization, but we definitely put people experiencing disability to the forefront, even though you may not

be able to tell. It's just something that's important to us. And [market] testing wise, that's what our customers are saying. That's what makes us unique and special.

Staff members are also continuously consulted through organizational surveys for their feedback on customer relations. As the manager explains,

> We have some pretty in-depth communication with our staff, because we know that our staff are not only our biggest selling point, but also our best advocate. So, we're continuously asking them to get a pulse on what's going on in the community. Share frustrations. What can we do to better communicate with customers? We're trying not to be as top-down, so with our ads too we pitch ideas to staff. We come up with concepts for in-depot video display advertising, which is our captive audience advertising. We do user-generated content there, so (we ask) "what do you think customers want to see?"

SARC's Other Ventures and Procurement Experiences

Until recently, SARC operated other social enterprises in addition to SARCAN. One of SARC's other longest running businesses was a marketing department that supported the businesses of its member agencies. For the agencies that ran training workshops and produced goods such as wood products, SARC would assist in bringing the products to markets across the province, using the recycling system as logistics to transport products from agencies to warehouses. Although SARC was able to provide members with a cost-effective shipping system, other issues emerged. Consequently, the venture became too difficult to sustain when SARC had to address the need for additional funding to cover the salary of the coordinator who oversaw the business and other external factors such as increasing lumber prices and changing consumer practices. SARC decided to redirect its efforts to provide other support services that would better serve its member agencies.

While it was in operation, the marketing department had the responsibility of supporting member agencies in their effort to submit joint proposals in response to provincial tenders. The idea to pool the resources of smaller social enterprises by forming consortia to bid on tenders is well-understood (Muñoz, 2009; Revington et al., 2015). However, the member agencies are competitive with each other in the market, and this made it difficult for SARC as an umbrella organization to assist one group of member agencies when another group was also bidding for the same contract. As an umbrella agency, "we took the approach of making sure the entire sector is healthy, as opposed to [having] individual agency pitting against agencies," the manager explains.

Furthermore, the overall bidding experience at the time suggests that the social value through procurement was not broadly recognized. Organizational purchasers including the provincial government came across as predominately price sensitive and did not always recognize the social benefits of purchasing from the member agencies of SARC, especially when the purchasers could instead outsource to cheaper vendors. Bidding was an especially difficult task for SARC since there was no in-house expertise on (social) procurement within the organization.

An Exception in the Field

In a 2013 Canadian environmental scan of social enterprises that are mission driven to provide employment or training to people with intellectual or developmental disabilities, recycling was the most common business activity of the sixty-one businesses identified (Lysaght, Krupa, & Bedore, 2014). But even within this group, SARCAN remains a distant outlier considering the magnitude of its staff size and annual revenue.

Alongside the case of BUILD in this part of the book, the experiences of SARCAN demonstrate that the initiative on the part of the Saskatchewan government in awarding that initial contract to SARC/SARCAN underscores the importance of decisive and systematic action on the part of the government if successful procurement arrangements with social enterprises are to be forged. SARCAN as a social enterprise had been established in order to take on a specific government contract. This is precisely why SARC's more recent attempts at government procurement stand in stark contrast to the concerted, collaborative effort from the province and the community that went into SARCAN's founding. Interest towards green and social procurement is spreading across Canada at all levels of government, and formal policies are increasingly being implemented. In Saskatchewan, SaskPower established its Aboriginal Procurement Policy in 2012, and more recently in late 2018, the city of Saskatoon updated its purchasing policy to include social and environmental sustainability as criteria for evaluating bids that would provide "best value" (City of Saskatoon, 2018). At this time, it is not yet clear whether more procurement policy updates will emerge and the extent to which these policies will lead to leveraging procurement for social and environmental value in the community.

Conclusion

The concentration of SARCAN's revenue through a single contract with the Ministry of the Environment is something important to consider. Resource dependence theory suggests that a non-profit organization's pursuits and maintenance of its resources hold large influence over its behaviour, the implication being that an organization's autonomy is limited by its financial viability for survival. Hence, non-profit organizations need to diversify their revenue strategies (e.g., seeking donations, applying for government grants, undertaking commercial activity) in order to manage resource dependency or over-reliance on any single revenue stream (Froelich, 1999). Technically, commercial service contracts with the government (i.e., [social] procurement) offer an alternative to the traditional reliance on government grants of many non-profit organizations. If (social) procurement makes government spending on goods that also add social value more palatable to people who ordinarily object to public spending on support for vulnerable populations, then perhaps all the better. However, it is important to acknowledge that the overall reliance on government money still requires a full discussion on issues affecting the well-being and sustainability of social enterprises.

Through extensive relationship building, both SARCAN and BUILD have developed their organizations and then diversified their revenue strategy from grants to commercial activity, even though the revenue source remains one and the same (i.e., governments). In the case of SARCAN, it has expanded its business with its non-legislated recycling program, which at this time remains only a fraction of its overall revenue.

Lessons Learned

1. Consider your organization's unique assets when deciding which social enterprise opportunities to pursue. SARC's network of member organizations across Saskatchewan was an important advantage to a province-wide recycling program start-up.
2. Champions on both the side of the purchaser and the seller are needed to sustain a long-term relationship through political, socio-economic, and organizational-level changes.
3. Social enterprises may not be the best solution to social/economic value creation in all instances. It is challenging for organizations to frankly evaluate the viability of their social enterprises. Changing markets, funding challenges, and broader sector well-being all factored into the assessment that led SARC to close its marketing social enterprise and redirect its efforts to support its member agencies and communities in other ways.

REFERENCES

City of Saskatoon. (2018, December). *Purchasing policy C02-C45*. https://www
.saskatoon.ca/sites/default/files/documents/new_purchasing_policy_c02
-045.pdf

Froelich, K.A. (1999). Diversification of revenue strategies: Evolving resource
dependence in nonprofit organizations. *Nonprofit and Voluntary Sector
Quarterly, 28*(3), 246–68. https://doi.org/10.1177/0899764099283002

Lysaght, R., Krupa, T., & Bedore, M. (2014, April). *Social enterprise as an
employment option for adults with intellectual and developmental disabilities.*
https://www.mapsresearch.ca/wp-content/uploads/2016/01/Social
-Business-in-IDD_Environmental-Scan.pdf

Muñoz, S. (2009). Social enterprise and public sector voices on procurement. *Social
Enterprise Journal, 5*(1), 69–82. https://doi.org/10.1108/17508610910956417

Revington, C., Hoogendam, R., & Holeton, A. (2015). *The social procurement
intermediary: The state of the art and its development within the GTHA*. Learning
Enrichment Foundation. https://ccednet-rcdec.ca/en/toolbox/social
-procurement-intermediary-state-art-and-its

Smith, S. (2018, July). *The SARCAN story – Crushing it since 1998*. SARC. https://
www.sarcsarcan.ca/2018/07/12/the-sarcan-story-crushing-it-since-1988/

OTHER SOURCES

Interviews with SARCAN.
SARCAN, https://www.sarcan.ca/
SARC, https://www.sarcsarcan.ca/home/
SARC – Annual Report 2013–2014.
SARC – Annual Report 2017–2018.

6 Ever Green Recycling

YASMIN HARIRI

Introduction

The case of Ever Green Recycling provides an example of the importance of relationship building in social enterprises engaging in long-term and continued social procurement and purchasing in Canada. Ever Green Recycling is a bottles and materials recycling corporation located in St. John's, Newfoundland & Labrador. It operates four beverage recycling depots and is one of the largest recyclers of beverage containers in the province. Ever Green is managed by Mike Wadden, the organization's current president and chief executive officer (CEO); he has been with the company since 2003. The company has just under sixty employees and generates $4 million in annual revenue. Ever Green's long-term relationship with the province's largest health authority (Eastern Health) has been a critical support in their nascency, growth, and development.

Social and Environmental Mission

Ever Green's mission is twofold. First, it is concerned with assisting individuals experiencing chronic mental health problems and addictions by providing access to meaningful employment as part of their plan to enter or re-enter the workforce. This social mission, however, is not widely promoted because those employed at Ever Green are sensitive to being exposed as having mental health and addiction challenges. Second, its better-known environmental mission is to reduce waste going to the landfill through recycling a variety of materials and assisting companies to develop their recycling programs.

Recycling in Newfoundland & Labrador

In 1996, the Government of Newfoundland & Labrador established the Multi-Materials Stewardship Board (MMSB). Its mandate is described as the following:

> MMSB derives its mandate from the Environmental Protection Act and accompanying Waste Management Regulations. MMSB is mandated through these legislative and policy instruments and guided by the Provincial Waste Management Strategy to advance sustainable waste management in Newfoundland and Labrador with a focus on waste diversion and reduction to protect the long-term health and well-being of our environment and communities. (MMSB, 2019)

In 1997, MMSB established the Used Beverage Recycling Program. Consumers are charged a beverage container deposit upon purchase of any beverage, a portion of which is refunded when consumers return the containers to a recycling facility. This recycling program created opportunities for businesses to form around the collection and recycling of these cans and bottles at MMSB-branded Green Depots (Government of Canada, 2012).

History

Ever Green began in 1993 as a clinical mental health program in partnership with Eastern Health. The aim of the program was to provide an opportunity for individuals with moderate to severe mental illness to graduate into the workforce. The program originally consisted of two parts: Green Depots specialized in containers and Mill Lane focused on furniture and textiles. It operated as a partnership between Eastern Health and Ever Green, with each providing half of the overall budget. Participants in the program received employment experience at Ever Green alongside clinical support from Eastern Health's occupational therapists (OTs). This combined approach prepared participants to enter the mainstream workforce.

Transition to a Social Enterprise

By the early 2000s, after more than a decade of collaboration, Ever Green and Eastern Health had developed a rich partnership. Both parties, however, felt that the program needed some imagination and innovation to provide a more realistic employment experience for participants.

A number of problems also had emerged, many of which were causing immense inefficiencies in the business. First, the main goal of graduating individuals into the workforce was encountering difficulties. The expectations of the program more closely resembled a sheltered workshop with leniencies in sick-day allowances, breaks, and responsibilities. As such, employees were not fully equipped to enter more demanding work situations upon graduation. Second, the program was utilizing half of the province's OTs, many of whom had to closely support program participants as they completed their work, instead of the conventional model of OTs providing support and care. Lastly, the participants were paid a stipend, rather than market wages, which prevented them from experiencing financial independence. It became clear to both organizations that the program needed improvement. By 2005, Ever Green and Eastern Health decided to reinvent the program, rethink the nature of their partnership, and transition Ever Green to become an independent social enterprise, while continuing to maintain a strong relationship.

Driving Innovation

As the president and CEO, Wadden was faced with an enormous challenge in turning Ever Green into a sustainable social enterprise essentially running independently as a business. He needed to find a way to overcome the loss of Eastern Health's $2 million contribution to Ever Green's operating budget. His first step was to launch two studies evaluating all workplace and materials handling processes in the Green Depots. These studies were supported by grants from the National Research Council Industrial Research Assistance Program (NRC-IRAP) and a team of engineers at the College of the North Atlantic. The first sixteen-week study, completed in June 2005, redefined and simplified the workflow at Ever Green from an eighteen-step operation into a twelve-step operation, making the work easier to manoeuvre for employees. The second ten-week study, completed in March 2006, built on the results of the earlier workflow analysis and provided a prototype for a new dual-sort workstation. After being tested, the new workstation, along with the simplified workflow, provided the basis for a new computerized materials management system. These collaborative studies revealed opportunities for Ever Green to improve their operation and also allowed the team to propose highly innovative solutions. These innovations have assisted the social enterprise to overcome and subsidize any productivity shortfall related to its labour force through technology and operational systems. Furthermore, they have contributed to significant shifts in operational standards and practices throughout the industry. As Wadden observes, "Sometimes, problems can send you to find solutions before everyone else. And that's what's happened here with us."

TEXTILES AND FURNITURE

Ever Green's analysis revealed that the furniture business was encountering productivity challenges: employees needed a significant amount of support from OTs to complete their tasks and those tasks were taking longer than anticipated. The analysis revealed that this work was a poor match for employees with mental health and addictions challenges, so the first decision was to let go of the furniture portion of the business. The textiles business had similar challenges, but the workforce there was more skilled and the machinery used at Ever Green was excellent. As such, Ever Green decided to contract the textiles business to a local company, trading their equipment in exchange for the retention of Ever Green's skilled workforce. Many of these individuals remain working for that company today.

BEVERAGE CONTAINER RECYCLING

The workflow studies also revealed that beverage container recycling was the most appropriate in supporting Ever Green's labour force because the work itself was repetitive. What needed to be addressed were inefficiencies in operation, not the nature of the work. For example, some of the program participants had difficulty retaining information and yet they were asked to count and reconcile the number of bottles at six different points in the work process. Further, the employees only had informal and inconsistent descriptions of tasks they needed to perform, so they had a hard time following instructions and completing tasks. In collaboration with the team of professional operations engineers, Ever Green developed an innovative IT system for bottle counting and collection and divided tasks into smaller, more achievable, and clearly defined steps.

By rethinking the operational process and incorporating IT systems to increase accountability and job-tracking, Ever Green was able increase productivity immensely without a single layoff. Since implementing the workflow changes, absentee rates decreased from 25 per cent to 3 per cent and productivity increased by 300 per cent. Tasks that twenty people used to do were now completed by five resulting in more tasks being completed by the same staffing complement. Nonetheless, even now, Ever Green still operates at a slight disadvantage compared to other non-social enterprises because the work that five people do at Ever Green would take just over three in other companies.

MATERIALS RECYCLING FACILITY

Ever Green ran a purely profit-driven business through its materials recycling program for fibre, plastics, and glass. Materials were collected largely from other businesses, baled, refined, and sold to an aftermarket for use in manufacturing new materials. While this program did not generate many employment opportunities for Ever Green's participants, the program provided a surplus to help cross-subsidize other lines of business. Ever Green decided to maintain this product offering as a means to offset productivity shortfall in its other areas of the business.

INTELLECTUAL PROPERTY

In the process of improving operations, Ever Green came up with a number of technological innovations. One example is a digital consumer interface at bottle recycling depots, which considerably simplified the drop-off process for consumers. To undertake the software development, Ever Green engaged Blue Communications, a St. John's-based firm specializing in software design. Together, they developed an IT-based platform, which, in combination with the dual-sort workstations, streamlined the entire process of sorting, counting, storing, and accounting for the empty containers and allowed for remote management of work locations (making the process less burdensome and more efficient for employees). The integration of this IT platform with back-office financial reporting systems also provided Ever Green with a reliable and verifiable tracking and accounting system, supporting its interactions with customers, suppliers, and regulators.

During these changes at Ever Green, concerns were raised about the adjustments program participants would need to make as they had to transition to a technology-heavy work environment. Wadden and his team had faith in the capacity of Ever Green's employees and found that the new systems improved the employees' experience with consistent job expectations. The simplicity and ease of these new systems eventually increased sales, allowing Ever Green to retain and transition the entire workforce to these new operational processes.

Ever Green has been able to further offset its costs through selling these innovative solutions to other businesses. Unusual for social enterprises that work with individuals who are marginalized, Ever Green holds a number of patents on its technological innovations and has sold royalties to numerous businesses, including the governments of Newfoundland & Labrador and the Northwest Territories. Its technology has since become the industry standard on the east coast of Canada in beverage recycling.

Employment

About 75 per cent of Ever Green's employees experience some form of mental illness. Prior to becoming independent, Ever Green relied heavily on Eastern Health to assist in identifying individuals who were employment ready. Eastern Health also provided case managers and close support to every individual in the program. Since becoming an independent social enterprise, Ever Green still has a relationship with Eastern Health, but also has partnered with other local organizations with a focus on assisting people with mental illness to become employment ready by offering literacy and job coaching. Some of the partner organizations include Stella Burry Community Services, Mac-Morran Community Centre, Partners for Workplace Inclusion, and the Autism Society of Newfoundland & Labrador. Once individuals have gone through partner programs, Ever Green is able to train and hire them, then support their employment. However, it has become increasingly difficult to maintain regular rosters of participants in recent years because of persistent absenteeism resulting from the lack of close support of case workers. Wadden attributes the change to the changing nature of the participant population over time. In the earlier years of Ever Green, those with mental illness were largely experiencing mental health disorders, such as anxiety, bipolar disorder, or schizophrenia. More recently, the number of individuals suffering from addiction has grown, likely leading to higher absenteeism. Despite all these challenges, Ever Green remains committed to supporting this population and continues to find innovative solutions to overcome challenges.

Ever Green's commitment goes beyond investment in its own business. For example, Ever Green recently contributed $100,000 to an annual scholarship fund with Memorial University of Newfoundland. The *Ever Green Environmental Scholarship in Social Enterprise and Mental Health in Memory of Edwin M. Drover* is intended to promote innovation and entrepreneurship in the areas of both mental health and social entrepreneurship. Wadden talks about how he hopes this scholarship will contribute to the continued development of more social enterprises to support individuals with addiction and mental health challenges.

Marketing and Advertising

Ever Green has minimal engagement in advertising and marketing. It has a website and Facebook page, but these are infrequently updated. It also has TVs in each of its depots that advertise its products. Due to the sensitive nature of the illness of its employees, Ever Green has been reluctant to promote its social mission in marketing efforts. Individuals would need to research into the company to discover how it was different from other bottle depots in the province.

Considering the potential advantages of Ever Green's social benefits, the board of directors at its most recent retreat reflected that the social context around mental health has changed significantly since the social enterprise's early years. Most notably, there is significantly less stigma towards people with mental health disorders and addictions. Ever Green feels that it is time to begin telling the stories of its employees more proactively and supporting employees to be proud of their accomplishments as a business.

Social Procurement

In 2018, Newfoundland & Labrador released a *Social Enterprise Action Plan* outlining policy objectives and action plans to support the enrichment and development of social enterprises in the province. The plan describes how social enterprises "enrich our communities by conducting business in an innovative way that furthers social, community economic, cultural and environmental goals" (Government of Newfoundland & Labrador, 2018). Among a number of goals are specific measures for increasing social procurement opportunities for social enterprises and increasing collaboration between the social enterprises and government agencies.

Wadden remarked that such a plan represents a tremendous opportunity to realize the government's aspirations to support employment-challenged workers. For example, the government may engage a social enterprise for a service that would otherwise be provided by a private-sector company. The government may recognize that, although sometimes bidding at a higher cost, social enterprises can save more money by decreasing social subsidies through meaningful employment for vulnerable populations. Wadden believes that the government needed to "de-risk" these decision-making processes for employees by recognizing the financial benefits of social subsidies.

Wadden, however, also remarks that the responsibility does not rest on the shoulders of government alone. He believes social enterprises have their own responsibility to capture the opportunity by matching the productivity of their competitors, despite the limitations they might face. To accomplish this, social enterprises can quantify their social value to help justify the procurement decisions. For example, one of the reasons Ever Green has been successful in maintaining a long-standing relationship with Eastern Health is their ability to provide benefit to populations Eastern Health is concerned about. In fact, Eastern Health has been able to quantify exactly how much strain on the health-care system is being alleviated by Ever Green's training and employment of individuals with mental illness and the subsequent support towards meaningful employment.

Social Purchasing

As Ever Green works with a vulnerable population, most employees prefer that the social mission of the business remain quiet. Therefore, Wadden believes that most individual customers remain unaware of the social mission of the business, which in some ways limits the possibilities for social purchasing. Internal industry reports also have indicated that customers in the beverage recycling industry are primarily driven by convenience and location, and not by social impact. These findings stand in contrast to SARCAN's experience (chapter 5). As Wadden explains, "We've got to do it competitively. It's not a blank cheque. We've got to be just as good if not better as our competitors."

Organizational purchasers, however, tend to be better informed about the social mission of Ever Green and are more likely to make purchasing decisions based on social impact, compared to individual customers. It is a significant part of the sales process for Ever Green to share its story with organizational purchasers and appeal to the social value that the social enterprise offers to the Newfoundland & Labrador community.

Customers

Ever Green prides itself on running a competitive business and attracting a wide range of customers through its high-quality operations, rather than its social mission. Its sales come from both organizational purchasers and individual customers (see supplemental information).

Organizational Purchasers

Ever Green's history is one of partnerships with large organizations. It has had opportunities to participate in procurement provided by both government agencies and private businesses. Sales from organizational purchasers make up 14 per cent of its total revenue. These organizational purchasers are largely buyers of recycling service contracts. Ever Green assists them to develop a recycling program and regularly retrieves recyclable materials to be processed and sold to the aftermarket. In some cases, the organizational purchasers will even receive a rebate on what these materials net in the aftermarket, depending on current market value.

Ever Green has secured contracts with organizational purchasers through formal procurement processes, such as bidding. However, it attributes its successful acquisition of contracts largely to relationship building. Ever Green's longest-standing and largest customer, Eastern Health, was established through a well-cultivated relationship. From this partnership, Ever Green has secured two additional government contracts. Ever Green has focused more on corporate organizational purchasers since it has found them easier to work with and more appreciative of its social mission.

While many of its organizational purchasers are aware of Ever Green's social mission, Wadden feels it has limited impact on their purchasing decision. He points out that the recycling business is highly competitive, operating primarily on cost and quality. As a result, Ever Green is competitive because its services are high quality and its prices are attractive.

EASTERN HEALTH

As Ever Green transitioned to a social enterprise in the early 2000s, Eastern Health made a point of finding opportunities to support Ever Green as an independent social enterprise. Primarily, this included working with Ever Green to design a comprehensive recycling program and providing Ever Green with a large percentage of Eastern Health's recyclable goods for processing and resale. Ron Johnson, vice president of Information Services and Rural Health at Eastern Health, shares that the original partnership allowed Eastern Health to intimately understand the employment opportunities that Ever Green was providing for those with mental illness. This was a strong motivating factor for Eastern Health to continue purchasing Ever Green's services and remains so to this day.

Eastern Health has a strong desire to support organizations with social missions, as Johnson explains: "In the past couple years, we are starting to see the value of social enterprise and we are seeing the value and looking for partnerships in that area." This has led Eastern Health to work with a number of large organizations in the social-economy sector, such as The Gathering Place and Voices for Youth on the East Coast as well as engaging in a collaboration with Mars Discovery District in Toronto on a social bonds project. While Eastern Health has developed a culture of seeking out opportunities to support social enterprises and other non-profit organizations, it is yet to develop a formal internal social procurement policy. With a $1.5 billion budget (accounting for 20 per cent of the provincial budget), Eastern Health is aware that its spending decisions can have a profound impact on the community and the province. This awareness has led it to more regularly seek out opportunities for social innovation and to find creative ways to partner and collaborate with social enterprises.

Individual Customers

The beverage recycling portion of Ever Green, which constitutes 86 per cent of total revenue, is largely driven by 25,000 to 30,000 individual customers. It collects thirty-eight million containers per year, estimated as 22 per cent of the provincial market. However, Wadden believes the majority of individual customers are not social purchasers because they are largely unaware of the primary social mission of Ever Green (a result of the social enterprise's effort to protect the privacy of its employees). Some are driven by a desire to contribute to environmental benefits through recycling. On the whole, however, most customers are driven by the financial return on their recyclables. As such, Ever Green has found ways to streamline and automate the process for these customers and make their quality of service more appealing than that of their competitors. One example is the automated depot systems where customers can create an account, print personalized stickers to tag their deposit bags, and receive refund information by email.

Competition

Ever Green currently only serves the province of Newfoundland & Labrador, where it competes with three to four other companies in the recycling industry. These businesses are all much larger than Ever Green. That said, Wadden estimates that Ever Green's prices are all within one to two cents per can of the other companies, making it a strong competitor. Shortfalls in its beverage recycling business are made up for in materials recycling, ensuring that Ever Green can retain its ability to provide employment to individuals who are marginalized and also operate competitively in the market.

Summary: Lessons Learned

I talk to social enterprises all the time and they think we are a charity and people are going to support us because of our mission ... I'm a reality guy, and I've been doing this thing for fifteen years. If you are not as good, if not better, than the guy next to you, customers are going to be going to the guy next door. – Mike Wadden

The case of Ever Green is in many ways a common story of social enterprises in Canada: a successful, local business struggling to compete in the broader context of the Canadian economy. Ever Green, however, has in many ways escaped the small business conundrum and made significant efforts to move into a more competitive position. What stands out as a driving force at Ever Green is its self-image. Wadden and his team do not use their status as an employer of individuals with mental health disorders and addiction as an explanation for lower productivity, but instead see it as an opportunity to drive innovation. The importance and impact of identity on the success of social enterprises is well-documented. Wry and York (2017) explore how a social enterprise's identity can have a profound impact on the logical frameworks that influence management decision-making. They describe how many social enterprises face a duality of identity that puts social and financial aims in conflict with one another. They add that individual founder identities (in particular, social entrepreneurs) greatly shape the identities of social enterprises as a whole. Smith, Knapp, Barr, Stevens, and Cannatelli (2010) also describe that many non-profit organizations that create social enterprises will face an ideological tension between their social and business missions. They explain how many social enterprises that emerge after a parent non-profit has operated for some time often face stronger ideological tensions than those formed at the same time as the parent non-profit. Ever Green, which has transitioned itself into an independent social enterprise from a governmental partnership, appears to have overcome these ideological challenges through the leadership of Wadden and his balanced financial and social identity. Although Ever Green still faces challenges to becoming more engaged in social procurement, its long-standing relationship with Eastern Health helped to bring it to the forefront of recycling – and social-enterprise development – in Newfoundland and Labrador.

A few key lessons can be gleaned from the case of Ever Green Recycling:

1. In order to reach a large scale, social enterprises may benefit from structuring and operating the same as a for-profit business. In its

earliest days, Ever Green's identity was primarily attached to its social mission. In reality, this limited the scope of impact on their social mission and held them at a small scale of operation. As Ever Green shifted to become more focused on operating as a for-profit business, the operation rapidly grew, and they discovered more efficient methods of running the business, expanding their impact on their social mission.

2. The restrictions placed on social enterprises can be seen as opportunities for innovation that competitors are not considering. Ever Green's growth and productivity can largely be attributed to its innovative posture. The innovative strategy of Ever Green has even allowed the social enterprise to identify an unusual and lucrative revenue source: intellectual property. Utilizing government grant programs and working with local universities and colleges to provide real-world work experiences is an approach that Ever Green uses to drive its innovation. It is inevitable that social enterprises will run into productivity challenges that other for-profit competitors are not faced with. However, Ever Green is an example of how these challenges can be seen as opportunities to discover innovative solutions before competitors are forced to seek them out. These solutions can become competitive advantages and drive the industry forward.

3. Relationships are a critical piece of maintaining government contracts and engaging in social procurement. Ever Green began through a partnership with Eastern Health, a relationship that proved invaluable as Ever Green branched out on its own. This relationship allowed them to continue to engage in social purchasing and procurement and ensured that the business was constantly aware of opportunities for contracts from government institutions. Ever Green has established similar relationships with other large institutions, such as universities, that has allowed them to take advantage of unique opportunities for the business to grow and develop. This case points clearly to the importance of relationships, not just with institutions, but also individuals in those institutions, as a critical element of engaging in both social purchasing and procurement.

REFERENCES

Government of Canada. (2012, April 27). *Beverage container recycling program.* http://www.ec.gc.ca/gdd-mw/default.asp?lang=En&xml=5269B114 -FCAC-45E1-A50F-7B8D950A3BDC

Government of Newfoundland & Labrador. (2018). *The way forward: Social enterprise action plan.* https://www.gov.nl.ca/thewayforward/

Multi-Materials Stewardship Board (MMSB). (2019). *Find a green depot.* http://greendepotnl.ca/find-a-green-depot/

Smith, B.R., Knapp, J., Barr, T.F., Stevens, C.E., & Cannatelli, B.L. (2010). Social enterprises and the timing of conception: Organizational identity tension, management, and marketing. *Journal of Nonprofit & Public Sector Marketing*, 22(2), 108–34. https://doi.org/10.1080/10495141003676437

Wry, T., & York, J.G. (2017). An identity-based approach to social enterprise. *Academy of Management Review*, 42(3), 437–60. https://doi.org/10.5465/amr.2013.0506

OTHER SOURCES

Interviews with Ever Green Recycling and Eastern Health.
Ever Green Recycling, https://www.greencan.ca/

SUPPLEMENTAL INFORMATION

Revenue by Purchaser Type: Ever Green Recycling

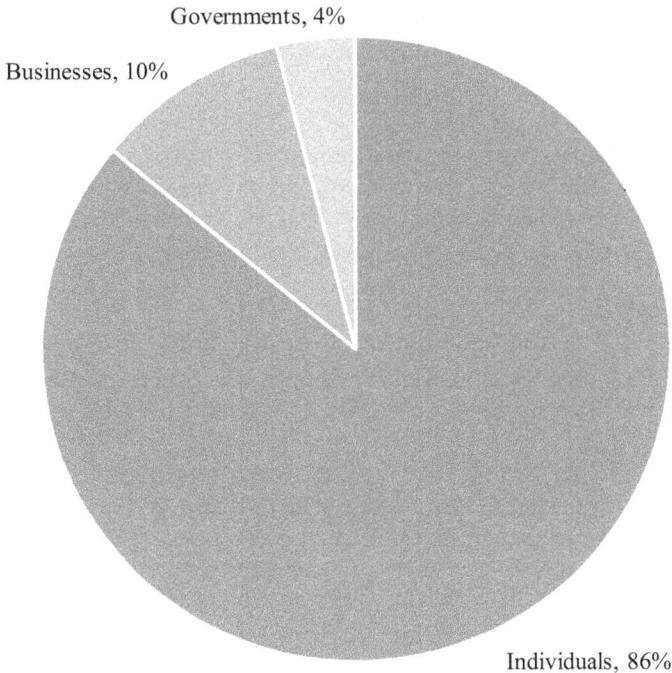

Governments, 4%

Businesses, 10%

Individuals, 86%

7 EMBERS Staffing Solutions

MARTY DONKERVOORT AND MARCIA NOZICK

Introduction

EMBERS Staffing Solutions (ESS) is a Vancouver-based non-profit work integrated social enterprise (WISE) and a division under EMBERS (Eastside Movement for Business & Economic Renewal Society), a community economic development charity. ESS is located in Vancouver's Downtown Eastside, a neighbourhood known for its struggles with social issues such as homelessness and substance abuse. Since its inception as a temporary staffing agency in 2008, ESS has provided employment to thousands of people by securing large contracts through relationship building. In 2019, ESS was placing more than three hundred workers into jobs on a daily basis, with over 90 per cent of the jobs in the construction sector. ESS's revenues increased from $1.6 million in 2013 to $8.8 million in 2018, and it was expected to gross over $16 million in 2021. This case documents EMBERS Staffing Solutions' mission, history, and social purchasing relationships with some of its organizational purchasers.

History and Mission

ESS's parent organization, EMBERS, began as a community economic development charity in August 2001. Its mission is to empower people living on low incomes to become economically self-sufficient and develop meaningful futures. More broadly, EMBERS works to reduce poverty and contribute to the revitalization of Vancouver's Downtown Eastside.

The charity works with thousands of people each year, connecting them with work opportunities, training, and support through four key initiatives:

1. EMBERS Ventures (2003–19) provided accessible and affordable business training and support to low-income entrepreneurs.

2. EMBERS Eastside Works facilitates connections for residents of the Downtown Eastside who face barriers in pursuing employment opportunities.
3. EMBERS Community Employment Services is funded by Corrections Services Canada with an aim of providing employment counselling to parolees in the Vancouver West and Fraser Valley region.
4. ESS is a non-profit social enterprise that connects employers with workers while offering successive opportunities for those workers to secure employment and gain skills. ESS provides temporary workers on a monthly, weekly, or daily basis to a variety of positions in offices and industrial settings. Although ESS places most of the employees in the construction sector, it also provides staffing for special events, warehousing, and manufacturing.

The idea for ESS emerged when EMBERS was searching for a new source of revenue. A community member suggested that EMBERS establish a day-labour company to employ Downtown Eastside residents in a way that, unlike conventional employment agencies, recognized the needs and abilities of this particular demographic. The result was a social-enterprise model that fully blended financial and social objectives. In 2008, EMBERS launched ESS, hoping to tap into the bustling hum of construction in Vancouver as well as other activities leading up to the Vancouver 2010 Winter Olympics.

As a new business with no brand recognition, ESS was slow to gain traction. Aside from business generated by the upcoming 2010 Olympics, ESS was launching in the midst of a global recession. The 2008 financial crisis had significantly slowed housing construction and commercial development. During the months leading up to the Olympics, ESS was placing fifteen to twenty people a day in jobs, with business coming from a few key employers. However, once the Olympics ended, the jobs all but disappeared, and by the end of 2012 ESS could only place eight to ten participants a day on average. With insufficient revenue to cover its overhead costs, ESS considered shutting down.

Convinced the model still had potential, Marcia Nozick – EMBERS's CEO and founder – persuaded her board of directors to let her run a pared-down version of ESS as a pilot for six more months. ESS's new business development strategy and a multi-year contract with an important new client helped turn the enterprise around, and it has continued to grow at an astounding rate. One of the drivers for the impressive growth at ESS was a provincial social procurement contract: in 2012, BC Housing initiated the SRO (Single Room Occupancy) Renewal Project – a contract over three-and-a-half years to renovate thirteen SRO hotels as affordable housing in Vancouver's inner city (BC Housing, n.d.). The contract specified the use of local labour for a portion of the construction. ESS was a labour-provision partner in this project, meaning that ESS finally had an anchor customer with a steady flow of job placements, thus enabling the social enterprise to grow, hire sales staff, and generate a surplus. At the end of 2014, ESS surpassed other programs at EMBERS both financially and in terms of program impact. By 2019, ESS was employing more than three hundred workers on a weekly basis and recorded revenues of $11.6 million by year's end.

ESS is Canada's only non-profit temporary staffing agency, providing socially responsible temporary services for companies in Vancouver and the Lower Mainland. ESS currently runs out of four different locations. Its mission is to provide its customers with high-quality, reliable, professional workers who exceed their expectations, and to support its workers in improving their skills and advancing their careers. ESS also has the objective to educate, advise, and help its workers succeed in the long term and to assist employees in transitioning from temporary service positions to permanent full-time positions. In addition to employment, ESS also provides its workers with boots and equipment for loan, extended medical and dental benefits for long-time workers, breakfast snacks in the morning, counselling and support services, and – most importantly – certified training opportunities to advance participants' careers in construction and other industries (Taylor & Svedova, 2015).

In 2013, ESS achieved international recognition with the Social Enter-Prize Gold Award presented by the Trico Foundation at the Social Enterprise World Forum in Calgary. In 2015, ESS won the City of Vancouver Award of Excellence for providing low-barrier, meaningful employment opportunities and contributing to a healthy city for all. In 2020, ESS won the Governor General's Innovation Award.

Social Purchasing Customers

ESS has developed strong relationships with a number of large and small developers and contractors in Vancouver. Between 2013 and 2019, the four largest organizational purchasers described below accounted for 35 per cent of ESS's total revenue.

Icon West Construction (ICON)

ICON is a construction company with an interest in sustainability. Having constructed significant projects in Canada including Fairmont Pacific Rim and Shangri-La Toronto, in 2018 it was building Vancouver House, a significant complex that includes apartments, office space, and retail at the foot of the Granville bridge in Vancouver. In 2018, ICON was ESS's largest organizational purchaser, accounting for 25 per cent of ESS's total revenue. During 2019, ICON hired approximately seventy-five ESS workers including carpenters, labourers, crane/hoist operators, forklift operators, elevator operators, and safety personnel on a daily basis. At the time of writing, it is estimated that ESS staff represented more than half of all labour on the Vancouver House project. This project alone has been responsible for creating more than 75,000 person-days of work spread over four years for ESS.

EllisDon Corporation

EllisDon is one of the largest construction and building services companies in the world. The company completes over $4 billion worth of contracts annually, in every market sector and across the globe. EllisDon is a privately owned company with more than one hundred employees. In Vancouver, EllisDon provided reconstruction and construction management services for Parq Vancouver. This new development at 39 Smith Street is a multi-use facility, including a parkade and an urban resort with two luxury resort hotels (over five hundred rooms), a conference centre, eight restaurants, retail space, and a new home for the existing Edgewater Casino.

During Vancouver's approval process for this development, the City of Vancouver imposed a Community Benefit Agreement (CBA) on the project. The city uses CBAs to require developers to commit "to actions, targets and/or outcomes relating to employment and local or social procurement … [in] a community where the development is occurring or in nearby communities in where equity-seeking groups, including low-income people and others, can be found" (City of Vancouver, 2018, p. 3). Vancouver is one of the first major cities in Canada to introduce a formal CBA, following community benefit frameworks introduced at the provincial and federal government levels in 2018. The policy adopted by the city aims to reduce poverty and meet established community economic development goals. Groups participating in a CBA may include people who are under-represented based on gender, faith, immigrant status, education level, economic status, or sexual orientation. With a CBA, developers in Vancouver with projects larger than forty-five thousand square metres are required to

1. Designate 10 per cent of new entry-level jobs as available to people in Vancouver, especially to individuals facing marginalization and barriers to employment

2. Purchase a minimum of 10 per cent of goods and services from
   local businesses, contributing to the positive social and environmental impacts of social procurement

The Parq Vancouver project and the related CBA is where the relationship between EllisDon and ESS developed. In order to comply with
the CBA, EllisDon agreed to hire 10 per cent of its workforce from the
identified groups. The company also hired Jeff Waters as an information coordinator to oversee the implementation of the CBA and monitor
its progress and commitments. The City of Vancouver had a consultant assigned to monitor both the process and the outcomes from the
CBA. The consultant made introductions between EllisDon and various
community groups representing individuals who could benefit from
the CBA. ESS presented a relatively easy solution for EllisDon to meet
many of its CBA commitments. In addition to ESS, EllisDon also developed relationships with three nearby First Nations to secure workers.
In the end, EllisDon surpassed its imposed CBA requirements by hiring twice as many as required on the project from local communities
and designated groups. In fact, EllisDon was so impressed with ESS
and its workers that it has continued working with ESS on subsequent
projects even without CBA requirements. Further, the subcontractors
on the Parq project were equally impressed and have since hired ESS
workers as well.

One of the reasons why EllisDon was so impressed with ESS was
the social enterprise's commitment to training and regular site visits by
ESS's management team. Jeff Waters, the EllisDon information coordinator responsible for the CBA, points out that ESS "provided a higher
level of service."

Darwin Construction (Canada) Ltd.

Founded in 1987 on Vancouver's North Shore, Darwin is a family-
owned construction and development company. Darwin's relationship with ESS first started in 2012. Like other contractors, Darwin hires
workers from ESS on a project-by-project basis. Quality is the most
important factor in its purchasing and hiring decisions. Darwin has
been impressed with the quality of work by ESS workers and has hired
three former ESS employees as permanent Darwin staff. ESS's social
mission is also an important factor for Darwin, which gave it a high
rating in our study. Darwin is also extremely satisfied with ESS's service. Darwin was one of the major construction companies on the SRO
Renewal Project from 2012 to 2015.

Wesgroup Properties

Wesgroup Properties is a family-owned real-estate company that has been operating for more than fifty years. The company leases commercial properties to long-term tenants and also designs and develops residential communities, from single communities to master-planned neighbourhoods. Wesgroup owns, develops, manages, and leases over sixty commercial and mixed-use properties within BC's Lower Mainland. With purchases just under $1 million, in 2018, Wesgroup was ESS's second-largest customer, hiring ESS workers exclusively on projects wherever possible. Wesgroup is extremely pleased with its relationship with ESS and has hired at least twelve ESS workers as permanent staff. Wesgroup continues to hire ESS workers for site supervision and safety, as well as carpenters, crane operators, and other construction positions. Although the cost for hiring ESS is slightly higher than other employment agencies, Wesgroup is supportive of ESS because of its social mission, training, and quality service. Although Wesgroup does not have a formal company policy to buy from social enterprises, it has also purchased services from BladeRunners, another community-based social enterprise in the Vancouver area providing life skills, job-readiness skills, work experience/on-the-job training, job coaching, and ongoing supports to youth who are unemployed. Long before Wesgroup started buying from ESS, Beau Jarvis, Wesgroup's current president, was a volunteer with ESS, driving its workers to job sites before starting his own workday.

Summary: Lessons Learned

The success experienced by ESS offers valuable lessons and provides important insights into the challenges and opportunities facing social enterprises trying to develop relationships with organizational purchasers.

1. Relationship building with developers and contractors takes time, patience, and perseverance. ESS struggled for years before finally breaking through and getting access to major developers and contractors.
2. Champions who believe in the social enterprise and its mission are critical. EMBERS's founder Marcia Nozick is that champion for ESS. She persevered even when things were gloomy and was able to eventually turn ESS into a successful social enterprise with annual sales over $16 million (2021).

3. The development of a Community Benefit Agreement (CBA) by the City of Vancouver played a significant role in getting ESS hired by EllisDon on the Parq Vancouver project. The fact that EllisDon doubled the CBA requirements illustrates that once given a chance to prove themselves, ESS and other social enterprises can develop long and lasting relationships with organizational partners.

4. This case demonstrates the importance of a demand for the service provided by social enterprise. At the time ESS was founded, Vancouver was experiencing a development and construction boom which resulted in a labour shortage in the construction industry. This shortage, coupled with a non-unionized construction trades labour force in the province of BC, presented an opportunity for a social enterprise like ESS to enter the market and prove itself.

5. The organizational purchasers interviewed for this case ranked ESS's social mission as important or very important, which is inconsistent with previous research showing that social mission is often ranked behind quality, service, and price (Loughheed & Donkervoort, 2009). Nonetheless, quality and price remain important components in the buying decision. All four organizational purchasers rate these components as critical to their purchasing decisions. Quality cannot be compromised; however, price is more flexible since most developers are willing to pay slightly more for dependable and well-trained workers. All four organizational purchasers in this case identify the training and support services provided by ESS to its workers as key reasons for procuring labour from ESS.

6. Building relationships with developers and contractors has led to ESS workers being hired directly by the contractors as permanent staff. Companies are free to hire ESS workers after three months without paying a placement fee to ESS (a standard practice among temporary employment agencies).

7. This case illustrates the importance of relationship building for social enterprises selling their goods and services. ESS builds these relationships through fundraising golf tournaments and corporate volunteering initiatives.

REFERENCES

BC Housing. (n.d.). *Vancouver – SRO renewal initiative*. https://www.bchousing
.org/projects-partners/development-projects/sro-renewal
City of Vancouver. (2018). *Administrative report: Community benefit agreement
policy*. https://council.vancouver.ca/20180918/documents/rr2.pdf

Loughheed, G., & Donkervoort, M. (2009). Marketing social enterprise: To sell the cause, first sell the product. *Making Waves, 20*(2), 16–19.

Taylor, K., & Svedova, J. (2015). *Embers Staffing Solutions: Social enterprise case study*. Sauder Centre for Social Innovation and Impact Investing, Sauder School of Business, University of British Columbia.

OTHER SOURCES

Interview with EMBERS, Icon West Construction, EllisDon Corporation, Darwin Construction and Wesgroup Properties.

EMBERS, https://www.embersvancouver.com/; https://emberscanada.org/

PART 3

The Importance of Parent Organizations

Parent organizations can play a significant role in the viability of work integration social enterprises. The majority of social enterprises in our study – nearly 80 per cent – have parent organizations. Even though these social enterprises generate revenue through sales, many of them are dependent on their parents for significant support in terms of administration, staffing, space, and funding (Chan et al., 2017).

Although the survey data indicates no statistically significant results with respect to the role of parent organizations in whether or not a social enterprise would bid for contracts, the cases in our data collection show that many parent organizations support their social enterprises by helping them initiate and maintain customer relationships. In part 3, we highlight this relationship with parent organizations through the following cases:

- Social Crust Cafe & Catering (Vancouver, British Columbia)
- ImagineAbility (Winnipeg, Manitoba)
- Wachiay Studios (Courtenay, British Columbia)
- Diversity Foods Services (Winnipeg, Manitoba)
- Rainbow's End Community Development Corporation (Hamilton, Ontario)

While these cases are not the only ones with parent organizations supporting them, they illustrate the different models of parental support and the varying degrees of integration that social enterprises use in their effort to sell goods and services. For example, Social Crust Cafe & Catering operates as a program within its parent organization. In contrast, Rainbow's End is a separate, independent corporation that originated as a program at St. Joseph's Healthcare Hamilton. In this case, although St. Joe's has evolved out of its role as a parent organization and become a champion for Rainbow's End, it continues to maintain a critical relationship with Rainbow's End. Despite being legally separate entities, Rainbow's End and St. Joe's remain closely associated through funding support and St. Joe's presence on the board of Rainbow's End. Another example is ImagineAbility, a parent organization that has strong ties to a separate for-profit social enterprise it created, called Opportunity Partners.

Among these cases, the parent organization is a major customer for the social enterprises. For instance, wholly owned by the University of Winnipeg, the University of Winnipeg Community Renewal Corporation is one of two non-profit shareholders of Diversity Food Services. Not surprisingly, 42 per cent of Diversity's revenue is earned from within the university campus. Similarly, much of the revenue earned by Rainbow's End comes from the on-site operations at St. Joe's or through customer referrals to the social enterprises by St. Joe's.

Space is one of the most common forms of support provided by parent organizations, as seen in the cases of Social Crust Cafe & Catering, Diversity Food Services, and Rainbow's End. Social Crust Cafe & Catering came into existence because Coast Mental Health saw an opportunity for its empty retail storefront. Initially part of the University's food strategy for students, Diversity Food Services began operating on the University of Winnipeg's campus and remains there to this day. The offices of Rainbow's End are located well outside St. Joe's premises; however, both Colours Café and the Bistro operate within the hospital and Rainbow's End does not pay rent for the space as would be the case had the hospital contracted the foodservices to a private, for-profit operator. In contrast, even though Wachiay Studio operates as one of the programs at the Wachiay Friendship Centre, the Studio pays rent for the space it uses, which helps support the activities of the parent organization.

Some of the parent organizations also cover wages and salaries of those working in the social enterprises, usually for those who work in administration and management. This is especially prevalent among social enterprises that are still in the early stages of development and/ or are still very much embedded as part of their parent organizations, such as Social Crust Cafe & Catering. Equally important, many parent organizations also support the social enterprises with their expertise in management and administration as well as connections in the community. For example, the board of Diversity Food Services includes two members selected by the University of Winnipeg Community Renewal Corporation. The University also provides opportunity for Diversity Food Services to test and demonstrate its capability in catering at high-profile events and large venues.

For the two organizations providing opportunities for individuals living with mental health challenges – Social Crust Cafe & Catering and Rainbow's End – their parent organizations offer ongoing emotional and healthcare support for the community members the social enterprise works with. The ability to offer program participants additional support as they receive training and secure employment at the social enterprise helps enhance the long-term sustainability of the social enterprises and the successes of participants who work there.

The most unique form of parental support is found in the case of ImagineAbility. As the parent organization, ImagineAbility set up a separate for-profit corporation – Opportunity Partners – to shield the non-profit organization itself from potential liability when Imagine-Ability decided to pursue a business opportunity. The arrangement allows ImagineAbility to leverage its assembly and packaging work (which is relatively common among social enterprises) into manufacturing and retail distribution.

The cases in this part of the book demonstrate that support from parent organizations is critical not only in the early stages of development but also as a form of long-term support for social enterprises. This is especially true for social enterprises that are small and lack capacity. Whether a social enterprise could eventually become completely independent from its parent organization is contingent to a large degree on market conditions. Regardless of how intertwined they are, social enterprises and their parent organizations can have mutually beneficial relationships over the long term.

Guiding Questions:

1. What are the contributions from the parent organizations in supporting the social enterprise demonstrated through these cases?
2. How important is the in-kind support received by the social enterprises in these cases? What would happen to the social enterprises if the in-kind support were to become unavailable?
3. Considering how crucial the support from the parent organization is, how would you assess the viability of these social enterprises? Should they work to become more or less closely tied to their parent organizations?
4. How do the relationships between these social enterprises and their parent organizations compare and contrast with other case studies in this book?
5. How should a social enterprise maintain a mutually beneficial relationship with its parent organization?

REFERENCE

Chan, A., Ryan, S., & Quarter, J. (2017). Supported social enterprise: A modified social welfare organization. *Nonprofit and Voluntary Sector Quarterly, 46*(2), 261–79. https://doi.org/10.1177/0899764016655620

8 Social Crust Cafe & Catering

YASMIN HARIRI

Introduction

Social Crust Cafe & Catering is a social enterprise initiated by its parent organization Coast Mental Health (CMH), a non-profit based in Vancouver, British Columbia, with a focus on supporting those with mental illness to "thrive in our community." While yet to engage in social procurement, Social Crust Cafe & Catering has developed social purchasing relationships through support from CMH that are critical to its function.

CMH provides a number of supports to those with mental illness or addictions, including housing, support services, employment, and education. The organization is large by most non-profit standards, managing a funding budget of over $36 million in 2018–19. CMH describes its mission as providing "training and develop[ing] businesses that reduce stigma and facilitate social connections, enabling people with mental illnesses to take on meaningful roles and progress towards recovery."

One arm of CMH – Coast Social Enterprise – operates two main social enterprises: Landscaping with Heart and Social Crust Cafe & Catering. Landscaping with Heart was started in 2005 when CMH began experimenting with social enterprise as a means of providing meaningful employment to residents of social-housing facilities. Landscaping with Heart was initially funded through grants; it transitioned to a social enterprise when enough contracts were secured to make it financially viable. The team is led by one individual with up to eight adult employees each season, all of whom identify with mental illness although not all are clients of CMH. The business runs only during the spring/summer season and primarily provides services to social-housing facilities in Vancouver. The business has maintained a steady $100,000 in contracts annually, largely through a relationship with BC Housing as well as a small number of individual customers. The second social enterprise associated with this arm of CMH is Social Crust Cafe & Catering, the focus of this case.

Social Crust Cafe & Catering was a long-time aspiration of the senior management of its parent organization, CMH. Understanding the challenges of mental illness and addictions, senior management was eager to find ways to direct youth towards a more productive path. The manager at CMH hoped that training, rehabilitation, and support for young people would mediate further mental-health and addiction problems in later life and assist them in finding and maintaining employment. In 2014, Social Crust Cafe & Catering was started as an experimental project, offering culinary training to youth with mental illness and addictions as well as employing and training them in a functioning cafe and catering company.

Established in an unused retail storefront beneath a CMH social-housing facility, the cafe offers a broad breakfast and lunch menu weekdays from 8:00 a.m. to 2:00 p.m. Alongside the cafe, the space is used to market and run a catering business, offering lunch, dinner, or appetizer packages, largely to organizational purchasers. While the cafe is the face of the operation, the catering business is the prime employer of those in the training program. Shortly after Social Crust began, the staff realized the skills required to run a cafe were ill-matched to the needs of those with mental illness because of the unpredictability in customer flow and work volume. Catering, on the other hand, with its regularity, repetitive production process, and flexibility, is an excellent fit. As such, most participants are employed in the catering business.

Culinary Skills Training Program

The Culinary Skills Training Program offers youth recovering from mental illness or with other barriers to employment with training, coaching, and work experience so that they can enter the labor force or continue further culinary schooling. (Social Crust Cafe & Catering, 2018)

Closely connected to the Social Crust Cafe & Catering business, the Culinary Skills Training Program is a four-month program offered exclusively to youth from the ages of nineteen to thirty. Youth apply to join the program and are selected based on their fit with both the program and the dynamics of the intake cohort. Participants engage in a four-month, intensive skills training program within the Social Crust kitchen before commencing a two-month practicum in the cafe where they put these skills to use. Participants are enrolled in three intakes or cohorts over the course of the year – Fall (September), Winter (January), and Summer (May). Social Crust aims to have eighteen participants per cohort; however, the cohorts at Social Crust have typically ranged from twelve to fourteen participants with demand steadily growing. Despite the demand for the program, recruiting can be challenging with a small support staff at Social Crust complicated by turnover among those responsible for recruitment.

The training program at Social Crust is tailored to the clients at CMH – i.e., youth facing mental illness or addiction challenges. The program assumes participants enter without any prior experience and begins with the basics of cooking and how a kitchen works. Alongside culinary skills, the program emphasizes basic elements of employment such as punctuality, professionalism, and collaboration. The initial work tasks are kept simple so participants can gain confidence in mastering a certain level of competency as they progress through the program. The aim is to build the skills and competencies for graduates to become employment ready. Oftentimes participants are ready in six weeks, but others remain at the cafe beyond two months as they continue to build their skills and proficiency. After completing the program, participants are supported by Social Crust in their job search in the culinary sector since the cafe cannot provide work for more than ten employees. Specifically, the staff help participants find employers that offer a good skills match alongside a supportive and inclusive work culture. Some of the places that have hired from Social Crust's training program include Joey Restaurant Group, MeeT on Main, and Granville Gardens Retirement Residence. Some participants who graduate from the training program also choose to pursue further culinary training through post-secondary programs. The program coordinator and chef instructors at Social Crust work closely with these participants to develop a post-graduation exit plan and check up on them one year after graduation.

Customers

Social Crust Cafe & Catering customers are largely split between individual customers who tend to purchase from the cafe and various organizational purchasers who primarily use the catering business.

Individual Customers

The cafe attracts a wide range of individual customers, largely from the local area. Most are walk-ins searching for breakfast or lunch near their home or workplace; however, some are regular local customers who frequent the cafe. Social Crust also offers a 10 per cent student discount to attract students from the three college and university campuses within walking distance of the cafe. Individual customers typically purchase a single breakfast or lunch meal, averaging five to ten dollars. The cafe recently partnered with Ritual, a pre-ordering mobile application, which allows the social enterprise to tap into an additional market.

Organizational Purchasers

Social Crust Catering primarily sells to private businesses and non-profit organizations. Some of its customers make one-off purchases of catering for lunch, dinner, or cocktail events. A lunch purchase includes a soup, sandwich, and salad combo. The catering business has also developed relationships with numerous institutions that provide recurring business. For example, Social Crust provides lunch for a seniors' living program at Douglas Park Community Centre every Tuesday and Wednesday. Another client, Mimic Studio, is a regular purchaser from Social Crust. Social Crust works with a variety of organizational purchasers and often seeks out other organizations with a social mission or purpose themselves. For example, a non-profit organization hosts a breakfast meeting in the cafe each month and Social Crust allows the use of the cafe, provided that the organization purchases coffee and food.

Social Procurement and Social Purchasing

Social Crust has not engaged in any form of social procurement to date. Among those interviewed for this case, the staff at Social Crust feel they lack the knowledge and experience to engage in the procurement process, including requests for proposals (RFPs) and bidding. The manager at Social Crust indicates that while they are always seeking opportunities for new and stable contracts, they are already at their maximum operational capacity and cannot handle more growth without increasing the size of their physical space and the number of their support staff.

To encourage social purchasing, the manager at Social Crust actively promotes the story of their social enterprise, for example, by sharing the impact a purchase makes in the lives of those who work at Social Curst and those who participate in the training program. Approximately 75 per cent of customers purchase primarily for social impact, including a number of like-minded organizations. The manager at Social Crust believes the importance of their social mission is even more significant in the catering business, from which customers may initially make a purchase for social impact and be surprised by the quality of the product.

Social Crust has considerable experience with social purchasing from government purchasers through relationship building. The catering business has provided meals for meetings at the City of Vancouver and identified BC Housing as a potential customer. Since CMH has existing relationships with a number of provincial and municipal agencies (including BC Housing), Social Crust has been exploring opportunities to provide catering through these networks.

Marketing and Advertising

Social Crust has heavily invested in developing a manageable, yet ambitious, marketing strategy to grow its business. In 2017, CMH engaged a consultant to create a marketing plan; however, conversations with the consultant made the manager at Social Crust realize the social enterprise was unprepared to meet a surge in sales. Consequently, a less ambitious marketing plan was developed to modulate a more gradual influx in customers. At the time of writing for this case, the manager at Social Crust hopes to engage in a more robust and ambitious marketing strategy once the social enterprise has expanded the kitchen and grown the training program and team to meet the higher demands.

The message of Social Crust is primarily built upon its social purpose, as the manager at Social Crust explains:

> We believe [our social impact] is our competitive edge. What we believe is, if you have a choice to spend your money on a business that is just going back in the owner's pockets or back into the business, why would you do that if you can help somebody's life?

As such, marketing materials from Social Crust proudly articulate and demonstrate the impact of customers' purchases and share details of the Culinary Training Program.

Social media is a primary focus in Social Crust's marketing strategy. A carefully designed website showcases the cafe and catering businesses as well as the social mission and training program. Instagram, Facebook, and Twitter accounts keep customers and followers up to date with events, news, participant stories, and food images. Even the cafe's storefront is part of Social Crust's robust marketing endeavour. The walls feature stories of the participants in the training program, and flyers for the catering service are prominently displayed near the cash register. Catering customers receive print materials describing the impact of their purchase. Another creative marketing initiative is a partnership with Foodie to host evening events with guest celebrity chefs. Celebrity chefs come and cook a meal with the participants of the training program, and customers pay to enjoy a four-course meal. In addition to bringing in revenue, the evenings also serve as a promotion for Social Crust since these events take place in the cafe, and the staff ensures that the customers are aware of the social mission and the benefits of the events.

Adding to Social Crust's own marketing strategy are the supporting efforts of CMH. For example, the parent organization sends corporate volunteer groups to the cafe to assist with meal preparation alongside participants in the training program. At the conclusion of the volunteer experience, Social Crust shares a meal as well as information about its catering program with the volunteers to promote its use for corporate events.

Financial Sustainability

CMH is intimately involved in the operations of Social Crust. CMH has a social enterprise board as well as a foundation board, both of which oversee and provide managerial and strategic support to Social Crust. CMH also provides a number of assets and supports to the cafe. First, Social Crust is given its space completely free of charge, since the space is in a facility owned by CMH. Furthermore, CMH covers the wages of all support staff, including the chef instructor, catering chefs, managers, and mental health worker for the training program, the cafe, and the catering service. However, the wages of Social Crust's management group are funded entirely by donations. The costs associated with the Culinary Training Program, including its staff, are 100 per cent funded by donors to CMH. The manager at Social Crust hopes that the cafe can begin to break even while the catering service starts turning a larger surplus. However, it remains unlikely that the entire social enterprise will become fully independent from CMH's various kinds of strategic, financial, and in-kind support.

Social Crust Cafe & Catering has been experiencing steady growth since its inception, more than doubling its revenue over the last three fiscal years (see supplemental information). The social enterprise is responsible for covering the cost of food, marketing, and junior labour force whereas the support from CMH covers a number of in-kind expenses. Social Crust has been able to turn a small surplus since 2015 (see supplemental information); however, the catering service has not yet been able to generate a surplus, meaning the social enterprise still relies on the cafe to cover all the expenses. The cafe initially accounted for nearly two-thirds of the total revenue, but the catering service has grown significantly over 2018–19, making up nearly 50 per cent of total revenue.

Social Crust has made conscious efforts to expand the catering service, recognizing that catering not only offers a better fit for the participants at Social Crust but also presents advantageous market opportunities. The catering service experienced record-breaking growth in the 2018–19 fiscal year, which generated much excitement within CMH about possibilities for continued growth and expansion. For the fiscal year 2020, Social Crust forecasted a 20 per cent year-to-year increase in catering sales based upon its targeted marketing efforts. While Social Crust actively seeks growth and generates surplus, the social enterprise expresses fear that its facilities and labour force may not be suited to significant growth. The kitchen facility at Social Crust was originally outfitted to support the cafe only and does not actually provide adequate preparation space to assemble large-scale catering orders. Should the catering service at Social Crust begin to expand and experience multiple daily orders, the current kitchen space would be inadequate. The manager at Social Crust is conflicted over the need to expand while feeling uncertainty over the ability to meet that demand.

Summary: Lessons Learned

Social Crust Cafe & Catering falls under the category of a supported social enterprise because of its closely woven relationship with CMH (Chan, Ryan & Quarter, 2017). While Social Crust independently shapes its brand and develops a uniquely robust marketing program, it still relies heavily on CMH for many aspects of its work. CMH provides space, managerial support, and sales opportunities to support operations at Social Crust. CMH also gives strategic support, including consulting services and board advisory services, to shape and drive the growth of the social enterprise. Without the financial, managerial, and strategic support of its parent organization, Social Crust could not be an independently viable business.

This parental relationship provides several opportunities to small social enterprises. Below are some of the lessons that can be gleaned from this case study around the role of parent organizations in the viability of social enterprises:

1. Parent organizations can support small social enterprises to gain access to social purchasing and make important business

relationships. Developing relationships with large organizations that are interested in opportunities for social purchasing
is not an easy task for a small social enterprise. Several larger
contracts and regular customers of Social Crust, however, have
come from the extensive reach and network of CMH, including connections to the government sector. Social Crust directly
attributes this to the support of their parent organization and
believes this to be an important benefit of being linked to a
larger organization.

2. Growth can also be limited by the support of the parent company. During the discussions about growth possibilities, the
manager points out that Social Crust cannot grow much further
without extensive renovations to the existing physical space.
They would like to see these renovations funded by CMH as
they do not have the revenue internally to fund these extensions.
It was clear in this case that the growth of Social Crust would
always be dependent on the support available from its parent
company (or at least until they became independently financially stable). While opportunities for growth existed, including
marketing plans and large contracts, its growth was limited and
dependent on CMH being able to extend the physical facility.
Without independent viability, social enterprises will remain
dependent on their parent company to seek out or take advantage of opportunities for growth.

3. Social procurement may be dependent on the scalability of business. Social Crust shared that they were looking into opportunities for social procurement but felt that the business was not yet
ready to meet the demands of larger, more consistent contracts.
This simple example may provide insight into why so many
smaller social enterprises are yet to engage in social procurement. Without the physical facility, human resources, or business
acumen to meet the demands of larger procurement contracts,
social enterprises may remain excluded from this form of growth
opportunity.

The situation at Social Crust raises questions about the function and
structure of social enterprise when it is significantly supported by a
parent organization. If a social enterprise's stability involves such close
ties and reliance on a parent organization for stability, can it be evaluated as an independent business? Or should it be considered a business
venture of the parent organization? Whatever the answer, this model

still demonstrates the immense opportunities for parent organizations to develop revenue-generating business units that can simultaneously train and employ the participants these organizations seek to support, while also generating additional revenue.

REFERENCE

Chan, A., Ryan, S., & Quarter, J. (2017). Supported social enterprise: A modified social welfare organization. *Nonprofit and Voluntary Sector Quarterly, 46*(2), 261–79. https://doi.org/10.1177/0899764016655620

OTHER SOURCES

Interviews with Social Crust Cafe & Catering and Coast Mental Health.
Coast Mental Health. (2019). *Coast Mental Health Annual Report 2018/2019* [PDF file]. Retrieved from https://www.coastmentalhealth.com/assets/media/2018/07/cmh_annual_report-2019-07-25.pdf
Social Crust Cafe & Catering, https://www.socialcrustcafe.com/
Coast Mental Health, https://www.coastmentalhealth.com/who-we-are/about/

SUPPLEMENTAL INFORMATION

Sales by Business Unit (2015–19): Social Crust Cafe & Catering

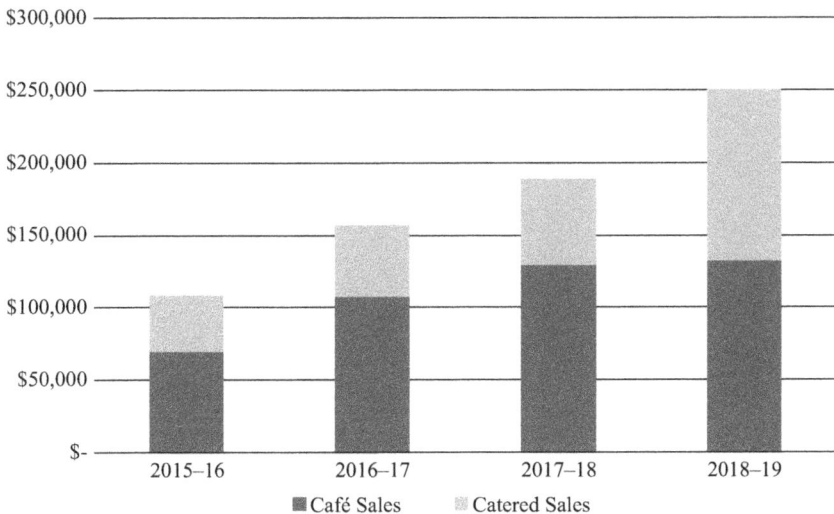

Financial Highlights (2015–19): Social Crust Cafe & Catering

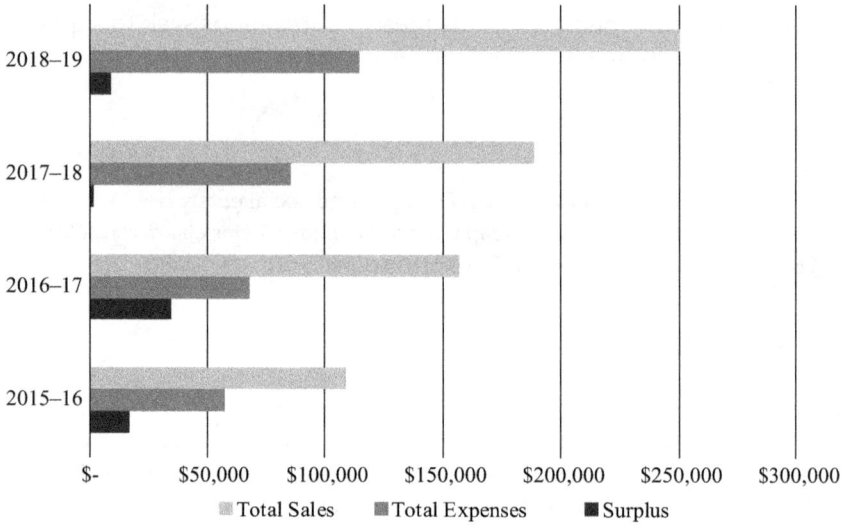

9 ImagineAbility Inc.

MARTY DONKERVOORT AND AUDRA PENNER

Introduction

ImagineAbility Inc. is a Winnipeg-based non-profit community organization with charitable status providing support services for people
living with intellectual disabilities. The organization was established
in 1962 as ARC Industries and renamed Versatech Industries in 1986.
The name was changed again in 2012 to ImagineAbility. Throughout
its decades-long existence, ImagineAbility has offered work experience
to individuals with intellectual disabilities. The staff of about 70 works
with approximately 240 individuals. Most of the revenue (approximately 81 per cent) to support its operations comes from government
grants, foundations, and donations. However, since the beginning,
ImagineAbility has also earned revenue through its packaging and
assembly services for customers in the community.

The contract manufacturing services are embedded in the organization
as a program, not a separate social enterprise. Out of the approximately
240 participants at ImagineAbility, about 30 per cent are engaged in the
packaging and assembly operations, which have grown to account for 19
per cent of total revenue in the fiscal year 2019. In addition to the contract
manufacturing program, ImagineAbility is the parent organization of a
separate for-profit social enterprise it created called Opportunity Partners.
The annual sales revenue generated by Opportunity Partners is approximately $350,000, slightly more than half the annual sales revenue from
the contract manufacturing services at ImagineAbility. For about twenty-
five years, ImagineAbility also was operating recycling and document
destruction (shredding) services. Unfortunately, these services gradually
became economically unviable and were withdrawn in 2012.

The mission of ImagineAbility is to support the aspirations of individuals living with intellectual disabilities along with its stated vision that

"All individuals are valued, accepted, and can realize their potential." Integrity, inclusion, advocacy, accountability, respect, empowerment, safety, and transparency are among the organization's stated values. All of ImagineAbility's services are focused on the participants' individual growth and development in areas of work, health, leisure, and learning. In addition to offering employment to its participants, ImagineAbility also provides support services such as individualized social and leisure activities as well as community-based services that can include volunteer or paid employment in the community. Currently, ImagineAbility operates out of two locations in Winnipeg.

Operating for close to sixty years, ImagineAbility is one of the oldest organizations featured in this book. The non-profit received its registered charity status in 1979 based on its recognition as a teaching institution. Parents of children with intellectual disabilities started the organization to provide meaningful employment and recreational activities. These parents believed that with some accommodation their adult children were capable of work. Throughout the many decades and several name changes, ImagineAbility has stayed true to its mission and vision. The governance of the organization consists of a board of directors and a management team of nine including the president and CEO who reports to the board. The board consists of ten directors, including some parents, professionals (lawyers and doctors), as well as representatives from local businesses.

Earned Revenue from Social Procurement and Purchasing

Earned revenue from packaging and assembly services provided to industry is an important part of ImagineAbility's financial viability as it helps reduce the organization's dependence on government funding and donations. In 2010, ImagineAbility actively explored options to increase earned revenue to offset this funding dependence. When an opportunity presented itself in 2012, ImagineAbility decided to embark on a completely new venture, acquiring the patent and the North American distribution rights to a product called Hold It. The product is part of wall-storage units that hold brooms, rakes, shovels, etc. in garden sheds or garages. Production of the components is contracted to independent suppliers while assembly and packaging of the product is contracted out to ImagineAbility. As a consumer product, Hold It poses a potential liability to the manufacturer/distributor. To protect ImagineAbility's assets, the non-profit organization made an unusual move – incorporating an independent for-profit corporation called Opportunity Partners Ltd. which is wholly owned by

ImagineAbility. The mission of Opportunity Partners is similar to that of its parent organization:

> To create a better business, community and world by recognizing that every single person has capabilities, abilities and gifts. Living a good life depends on whether those capabilities can be used, abilities expressed, and gifts given.

ImagineAbility fronted most of the start-up capital for Opportunity Partners in the form of loans. Opportunity Partners contracts 100 per cent of the packaging/assembly, warehousing, and distribution activities associated with Hold It to its parent ImagineAbility. Hold It is distributed across Canada by Canadian Tire and in select Home Hardware stores. Since its inception, Opportunity Partners has generated approximately $2.8 million in revenue from Hold It sales, allowing it to pay off the loans to ImagineAbility and to reinvest the profits in its parent organization.

ImagineAbility's earned revenue from its commercial operations in 2019 was $605,768. Approximately $335,000 (55 per cent of total earned revenue) was related to packaging and assembly activities, including those from Hold It. Major purchasers include Coghlan's Ltd., Vita Health, Cascades Containerboard Packaging Canada, and A. Adams Supply Ltd. The remaining 45 per cent of earned revenue came from contract-filling operations, which have only one purchaser, Amsted Rail (Griffin Wheel). Most of these relationships were initiated by the purchasers who were looking for contractors to provide their assembly or packaging needs and came to ImagineAbility because of the organization's capabilities.

Coghlan's Ltd.

Coghlan's is a Winnipeg-based distributor of outdoor accessories. It is a privately held family business founded by Norm Coghlan more than sixty years ago. Prior to forming his own company, Coghlan sold lanterns, camp stoves, and parts primarily to the hardware market in the United States and Canada. Today, Coghlan's is the largest single brand of camping accessories in the world.

Coghlan's relationship with ImagineAbility started in 1962 when Norm Coghlan needed someone to assemble the Camp Stove Toaster. Upon learning that the toaster manufacturer in the US was discontinuing its production, he purchased the entire American inventory. As a distributor, however, Coghlan's had no manufacturing capacity and searched for an entity to assemble the toasters. He ended up approaching ImagineAbility, and the relationship continues to this day. The Camp Stove Toaster is still in Coghlan's product line, but it is now one of over five hundred accessories offered by Coghlan's.

As Coghlan's product line expanded so did its relationship with ImagineAbility, which started assembling and packaging other products for Coghlan's. Currently, ImagineAbility handles about one hundred accessories in Coghlan's product line. Manufacturers ship the accessories directly to ImagineAbility where they are stored, assembled (where necessary), packaged, and then shipped to Coghlan's distribution warehouse in Winnipeg for shipment to over forty countries around the world.

As popularity grew for accessories and the line expanded, Coghlan's added a central warehouse in St. Paul, Minnesota, in the mid-1960s. Based on its relationship with ImagineAbility in Winnipeg, Coghlan's teamed up with Opportunity Partners Inc. (no relationship to Opportunity Partners Ltd. in Winnipeg), a non-profit community organization in the US offering meaningful work for people with disabilities. Coghlan's was the American organization's first large client and their oldest. According to Rob Coghlan, Coghlan's president and chief executive officer,

> Coghlan's relationship with ImagineAbility in Winnipeg and Opportunity Partners in St. Paul sets them apart, allowing them to give back to their community and provide meaningful work to those who take great pride in a job well done.

Rob Coghlan, Norm Coghlan's son, claims that the company could not have built its business without its relationship with ImagineAbility. He also states that the relationship was a business decision and not a charitable one. Quality and competitive pricing rank ahead of supporting ImagineAbility's social mission even though social mission is important to Coghlan's. Most importantly, Coghlan's is satisfied with the work done by ImagineAbility. Although Coghlan's does not have a formal social procurement or purchasing policy, it has purchasing relationships with not only ImagineAbility and Opportunity Partners, Inc., but also two more social enterprises: Epic de St. Malo Inc. in St. Malo, Manitoba, and Kindale Industries in Steinbach, Manitoba.

Coghlan's relationship with ImagineAbility has spanned nearly sixty years. There is no tendering process and prices are renegotiated and adjusted as needed. The relationship with Coghlan's accounts for approximately $60,000 in annual revenue for ImagineAbility, representing approximately 9 per cent of its total earned revenue.

Vita Health

Vita Health approached ImagineAbility in 2014 when seeking a new packaging partner for their protein bars, which are shipped to Costco stores across Canada. With annual revenues of almost $200,000, Vita Health accounts for 31 per cent of ImagineAbility's packaging and assembly revenue. The protein bars are extremely popular among ImagineAbility workers, who were integral to the process of setting up the initial production line. Vita Health is very happy with the business relationship. The responsibility of almost all the logistics including quality control, paperwork, shipping, and receiving is with Imagine-Ability. The contract with ImagineAbility allows Vita Health to increase its capacity, to reduce the associated risk by having this work done off-site, and to sustain a steady, consistent, and reliable supply.

Amsted Rail (Griffin Wheel)

In 2011, Amsted Rail needed a supplier to package its 3.5 and 4.0 oz. bags of rice hulls (the husks of rice). These bags are part of the production cycle in the manufacturing of train wheels for Canadian Pacific, Canadian National, and other brokered accounts that Amsted works with across North America. They were looking for a supplier who could manage eleven thousand to seventeen thousand bags a day. Imagine-Ability believed they could do the work if they could automate the process to meet the daily volume demand – they arranged a lease-to-own plan to acquire the machine necessary. ImagineAbility is responsible for all work necessary in the process including machine maintenance, shipping and receiving, and holding some back-up inventory. Since then, ImagineAbility has become an integral part of the Amsted Rail production process. The bags of rice hulls produced by ImagineAbility have helped reduce the number of defects in the manufacturing of train wheels. The Amsted Rail work earned ImagineAbility almost $270,000 in revenue in 2019.

A. Adams Supply (1969) Ltd.

This privately held company with twenty employees in Winnipeg started operations some seventy years ago. Although ownership has changed several times over the years, A. Adams Supply operates as a wholesaler specializing in fasteners (i.e., nuts, bolts and screws, washers, anchors, and threaded rods) and cutting tools. In addition, A. Adams Supply provides customized products to the aerospace and the oil and gas sectors. It is in the oil and gas sector where its relationship with ImagineAbility lies.

The relationship with ImagineAbility started more than twenty years ago when a company called the Dixon Group started buying from Versatech (which later became ImagineAbility). Dixon Group provided the equipment to Versatech to cut metal link chain in six- and twelve-inch lengths and attach S-hooks to both ends, then began delivering forty-five-gallon barrels filled with chain to start production. These pieces of chain were then sold to buyers in the oil and gas sector. Later, Dixon Group contracted A. Adams Supply to source and deliver the chain length pieces and sold the equipment to A. Adams Supply, which has maintained the relationship with Versatech (now ImagineAbility) for more than twenty years.

The finished pieces of chain are hung vertically in crates provided by A. Adams Supply and shipped to Dixon Group, which incorporates them into equipment destined for the oil and gas sector. Since the very beginning, the work completed by ImagineAbility is priced on a piecework basis. ImagineAbility was initially approached for this contract due to the tedious nature of the work. Jack Enns, A. Adams Supply general manager, has managed this contract with ImagineAbility since joining the company fifteen years ago. He is extremely pleased with the "very easy [working] relationship" with ImagineAbility: "I have never had an issue with the quality or delivery of the work done by ImagineAbility." The contract with A. Adams Supply represents approximately $3,000 revenue for ImagineAbility. Although without a formal policy on social procurement or social purchasing, A. Adams Supply also purchases from another social enterprise, Kindale, in Steinbach, Manitoba.

Hold It and Opportunity Partners

The product Hold It and Opportunity Partners account for approximately $20,000 (less than 4 per cent of total earned revenue) for ImagineAbility. Opportunity Partners distributes Hold It across Canada through relationships with Canadian Tire Corporation and Home Hardware Stores Ltd. Founded in 1922 and headquartered in Toronto, Canadian Tire Corporation is a Canadian retail company selling a wide range of automotive, hardware, sports and leisure, and home products. Since 2010, Canadian Tire has been distributing Hold It. The sales to Canadian Tire bring in approximately $300,000, representing roughly 85 per cent of total annual Hold It sales revenue. Another long-standing Canadian retailer, Home Hardware Stores is a privately held Canadian home improvement, construction materials, and furniture retailer founded in 1964 and headquartered in St. Jacobs, Ontario. Home Hardware Stores started distributing Hold It in 2009. The annual revenue from Home Hardware Stores for Hold It is between $40,000 and $50,000, representing approximately 15 per cent of annual Hold It product sales revenue.

Summary: Lessons Learned

The success experienced by ImagineAbility offers valuable lessons and important insights into the challenges and opportunities facing social enterprises.

1. It is important to offer a service that can be difficult to source. One of the main reasons for customers initiating a relationship with ImagineAbility is related to the difficulty in finding workers/companies who can meet their specific needs.
2. Offering a quality and timely service is key to developing long-term relationships with organizational purchasers. Many of the relationships with ImagineAbility have been maintained over many years, for example, Coghlan's (more than fifty years), A. Adams Supply (more than twenty years) and Amsted Rail (almost ten years).
3. Excellent quality and competitive pricing are both more important than the social mission. Businesses currently purchasing services from ImagineAbility identify quality and competitive pricing as the two main reasons for supporting ImagineAbility, with its social mission ranking third.
4. Regardless of the level of earned revenue, many non-profit supported social enterprises (including ImagineAbility) that provide local employment and training programs require grant or government funding. Earned revenue alone is not sufficient to sustain them. Earned revenue at ImagineAbility accounts for only 20 per cent of its total annual revenue.
5. It is important to align potential work with participants' abilities and interests. ImagineAbility only enters into relationships with potential purchasers once participants and staff have reviewed the work entailed and determined that participants are not only able to do the work but also have expressed an interest in doing it.
6. Even with more than thirty-five organizational purchasers in the private sector, ImagineAbility has not yet been able to sell to the government. Only the City of Winnipeg and the provincial Crown

corporation Liquor and Lotteries have made small, isolated purchases, representing less than 1 per cent of sales revenue over the years.

7. Starting a stand-alone business like Opportunity Partners is challenging for the parent organization. It can take considerable resources including funds, time, and expertise to start a new social enterprise.

SOURCES

Interviews with ImagineAbility, Coghlan's Ltd., and A. Adams Supply (1969) Ltd.

ImagineAbility, https://imagineability.ca/

10 Wachiay Studio

YASMIN HARIRI

Introduction

Wachiay Studio is a screen-printing social enterprise located in Courtenay, British Columbia, on Vancouver Island. It began in 2012 as an after-school program at the Wachiay Friendship Centre, teaching Indigenous youth (fifteen to twenty-nine years old) the art and technique of screen-printing. After experiencing growth and success selling at local events, Wachiay Studio saw an opportunity to expand into a stand-alone operation and become a business, progressing from offering classes to printing and selling original goods and services. In 2015, the Friendship Centre opened a 2,500-square-foot studio, fully equipped with commercial screen-printing equipment and materials. Wachiay Studio became a corporation, owned by its parent organization Wachiay Friendship Centre, with a social focus. Any profits are reinvested into the studio to expand programming and grow the business, creating jobs and opportunities in the small community while reducing the parent organization's reliance on grants to operate. Despite being interested, Wachiay Studio has not yet engaged in social procurement.

Sales and Marketing

Wachiay Studio is a small business with gradually increasing annual sales, which approached $250,000 as of 2018. The studio operates two main product lines: production of screen-printed goods for customers and screen-printing services consisting of workshops and classes. Those interested in the services can participate individually or in a group, committing to a single class or multiple workshops. The main source of income for the studio comes from the screen-printing business, producing prints on items such as clothing and paper. Although

Wachiay Studio runs an online store for purchasing goods and services (e.g., original t-shirt designs, limited-edition art prints, courses and workshops, etc.), online sales account for less than 15 per cent of total sales. The studio earns the majority of its revenue from direct sales to local businesses, organizations, and individuals.

Wachiay Studio has been run by Andy MacDougall since its inception. MacDougall had over thirty-five years of experience in the screen-printing industry in Edmonton, Vancouver, and elsewhere around the world when he returned to Vancouver Island to help the Wachiay Friendship Centre establish Wachiay Studio. He is responsible for managing the social enterprise along with two to three support staff who assist in art production, printing, teaching, and administrative functions.

Wachiay Studio's marketing is fairly limited, with most of its sales driven through social networks and referrals. The studio intentionally promotes its social mission in its print and online marketing materials, but MacDougall himself indicates that the marketing content is infrequently updated. Its Facebook page is more active and regularly includes business updates and news. Beyond this, Wachiay Studio does not actively engage in conventional marketing to grow its business.

Parent Organization

The Wachiay Friendship Centre, the parent organization of the studio, has been serving the Indigenous community in the Comox Valley (K'ómoks First Nation's Unceded Traditional Territory) on the east side of Vancouver Island for over twenty-five years. The Friendship Centre offers its services to Indigenous people in the urban area although it is open to anyone in the community. These services include youth activities, Elders programming, legal advocacy, housing, tax assistance, the Helping Hands dry food program, the Roots program, services on behalf of the Ministry of Child and Family Services, and the FASD (fetal alcohol spectrum disorder) Keyworker program. Recently, the Wachiay Friendship Centre purchased the building where it has been operating and installed a large childcare centre, youth centre, and additional office space.

Wachiay Studio was initiated to support the Wachiay Friendship Centre by contributing to its financial stability and functioning. Wachiay Studio pays rent and utilities to the Friendship Centre for use of the facilities. The studio also collaborates with the Friendship Centre to offer customized programming for youth and adults. Alongside training programs, the studio fosters the health and growth of Indigenous culture and individuals through employment and artistic expression. The studio gives priority to hiring Indigenous youth as summer students and promotes Indigenous arts and crafts in its business.

Social Mission and Programming

The mission of Wachiay Studio is to

> create opportunities and provide skills training for Aboriginal youth and artists in the graphic arts and screen-printing. Profits from our operations will be reinvested in the ongoing operations and programs of the Wachiay Friendship Centre.

While this statement highlights Wachiay Studio's social aims, conversations with MacDougall and Wachiay Studio's purchasers reveal other dimensions to the social enterprise's community focus.

One Tribe

Wachiay Studio provides training and employment to urban and rural Indigenous youth through One Tribe, a collaborative initiative with the Friendship Centre. In One Tribe, youth participants learn how to create original designs, apply screen-printing techniques, and print their designs on clothing and paper goods. Their work is showcased and sold through a mobile booth that Wachiay Studio brings to festivals and events around Vancouver Island. A portion of the profits from their designs goes back to the studio while the rest are given as a commission to the young artists themselves. Wachiay Studio has created an online store and a Facebook page to promote its artwork and events.

Environmental Aims

Wachiay Studio is also a promoter of environmentally conscious printing practices. In its own studio, it uses water-based inks and trains participants to make conscious choices in their printing practices. MacDougall is actively engaged in a global discourse on environmentally conscious printing practices, including making trips to Mexico and Spain to demonstrate and train screen-printers in the use of environmentally friendly printmaking materials. Wachiay Studio promotes its environmental choices to customers as a purchasing factor.

Economic Development

Wachiay Studio is also proud of its contributions to the local economy in the Comox Valley. The studio has supported a number of new artists and screen-printers to develop small businesses on Vancouver Island and beyond. The studio supports the growth of the local economy by developing sustainable small businesses and training a skilled labour force to help these local businesses grow. MacDougall estimates that Wachiay Studio has assisted in the establishment of fifteen small maker businesses in the Comox Valley. In a desire to create favourable conditions for a differentiated marketplace, Wachiay Studio makes a point of not infringing on the business of like-minded enterprises in the Comox Valley region, especially those run by individuals trained and supported by the studio. Instead, the studio seeks opportunities to generate sales from outside the community through attracting new markets to its business.

Social Purchasing

Supported in its tight-knit community, Wachiay Studio primarily earns its revenue through social purchasing. As a business, the studio offers a high-quality product and delivers a consistent experience to its customers. MacDougall believes that customers are largely purchasing the studio's goods and services because of their quality. He indicates the social mission is a partial factor for purchasing, estimating that around 40 to 50 per cent of a customer's purchasing decision may be related to the social value of the studio. MacDougall remarked that

> most of our [business-to-business] customers use us because we are good at what we do, we are friendly to work with, and we use environmentally friendly materials. The fact we are a social enterprise is secondary to the quality of the product and service delivered.

Wachiay Studio's customers are a mix of organizational purchasers and individual consumers, the majority of whom are local to Vancouver Island. Organizational purchasers mostly place orders of custom-printed goods (e.g., t-shirts, paper materials, bags, etc.); however, some also buy group workshops or classes. The average order is between $500 and $1,000. These organizational purchasers do not put forth a tendering process but often ask the studio to provide price quotes before purchasing. To a degree, Wachiay Studio has catered the screen-printing business towards working with organizational purchasers since the studio has noticed that organizational purchasers are more likely to place orders regularly, whereas individual customers tend to purchase one-off orders. In contrast, workshops and online sales are largely driven by individual consumers. Some of its customers include a school board, an art and clothing business, and an FASD treatment organization.

District Principal, Indigenous Education (Comox Valley, British Columbia)

The school board became acquainted with Wachiay Studio through connections in their shared small-town community. The school board purchases from Wachiay Studio between ten to twenty times per year for its roster of schools. A typical purchase from the school board includes both goods (around twenty to three hundred items) and classes for students. Each purchase ranges between $300 and $3,000. Bruce Carlos, the district principal, indicates that he purchases from Wachiay Studio because of the strong relationship that he has with MacDougall and his team, and the specific nature of the classes and training the studio offers. While there are other studios in town, he goes to Wachiay Studio because it allows students, many of whom are Indigenous, to engage in a hands-on way with tasks such as t-shirt design and printing. While the social mission of Wachiay is not a primary purchasing factor for Bruce, it is certainly an added benefit. He is primarily drawn to the quality of the product, its competitive price point, and the benefit of supporting a local business. The district principal speaks very highly of working with Wachiay Studio and mentions how well the studio trains the school board staff in supporting students.

West Coast Karma

West Coast Karma – an art and clothing business – is a regular customer of Wachiay Studio, purchasing about twice a month. A typical purchase involves custom-printed goods (e.g., wood pieces, t-shirts, etc.) and averages $350 per order. West Coast Karma became connected to the studio through a referral from another customer. They are primarily attracted to the competitive pricing, the charitable status of the business, and the ability to support the local community. Gabby Mason, the owner of West Coast Karma, indicates that the social mission of Wachiay Studio is definitely a factor in the purchasing decision. He says he has not been able to find any other business with a social mission that is able to offer comparable pricing. Mason notes that he would characterize his social purchasing as "marketable" since he likes the fact that he can promote his decision to purchase from a social enterprise in his own marketing. As a business, Mason expresses a distinct interest in buying more exclusively from socially minded businesses. However, he still feels that it is often difficult to find these businesses. Mason would like to see a central repository on social enterprises in Canada, by industry and category, to make social purchasing more accessible.[1] He believes there should also be a means of quality control to support social enterprises in offering as high-quality goods as large corporations, allowing them to compete on par in the marketplace. Mason hopes to expand his purchasing to include occasional rental of Wachiay Studio's facilities.

Whitecrow Village

Whitecrow Village is an FASD treatment organization and an intermittent customer of Wachiay Studio, having purchased twice in 2017. Its orders were entirely printing services and averaged $1,100 each. The organization learned about Wachiay Studio through its connection to the Wachiay Friendship Centre. Kee Warner, the executive director, states that the social mission of Wachiay Studio was a significant factor in the non-profit organization's purchasing decision and that the studio's shared worldview around the engagement of individuals with symptoms of FASD was incredibly important. Their primary reasons for purchasing from Wachiay Studio were the employment of FASD participants, support for the local community, and reduction of community vulnerability. As an organizational purchaser, Whitecrow Village tries to purchase from socially aligned organizations on a regular basis. Warner indicates that the organization referred other people to Wachiay Studio about five times in 2017.

Social Procurement

Despite a keen interest in the new business opportunities procurement may afford, Wachiay Studio has not yet participated in formal procurement of any kind. MacDougall talks about two of the barriers that make him hesitant in seeking procurement opportunities: lack of human resources and production capacity.

---

1 Editors' note: While such information is available through sources including Buy Social's Certified Social Enterprise Suppliers, Social Enterprise Toronto, and Chantier de l'économie sociale in Québec, compiling a list of social enterprises that serve one's own local community still requires considerable effort.

Lack of Human Resources

One of the most significant barriers for Wachiay Studio to pursue social procurement is securing the human resources required to seek out and produce large-scale orders. Located in a rural town with a limited labour force, Wachiay Studio struggles to find or train screen-printers who can produce prints at the requisite quality. There is little margin for error or spoilage in the business, so the studio requires individuals who can produce consistently high-quality prints. Mac-Dougall points to the significant difficulty in attracting highly skilled individuals to live and work in a small town on Vancouver Island. As a social enterprise, Wachiay Studio prefers to hire and train local people, particularly Indigenous youth, with the necessary training taking approximately six months. The studio has applied for various grants or funding programs from local organizations, but it rarely receives timely responses. The lengthy application process means the youth participants willing to be trained often end up finding other low-skill employment, which translates into a lost opportunity for local human-resource development. This labour shortage could cause a major bottleneck in the business. At the same time, Wachiay Studio is so overwhelmed with existing business from social purchasing that it is unable to pursue procurement opportunities at this time. MacDougall stresses that without additional production support, he becomes consumed in production himself and has little latitude to focus on growth opportunities.

Production Capacity

Beyond human resources, MacDougall does not believe Wachiay Studio's physical infrastructure and craftsmanship would be suited to meet the consistency demands of larger-scale procurement. The studio produces handcrafted goods – a contrast to what MacDougall believes procurement contracts would require, i.e., machine-made products to ensure consistency in production. MacDougall's insight is based on his experience in other Vancouver screen-printing businesses that engaged in public procurement. He has not yet explored what kinds of procurement opportunities exist and whether Wachiay Studio may be suited to any of them.

Summary: Lessons Learned

Wachiay Studio raises a number of questions about the opportunities afforded to small social enterprises looking to scale up and participate in the greater Canadian and international economy. While Wachiay Studio produces high-quality and consistent goods, operates sustainably, and has an interest in expansion and growth, it perceives itself as unable to expand much further. While some social enterprises may wish to remain local and community oriented, Wachiay Studio has aspirations of expansion and growth to new markets and opportunities.

A few key lessons can be learned from the case of Wachiay Studio:

1. Wachiay Studio is a clear example of the complementary relationship of a social enterprise and a parent organization. The studio is dependent on the Wachiay Friendship Centre for space, participants, and a connection to Indigenous culture and Elders. On the other side, Wachiay Studio helps contribute to the missions of the Friendship Centre, provides a source of income through rent and utilities, and supplies specialized, high-quality training to members of the Centre in the art of screen-printing that allow them to showcase their art. Neither appears to be over-reliant on the other, but rather, symbiotically enriched by the partnership.

2. The barriers Wachiay Studio articulates surrounding social procurement point to the challenges around the capacity of rural social enterprises to participate in urban markets. There appears to be an inflection point where a social enterprise reaches a stage of success in the context of its local community but needs significant changes to scale up and participate in the broader economy (Corner & Kearins, 2018; Lyon & Fernandez, 2012). In the local community of the Comox Valley, Wachiay Studio has a strong reputation and loyal consumer base. In order to expand beyond the local market and pursue large-scale contracts and procurement opportunities, the studio is likely to require a significant shift in its business operations. For small social enterprises like Wachiay Studio, making the decision to expand requires significant adjustment to both business operation and organizational identity.

3. Although Wachiay Studio thrives on social purchasing, it faces barriers to social procurement. This confirms our overall finding that, in general, only social enterprises with significant income and a high assessment of their marketing capacity end up engaged in social procurement. The rest, like Wachiay Studio, rely on social purchasing to stay viable. That said, its social purchasing helps to support not only its own success, but also that of its parent organization, the Wachiay Friendship Centre.

4. While the focus on procurement processes is important (Young & Chandra, 2017), the case of Wachiay Studio highlights the need

for support and intervention for social enterprises, as part of their overall strategic planning, before they even begin to consider competing for procurement bids. MacDougall does not believe that Wachiay Studio is prepared or equipped to pursue procurement opportunities. Much of his perception of what readiness looks like is based on past experience with other organizations. It is possible that suitable procurement opportunities already exist for Wachiay Studio, but that staff are unaware of them.

REFERENCES

Corner, P.D., & Kearins, K. (2018). Scaling-up social enterprises: The effects of geographic context. *Journal of Management & Organization*, 27(1), 1–19. https://doi.org/10.1017/jmo.2018.38

Lyon, F. & Fernandez, H. (2012). Strategies for scaling up social enterprise: Lessons from early years providers. *Social Enterprise Journal*, 8(1), 63–77. https://doi.org/10.1108/17508611211226593

Young, L., & Chandra, F. (2017). *Recommendations for evaluating social procurement policy within the Canadian federal government*. Retrieved from https://dspace.library.uvic.ca/bitstream/handle/1828/8655/Chandra _Felicia_and_Young_Louisa_MPA_2017.pdf

OTHER SOURCES

Interviews with Wachiay Studios, Comox Valley Schools, West Coast Karma, and Whitecrow Village.

Wachiay Studio, https://wachiaystudio.com/

Wachiay Studio, http://www.facebook.com/Wachiay-Studio-913089595408098/

Wachiay Friendship Centre, https://www.wachiay.org/

11 Diversity Food Services

MARTY DONKERVOORT AND KIRSTEN GODBOUT

Introduction

Diversity Food Services (DFS), a work integration social enterprise (WISE) in the foodservices sector in Winnipeg with two parent organizations, presents a unique dual aspect to social purchasing. First, customers purchase DFS's products and services in restaurants, cafes, and grocery stores; and second, DFS purchases more than 60 per cent of its supplies from local farmers and suppliers. DFS is, therefore, both a social purchaser itself and a recipient of social purchasing by its customers. Since its inception in July 2009 at the University of Winnipeg (UofW), DFS has grown from $1.25 million in annual sales revenue to more than $3.5 million and from twenty-five employees to more than one hundred. These employees tend to come from the inner city of Winnipeg, and many are new immigrants, refugees, or Indigenous people who have faced barriers in entering the labour market. In addition, DFS has increased its operational sites from three locations at the UofW to six on campus and three off campus. Overall, DFS has led the way on North American university campuses in providing sustainable, nutritious food. Along the way, DFS has earned numerous awards and recognitions (see supplemental information at the end of this chapter). DFS's social and environment mission has contributed to the well-being of the community with its social return on investment (SROI) calculated to generate a return of $1.68 for every dollar spent by DFS (Akerstream, 2017).

Structure and Mission

Unique among the cases featured in this book, DFS is incorporated as a for-profit corporation with share capital. These shares are held by its two parent organizations: The University of Winnipeg Community

Renewal Corporation (UWCRC) with 52 per cent of the shares and Supporting Employment & Economic Development Winnipeg (SEED) with the remaining 48 per cent. DFS's board of directors consists of two members selected by the UWCRC, two selected by SEED, and one from the DFS management team. The UWCRC is a non-profit, charitable organization whose mandate is to work towards developing a sustainable university community that is attractive to the faculty, staff, students, and the greater community. SEED is a non-profit agency with an objective to combat poverty and assist in the renewal of inner-city communities by providing capacity-building services that assist low-income individuals, groups, and organizations in improving their social and economic vitality. SEED works with individuals and groups to start small businesses and save money for future goals. By offering business management training, individual consulting, and asset-building programs, SEED has been instrumental in changing the course of many lives in the inner city.

At Diversity Food Services:

> Our Vision is to produce quality, nutritious, and flavourful food in an environment that champions all who contribute their energy and skill – from the farmer, to the chef, to the service staff. Our service is distinguished by our passion for food and our abiding commitment to sustainable environmental practices whenever possible. Whenever possible, we choose to use food that has been sourced in a socially responsible manner, which includes reducing transportation costs, supporting fair-trade practices, and decreasing the dependency on food grown with herbicides. Our commitment includes providing food services in a caring work environment that offers meaningful employment opportunities to all employees. Integral to our Vision is creating a positive and caring atmosphere for all who eat, work, and serve.

Organizational Development

DFS was created in 2009 when Dr. Lloyd Axworthy, then president of the UofW, tasked the UWCRC led by Sherman Kreiner to review foodservices on campus. As part of the change and growth plan initiated at the UofW in the first decade of this millennium, the UWCRC took over the foodservices responsibilities from a private-sector contractor and was committed to planning foodservices that embraced the university's Campus Development Plan.

The UWCRC developed a strategy for campus foodservices, including procuring from and supporting local businesses based in Manitoba, promoting employment of local community members with a focus on those marginalized from employment, and advocating strong standards of earth stewardship and environmental practices, all while producing attractive and nutritious food on campus with student-friendly pricing. Familiar with the UWCRC's mandate to actively develop partnerships with community, private-sector, and public-sector organizations, SEED Winnipeg led by Cindy Coker approached the UWCRC to propose a social enterprise restaurant on campus. SEED had already identified the downtown campus as a prime location and drafted a business plan to operate a small campus restaurant. In addition, both organizations shared values related to local, organic, and ethical ingredients, making for a natural partnership.

The attraction for SEED to partner with the UWCRC to address foodservices on the UofW campus came from the interest in working with a foodservice business willing to create a workforce intentionally designed to include the individuals served by SEED. Based on the intersecting goals of SEED and the UWCRC, these two non-profit organizations collaborated to create a joint venture that in turn created DFS.

In February 2009, the joint venture between the UWCRC and SEED selected Kirsten Godbout (formerly of Bread & Circuses Bakery Café) and Chef Ben Kramer (formerly of the Dandelion Eatery) to work as consultants with Lydia Warkentin of the UWCRC and a representative from SEED's business development department to craft a business plan for DFS. Godbout and Kramer brought their acumen in terms of local procurement, production of fresh food featuring local ingredients, community-driven service, and working with a community-based inclusive workforce. After the consultation and development period, Godbout became and continues to serve as DFS's executive manager of operations, and Kramer worked as DFS's executive chef from July 2009 to August 2015. As DFS grew over its first decade of operations, the management team expanded to include Ian Vickers serving as chief operating officer (since July 2013) and chef Kelly Andreas, who took on the executive chef position from November 2015 to November 2019. A team of middle managers rounds out DFS's management team with roles such as chef de cuisine, front of house managers, and catering managers at DFS's multiple locations.

The opening of DFS in the summer of 2009 coincided with the opening of McFeetor's Hall, UofW's first student residence to include a meal-plan program, thus increasing the demand for quality food on campus. Another impetus for a new approach to foodservices at UofW is that prior to the opening of DFS, the UofW received two consecutive reviews by Maclean's, a news magazine featuring an annual review of Canadian universities and colleges, naming it the campus with the poorest food in Canada.

In July 2009, DFS assumed the lease for campus foodservices, taking over the three existing foodservice outlets as well as the on-campus catering services. During the first year of operations, DFS received start-up funds from its two parent organizations as well as third-party support in the form of grants, including employment partnership funding from the Government of Manitoba, funding for on-site English instruction for staff from the provincial language support for new Canadians and private funding support (e.g., quality kitchen shoes for staff and a delivery vehicle). DFS also took out a business loan and a line of credit from Assiniboine Credit Union, and a low-interest loan backed by the Jubilee Fund (an ethical investment fund established to raise awareness of poverty reduction, financial assets, and access to credit). The Jubilee Fund's focus on poverty reduction was an ideal match as a loan partner for DFS.

The initial staff complement at DFS was approximately thirty-five individuals, twenty-two of whom were experiencing challenges marginalizing them from employment such as language barriers, lack of employment references due to no recent employment or being new to Canada, experiences with addictions, a history with the justice system, and poverty. Since its inception, DFS has employed people from more than forty-five countries and continues to work with a diverse workforce with 65 to 70 per cent of the staff being those previously marginalized from employment.

After the 2009–10 school year, DFS realized that the ebb and flow of students based on the academic calendar needed to be balanced with opportunities beyond the campus community in order to create reliable year-round employment and to minimize revenue fluctuations and DFS's financial vulnerability. Beginning in the summer of 2010, DFS actively sought catering outside the UofW community to supplement its income during the quiet months on campus. The catering business at DFS expanded quickly with both small and large catering functions. The slower spring and summer periods on campus have allowed DFS's kitchen to commit to large-scale catering orders over the years – for example, orders for the Truth and Reconciliation gatherings at the Forks in June 2010, the volunteers of the Winnipeg Folk Festival in 2014 and 2015, the 2017 Canada Summer Games participants, as well as various corporate and private events in Manitoba.

As student enrollment and campus facilities and operations grew at the UofW in the early 2010s, DFS was called upon to increase its on-campus services. In October 2011, DFS opened the restaurant Elements in the Richardson College for Science and the Environment. Elements offers the campus community and students using meal plans an opportunity to access table-service dining on campus just steps from the doors of McFeetor's Hall. Within DFS, Elements provides an opportunity to learn the skills and knowledge needed to work in a made-to-order restaurant in addition to the cafeteria model used at DFS's original locations. The additional training and skills increase employability for trainees in the hospitality industry. However, these new opportunities also made DFS financially vulnerable with new debt, again through a low-interest Jubilee Fund loan. Considering most new restaurants take four to five years to become profitable and repay initial investment, DFS took on a significant risk against possible future gains during these early years of operation.

In January 2013, DFS further diversified its revenue streams with the *Diversity To Go* product line initiated through a partnership with Winnipeg's Vita Health stores. The *Diversity To Go* line adds over $100,000 annually to DFS's revenue as well as additional year-round jobs. In November 2014, DFS expanded its operations beyond the UofW campus with a foodservice contract with FortWhyte Alive (FWA), an environmental, education, and recreation centre on Winnipeg's perimeter. At FWA, DFS runs the Buffalo Stone Café as well as the catering for all meetings, functions, and events. Spring 2017 saw the next step of growth for DFS when it assumed the lease for the foodservices at Players, an Indigenous-owned golf course just north of Winnipeg.

Social Purchasing

As mentioned in the introduction, DFS is both a social purchaser of supplies and a beneficiary of social purchasing for its products and services by its customers. In addition to its on-campus food services locations and catering, it has entered into a supplier relationship with a large local health-food chain and several partnerships with other organizations and corporations to provide foodservices on their premises.

DFS as a Social Purchaser

With annual revenue of $3.4 million in 2018, DFS is a major purchaser of fresh and organic vegetables, fruit, meat, poultry, and dairy products from approximately sixty local suppliers. Right from the start, DFS has been committed to local purchasing where possible. The purchasing relationships with local farmers and suppliers were developed by DFS's first executive chef and continue to this day.

Of DFS's purchase of approximately $1 million in supplies in 2018, 60 per cent was from local farmers and suppliers within one hundred kilometres from the UofW's campus. Of the portion purchased locally, approximately 30 per cent was purchased directly from farmers, and the remaining 70 per cent via intermediaries such as Pratts Wholesale Ltd., Sysco, and others to take advantage of economies of scale for transportation.

DFS's commitment to purchasing locally is part of its overall philosophy regarding social and environmental concerns. Its purchasing policy supports local small-scale farmers in a number of ways. Guaranteed purchasing contracts allow farmers to plan their growing season and harvesting schedule, thus eliminating waste. Based on the personal relationships and established trust levels, farmers can produce organic crops without third-party certification, thereby reducing overall expenses. Direct purchasing also increases profit margins for farmers and producers with the elimination of intermediaries. In addition, the environment also benefits from this arrangement since less packaging is required, thus reducing the carbon footprint related to shipping costs.

The local growing season has an undeniable impact on the ability to purchase locally, although buying from local greenhouses helps to offset some of the seasonal effects. DFS tries to minimize these effects by purchasing root vegetables locally during harvest and putting products in cold storage for up to six months. It also steam-blanches potatoes to increase their shelf life. Local tomatoes purchased in season are used to makes sauces that can be stored and used throughout the rest of the year. These practices increase DFS's ability to continue with local purchasing and to manage costs.

Customers at University-Based Restaurants and Cafes

Thousands of students, faculty, and staff, as well as community members outside of the university, patronize DFS's six on-campus restaurants and cafes daily. In addition, students living at McFeetor's Hall have a mandatory meal plan provided by DFS. Together, the on-campus facilities account for approximately 42 per cent of DFS's annual revenue. Although the convenient location of DFS's facilities is a significant factor in purchasing decisions, there is competition on campus such as

Stella's Café and Bakery. Since the UofW is located in the heart of the city, scores of restaurants and cafes are located within walking distance from the campus. This means that potential purchasers have a great deal of choice, and location is not necessarily the most important factor. Quality, variety of offerings, and price are important drivers in the purchasing decision. While DFS's social mission is an important consideration for some, it is ultimately less important than the others to most purchasers.

DFS actively promotes its social mission to its patrons by placing ads in the student newspaper, wall posters in student facilities, and information cards on tables, all in an effort to educate and to differentiate DFS from the competition. The social and environmental mission also serves to explain the slightly higher prices compared to other food operations nearby.

Customers of Diversity To Go Products at Vita Health Fresh Markets

Vita Health Fresh Markets (VHFM), Canada's first health-food store, started up in 1936. VHFM is a privately owned company in Winnipeg with six stores throughout the city. Like DFS, the company is committed to sustainability initiatives including food waste diversion, recycling, energy efficiency, decreasing food miles travelled, and the reduction of plastics.

In 2013, DFS developed a fresh-food line with forty-three different products under the brand name *Diversity To Go*, including salads, wraps, soups, hummus, fruit cups, sauces and dips, heat-and-serve bowls, and cook-and-serve items. Not all items are sold in all six of VHFM stores as store managers purchase based on customer preferences and display space in the store, but every store in the chain carries some of the *Diversity To Go* product line. All of the items in the product line are produced in DFS kitchens. In 2018, *Diversity To Go* products accounted for 5 per cent of DFS's total revenue. This product line is sold mainly on its convenience and quality.

Purchasers of DFS's Catering Services

At the beginning, DFS only offered catering on campus; however, DFS soon added off-campus catering to boost its revenue. Adding catering to its operations (especially off-campus catering) was an important element to deal with the seasonality of the academic year. By 2014, the catering services had reached the milestone of ten thousand orders since 2009. In 2018, the catering business completed four thousand catering orders, accounting for 21 per cent of DFS's total income. Purchasers of DFS's catering services include the Truth and Reconciliation Commission and the Manitoba Dairy Association annual dinners.

Buffalo Stone Café at FortWhyte Alive

FortWhyte Alive (FWA) is a non-profit organization operating a nature centre, wildlife refuge, and a place for education on 640 acres of protected urban greenspace located in the southwest corner of Winnipeg. It is an award-winning destination for outdoor experiences connecting humans with nature through a variety of programs and events that foster sustainability in the local community. Its mission states that FWA is dedicated to providing programming, natural settings, and facilities for environmental education, outdoor recreation, and social enterprise.

Buffalo Stone Café is located in the Alloway Reception Centre, a scenic location on the FWA premises. The café features light savoury meals, freshly ground coffee, and bakery treats in a relaxing lakeside setting. Before DFS assumed the operation of the cafe in 2014, it was run by FWA's staff.

FWA's decision to work with DFS was driven by DFS's reputation for high-quality food at competitive prices but also by their shared social and environmental values. For DFS, the partnership presents an opportunity to address the seasonal fluctuations of its operations on campus. The partnership provides work for DFS's employees who would otherwise be laid off during the summer months.

Taking over the cafe at FWA also gives DFS access to the Winnipeg wedding catering scene since FWA is a prime location and hosts dozens of weddings throughout the year. As a consequence, revenue generated from Buffalo Stone Café has increased steadily every year. This is the result of the quality of the food and DFS's ability to bring in extra staff when needed to cater large private events. DFS and FWA equally share the expenses related to a full-time year-round staff person who promotes and coordinates private functions.

Since the start of the relationship, DFS has been able to purchase some of the food that is produced right on the premises of FWA. The cafe menu has incorporated both pork raised and vegetables grown on the FWA farm.

Although DFS's social mission is important to FWA, the social value perhaps plays a smaller role for customers patronizing the cafe. Success is mainly related to the quality of the food, service, and pricing. Although DFS's commitment to environmental sustainability and social issues is mentioned on FWA's website, it is neither well known nor considered a driving force for cafe patronage. Although the partnership experienced some early growing pains related to menu changes, Ian Barnett, the director of operations at FWA, describes the relationship as "very positive," where customers are pleased, revenue is growing, and FWA does not need to worry about foodservices, which is outside its expertise. The popularity of FWA and the seasonal visitation increase during spring, summer, and fall makes the partnership ideal for DFS's goals to achieve year-round employment.

Eagle's Roost Café at the Players Course

The Players Course is an Indigenous-owned golf facility in northwest Winnipeg, operated by the Southeast Resource Development Council (SERDC). SERDC, incorporated in 1978, is the formal unification of eight First Nations in the southeastern portion of Manitoba. In addition to the Players Course, SERDC operates four more subsidiary companies, including South Beach Casino located just north of Winnipeg.

In 2017, SERDC was seeking a new contractor to operate its clubhouse, Eagle's Roost Café & Grill, and issued a request for proposals. Eagle's Roost serves guests of the golf course, residences, and businesses in the neighbourhood, and caters events such as tournament banquets and weddings. DFS stood out among a number of bidders and was ultimately chosen because of its alignment with SERDC's values, especially the employment practices. DFS started operating the Eagle's Roost Café in the spring of 2017 as its second off-campus location. Similar to Buffalo Stone Café, the seasonal nature of the operation fits well with DFS's on-campus operations.

According to the Players Course, the relationship has been very successful. DFS has reached out to the neighbouring commercial and industrial businesses to patronize the cafe. Revenue from golfers has increased as a result of the food quality and excellent service. In addition, the catering business (e.g., weddings and parties at the golf course) has increased including events in the off-season. Rob Damsgaard, the director of golf operations, is very happy about the work of DFS, stating "DFS is very professional ... [and] responsible for increased revenue at the cafe."

Summary: Lessons Learned

The success in social procurement and social purchasing experienced by DFS offers lessons and insights into the challenges and opportunities facing social enterprises trying to develop and maintain these relationships with their individual customers and organizational purchasers.

1. The support from the two shareholders or parent organizations of DFS reflects the importance of leveraging the resources and the connections parent organizations have for social enterprises even after their fledging stages. Having achieved a brand presence and success on the campus of the UofW, DFS has been able to launch itself to the rest of the city to take on substantial contracts that might have been difficult for those without the strong backing of well-known organizations.
2. Diversification of services and product lines contributes to growth and stability of the workforce. The diversity in DFS's operations, including offsite catering services and a prepackaged product line, allows the social enterprise to stabilize year-round employment.
3. As illustrated in other cases, champions who believe in the social mission of the social enterprise are critical in making success a reality. Early champions at DFS include Dr. Lloyd Axworthy, Cindy Coker, and Sherman Kreiner. Both Coker and Kreiner have a long successful history in the social economy developing co-ops and social enterprises in both Canada and the US.
4. DFS's success is in part based on pursuing the environmentally and socially conscious consumer trend to purchase locally, reduce waste through less packaging and biodegradable containers, and buy ethical food that includes free-range poultry and meat. It is important to be part of a customer-driven trend.
5. The social mission of the DFS was identified as very important by DFS partners, FWA and Players Golf Course (ranking it as very important). This contradicts research showing that social mission ranks behind quality, service, and price in purchasing decisions (Loughheed & Donkervoort, 2009), which is borne out by DFS customers at their on-campus locations as well as customers at their partnership locations where food quality, service, and price are more important factors in their purchasing decisions.
6. Social enterprises can be self-sustaining. Although it received some limited start-up grants from SEED, DFS has been self-sustaining.

REFERENCES

Akerstream, A. (2017). Diversity Food Services local impact analysis (unpublished project report from an MBA course on sustainability experiential offered at Asper School of Business at the University of Manitoba).

Loughheed, G., & Donkervoort, M. (2009). Marketing social enterprise: To sell the cause, first sell the product. *Making Waves, 20*(2), 16–19.

OTHER SOURCES

Interviews with Diversity Food Services, FortWhyte Alive, and the Players Course.

Diversity Food Services, https://www.diversityfoodservices.com/

The University of Winnipeg Community Renewal Corporation, http://uwcrc .ca/

Supporting Employment & Economic Development Winnipeg, http:// seedwinnipeg.ca/

SUPPLEMENTAL INFORMATION

Financial Highlights (2013–18): Diversity Foods Services (in thousands)

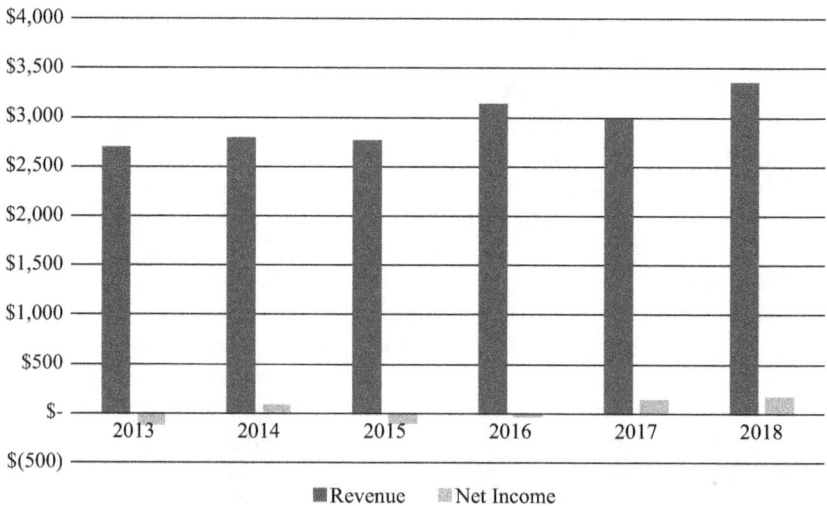

Revenue by Business Unit (2018): Diversity Food Services

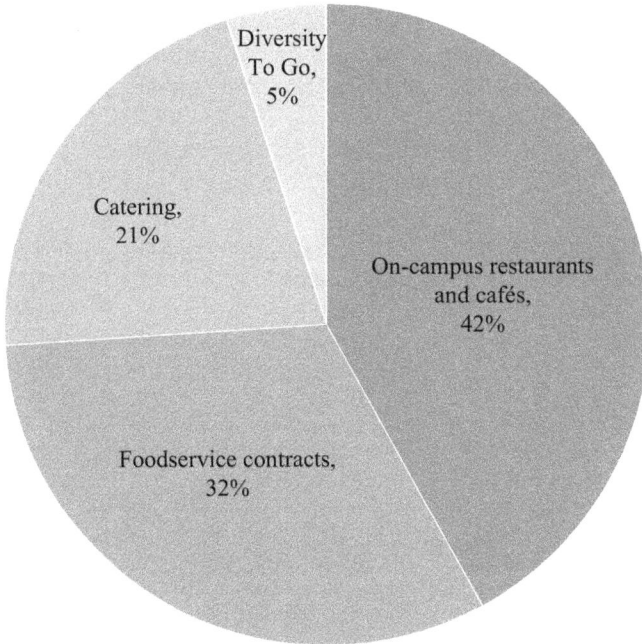

DIVERSITY FOOD SERVICES – RECOGNITION AND AWARDS

- 2010 – Golden Carrot Award for Business Community Food Champions
- 2010 – The Manitoba Round Table Award for Sustainable Development
- 2010 – Iron Chef Manitoba – Executive Chef Ben Kramer
- 2013 – Golden Carrot Award in Business – Executive Chef Ben Kramer (Awarded by the Physicians Committee for Responsible Medicine in the USA)
- 2013 – DEAM Manitoba Champion of Diversity Award
- 2013 – Gold Medal Plates GOLD – Chef de Cuisine Kelly Cattani
- 2014 – LEAF Level 2 Certification (Leaders in Environmentally Accountable Foodservice)
- 2014 – Winnipeg Chamber of Commerce Spirit of Winnipeg Award winner for the Social Enterprise category
- 2015 – Second highest scoring campus dining facility of Universities and Colleges in North America audited by the international AASHE-STARS sustainability campus index (top Canadian score)

- 2015 – CIAO MAGAZINE Restaurant of the Year
- 2015 – LEAF recognizes DFS as one of Canada's greenest restaurants
- 2016 and 2017 – Third highest scoring campus dining facility of Universities and Colleges in North American audited by the International AASHE-STARS sustainability campus index (only Canadian enterprise in the top five)
- 2017 – First place (tied) in Sierra Magazine's Cool Schools Ranking in the food category among 230 higher education institutions in North America
- 2018 – LEAF awarded Diversity Food Service's campus operations greenest Restaurant over 10,000 square feet in size in Canada
- 2018 – Excellence in Sustainability Award from the Province of Manitoba

12 Rainbow's End Community Development Corporation

ANNIE LUK AND DAVID WILLIAMS

Introduction

Located in Hamilton, Ontario, Rainbow's End Community Development Corporation is a non-profit, charitable organization that was established in 1997. It runs training programs and offers employment opportunities to individuals with mental health challenges through its social enterprises. With a vision "to provide opportunity where there was no opportunity," Rainbow's End strives to support its clients by helping them build skills and confidence through work. It is governed by a volunteer board of directors with eleven members and run by six full-time staff members. In the fiscal year 2016–17, Rainbow's End provided employment to seventy-six clients (or "team members" as Rainbow's End calls them) who worked nearly fifty hours each month.

The office of Rainbow's End is located in a light industrial area on Bigwin Road in Hamilton, a municipality approximately seventy kilometres south-west of Toronto. The organization began as a mental health program connected to St. Joseph's Healthcare Hamilton (commonly referred to as St. Joe's) in the 1990s. The program was conceived as a continuum of support allowing patients recently discharged from the hospital to further their recovery and well-being through social engagement found in the workplace. Today, team members at Rainbow's End come from St. Joe's, March of Dimes, the YMCA, and other community organizations in the Hamilton area. Although Rainbow's End was incorporated in 1997, it did not operate fully on its own (i.e., at arm's length from St. Joe's) until 2010 when an executive director was hired to expand the social enterprise. David Williams, the current executive director, began in 2011 as the operations manager. Williams came from a business background, having spent a career in the corporate world. Although Rainbow's End is now a completely separate corporate entity from St. Joe's, the two organizations maintain a very close relationship; the former parent organization has a representative sitting on Rainbow's End's board of directors and is one of its customers and partners. This close partnership with its former and now arm's-length parent organization is further detailed below.

Financial Information

The total revenue for the fiscal year 2018 for Rainbow's End was $971,262, of which $800,192 (82 per cent) came from the sales of goods and services. Unlike many charitable organizations, Rainbow's End received $171,070 as gifts and no funds as receipted donations. These funds came from St. Joe's and the Hamilton Niagara Haldimand Brant Local Health Integration Network (HNHB LHIN, a regional planning and funding body for health care on behalf of the Ontario government). The annual funding support from these two organizations is mainly to support the administration of Rainbow's End – i.e., office rent and the paid staff members who are primarily responsible for the overall coordination and administration of Rainbow's End. The funding arrangements are governed by memoranda of understanding specifying the requirements for Rainbow's End to qualify for the funding (e.g., employment for a certain number of team members each year). However, even though the funding is not sufficient to cover all the administrative costs (surpluses, if available, from Rainbow's End's six social enterprises also contribute to the overall administration), it is critical to the sustainability of Rainbow's End. As Williams states: "We would be sunk without the funding." While these funding supports have been consistent over the years, they are by no means certain for the future. With the ongoing discussion of eliminating the LHINs by the current provincial government (Crawley, 2019), the uncertainties around a considerable portion of funding for Rainbow's End are worrisome. Meanwhile, the funding from St. Joe's (a portion of St. Joe's base funding from the province) is backed by a strong commitment from the hospital's senior management. Despite the commitment, health care funding in Ontario is never completely secure. In the face of political and funding uncertainties, St. Joe's commitment to Rainbow's End remains consistent. One of the reasons behind this commitment is the strength of personal relationships between the two organizations, which is similar to the experiences of other social enterprises. In addition, Rainbow's End has established its reputation within St. Joe's over the last two decades, which helps reinforce the commitment from St. Joe's to Rainbow's End despite different personnel changes over the years.

Rainbow's End seeks additional funding when there are plans to expand specific aspects of the operations because the organization has only a limited financial reserve to support any expansion. For example, Rainbow's End has, in the past, accessed funding from the Trillium Foundation, Bell's Let's Talk Fund, ArcelorMittal Dofasco's Corporate Community Investment Fund, McMaster Students Union, Hamilton Community Foundation, and others.

Among the expenditures of Rainbow's End, compensation is the largest line item and accounts for 60 per cent of the total expenditures. The second largest line item is for supplies, constituting 27 per cent of the total expenditures. Each social enterprise within Rainbow's End operates with the objective to break even and, when possible, contribute to the administration of Rainbow's End. In fiscal year 2018, Rainbow's End recorded a small surplus of just under $30,000. Of note, Rainbow's End held few assets, most of which are in cash or short-term investments, suggesting the organization is able to operate its businesses without significant physical assets like buildings and equipment.

Social Enterprises

Rainbow's End currently has six social enterprises that train and employ people in the Hamilton-Burlington area. Williams calls the social enterprises "lines of business divisions" within Rainbow's End, as opposed to programs, because he sees them less as extensions of social or community services but more as workplaces that welcome those with mental health challenges. Each business division is responsible for its profit and loss and strives to break even with its revenues against wages and supplies. The negotiation of the contracts is generally set up to ensure that the wages and supplies are covered by the revenues. Nonetheless, Rainbow's End's more profitable businesses cross-subsidize the ones that are less so.

Prior to the establishment of these social enterprises, when Rainbow's End was still a program at St. Joe's, there was a sheltered workshop called Harp's Ceramics run by the hospital's vocational counsellors to provide support and programming for patients (who, in the 1990s, were paid around five to eight dollars per hour as an honorarium). Similar to many social enterprises, the sheltered workshop model evolved into social enterprises when the programming staff realized the importance of being able to offer market wages along with the sense of meaningful employment in an actual business (as opposed to being participants in a community program). As a result, in the late 1990s and early 2000s, Rainbow's End closed Harp's Ceramics, shifted its operating model from a sheltered workshop to a social enterprise, and became a separate entity from St. Joe's.

At present, two of the six social enterprises offer foodservices – Colours Café and Rainbow's End Bistro. These two social enterprises are the largest within Rainbow's End, employing seventeen to twenty team members. Sales from these two social enterprises account for about two-thirds of the sales revenue for Rainbow's End, with Colours Café at $272,000 and the Bistro at $267,000. Both are operated at the West Fifth Street campus of St. Joe's. Opened in 2014, Colours Café is located on the second floor and sells coffee, tea, baked goods, and snacks to inpatients, staff, and visitors at the hospital. It is an interesting arrangement that the inpatients are served by people who share their struggles with mental health. Colours Café offers training and employment for those who may have been patients at St. Joe's (Dunphy, 2014). The Bistro, started in 2015 on the ground floor of the hospital, offers meal service as well as catering (both on-site and off-site) using the cafeteria kitchen inside the hospital (shared with Tim Hortons, which operates beside the Bistro; the hospital operates a separate kitchen to supply meals for inpatients).

The Bistro is the newest social enterprise in the Rainbow's End port-folio. The way this opportunity came about highlights the importance of Rainbow's End's close relationship with St. Joe's. In 2014, after the current West Fifth campus was redeveloped, St. Joe's had to find a new cafeteria operator. Prior to the redevelopment, the hospital ran the caf-eteria, but they decided not to continue due to challenges in turning a profit. Once the redeveloped site opened, Aramark – a commercial food-service operator that also runs the cafeterias at the other locations of St. Joe's – ran the cafeteria for a time and then notified the hospital that it would pull out because it was also struggling to turn a profit. The hospi-tal issued a request for proposals but saw little interest from the private sector; the hospital suspected a general perception of unprofitability for the cafeteria was to blame. This was when St. Joe's decided that perhaps Rainbow's End could give it a try. This was a significant opportunity for Rainbow's End because of the size of the kitchen and the breadth of the skills required to run the only cafeteria that supports an 850,000-square-foot facility with more than 305 beds. Although some equipment was already in place at the hospital's kitchen (which would have been made available to whoever would take up the contract), Rainbow's End needed to purchase additional equipment on their own. The way Rainbow's End came into the opportunity to run the cafeteria is consistent with the mar-ket failure theory that posits how non-profit and voluntary organizations are able to meet the market demands for certain goods and services when the private sector is not (Young & Brewer, 2016).

The unique nature of the relationship between Rainbow's End and St. Joe's through the Bistro and Colours Café is best highlighted in contrast to how most hospitals (or most publicly funded institutions or facilities such as colleges, universities, and airports) handle food-services and other potentially profit-making offerings such as parking and gift shops. Private businesses usually operate as concessionaires inside these institutions or facilities, meaning that the private businesses would typically pay the public institutions a combination of rent/fee and a portion of their revenue for the right to operate the business. Because of the close relationship between Rainbow's End and St. Joe's, the arrangement for the Bistro and Colours Café is different from Tim Hortons, which operates as a more conventional concession adjacent to the Bistro at the West Fifth campus. The Bistro and Colours Café do not pay rent, and they also occasionally receive support for getting required certifications (e.g., for health and safety). While these in-kind contributions are important for the financial success of Rainbow's End, St. Joe's willingness to offer support and total commitment to the sustainability of Rainbow's End and the well-being of those who work there is, as Williams puts it, "undoubtedly more critical to Rainbow's End and our mission." This illustrates the importance of external support in terms of funding, expertise, labour, and other in-kind resources (provided by the arm's-length parent organization, St. Joe's, in this case) to the ability of social enterprises to fill the demand not met by the private sector (Young & Brewer, 2016).

Three of the other social enterprises at Rainbow's End are related to maintenance and janitorial services – Mow-Town (or Snow-Town in the winter months), the Clean-Up Crew, and R.E.A.L. (which stands for Rainbow's End Alternative Labour). They are based at the office of Rainbow's End, where all the equipment and trucks are stored. Mow-Town is the longest-standing social enterprise within Rainbow's End, with two to five team members. The crew for Mow-Town works mostly for residential customers, providing landscape and snow-removal services. They typically work in teams of two or more with their own truck and trailer of equipment. However, they do sometimes work individually after being dropped off, with their equipment (e.g., lawnmower or leaf-blower), at the customers' locations. The arrangement is similar for R.E.A.L., which offers casual labour to individual or institutional customers. Those who work as part of the Clean-Up Crew (about nine team members currently) provide facility maintenance services for commercial buildings such as offices, churches, or hospitals. They work individually or in small groups at a frequency specified by the customers (for example, once or twice a week).

Finally, Pins 'n Needles was established in 2005 and currently employs two women who use commercial sewing machines and sergers to carry out custom projects for customers. This social enterprise has been on contract since 2014 with Mylan Canada, a pharmaceutical company producing Dream Kits, a package including a pillow protector and terry cloth pillowcase, specifically for individuals who experience side effects from their medications for schizophrenia. The pharmaceutical company provides funds for the wages and the supplies (valued at around $30,000 a year for about three hundred kits) for Pins 'n Needles to produce the Dream Kits, which Mylan would mail its own customers across Canada. Each Dream Kit includes a card that explains to patients who made the kit for them. This relationship with the pharmaceutical company came about because of Rainbow's End's relationship with St. Joe's, since many of the patients were originally with St. Joe's.

With reference to training, those working in foodservices go through more formal training while the other social enterprises usually hire people who already have some experience with the equipment for the job. The training in foodservices includes job shadowing, specific coaching from the chef manager in the areas of food preparation, cash handling, customer service and communication, as well as certification processes for safe handling of food. As the number of team members grows, the training is becoming more formal and now includes WHMIS (Workplace Hazardous Materials Information System), occupational health and safety, etc. When hiring supervisors for the individual social enterprises, Williams emphasizes that it is far more important to hire people who have teaching experience instead of looking for those with only technical skills. This way, the supervisors of the individual social enterprises are able to work well with the team members rather than being solely focused on getting the job done.

Several team members have been working at the social enterprises for around five years or more. Rainbow's End offers the opportunity for team members to receive training and then transition to other employment, as well as to stay with Rainbow's End and continue with their work. Team members do not feel pressured to leave the social enterprises within a specific period of time, as may be common in some community programs.

Social Procurement and Social Purchasing

To those involved with Rainbow's End, the social mission is an important aspect of its identity and is clearly promoted on its website. It is sometimes easier for Rainbow's End to convince organizational purchasers to buy from it because many of these customers are already well aware of its social mission. As far as submitting bids is concerned, Rainbow's End finds it difficult to pursue procurement opportunities from government agencies partly because government contracts tend to be larger than what Rainbow's End could take on and partly because many of the government contracts are located in Toronto. There are some social enterprises in the Hamilton area, and Rainbow's End takes advantage of working with them as partners. However, the Hamilton area does not offer as many partnering opportunities as would exist in a larger city like Toronto. Even though Rainbow's End is open to collaboration with non-profit organizations or social enterprises, the level of effort and expertise to create a team to fit procurement requirements is not realistic (Muñoz, 2009). In addition, although Hamilton is definitely not a rural area, the geographic constraints of procurement opportunities being primarily present around large urban centres such as Toronto are similar to those experienced by social enterprises located in rural areas (Lang & Ferguson, 2012; Lang et al., 2016).

Although Rainbow's End does not engage in social procurement, a number of organizational purchasers buy from it on a less formal basis. One of these organizational purchasers is Eucharist Church, located in downtown Hamilton. Eucharist Church is under the denomination of the Canadian Baptists of Ontario and Québec, with about one hundred in its congregation. The church was established around 2010 with a social justice and community focus. Up until March 2018, Eucharist Church was renting other facilities for its services while it was raising funds to buy its own place. After purchasing a 125-year-old church from the First Romanian Baptist Church in March 2018 (Fragomeni, 2018), it also needed to purchase cleaning and maintenance services. The building committee had already heard about Rainbow's End and discussed different options – an example of word-of-mouth marketing typically used by social enterprises (Mitchell et al., 2016). The committee decided it would be important to hire someone who could benefit from the employment beyond the paycheque: "The main reason to work with a social enterprise is because we believe in their mission serving folks with mental health concerns." In fact, Eucharist Church rates the social mission as very important for its purchasing decisions. Supporting the local community and employment/training of a target population are the two top reasons for purchasing the services from Rainbow's End. Since the summer of 2018, Eucharist Church has been contracting two cleaners from the Clean-Up Crew at Rainbow's End to clean the church every Monday for four hours. The cost for the service is twenty-two dollars per hour plus supplies, which total roughly one hundred dollars each week. The pricing, according to Eucharist Church, is fairly "reasonable and typical" of other service providers. Pricing is the third top reason for choosing Rainbow's End. Not only is Eucharist Church satisfied with the pricing, it also gives high satisfaction as a purchaser. Despite emphasizing the importance of social mission, Eucharist Church does not have a formal policy to make social purchases. The church feels that it is still too small to need a policy.

A private facility management company is another organizational purchaser for Rainbow's End. The company hires Rainbow's End for janitorial services on an annual contract valued just under $25,000. The contract is for maintaining the grounds at St. Joe's West Fifth campus. Through the procurement process, this private facility management company was hired by the hospital and in turn, the private contractor subcontracts to Rainbow's End for janitorial services. Good service and good cause are the reasons behind this private company's purchasing decision for the services from Rainbow's End. The company finds it easy to work with the social enterprise and is highly satisfied with its performance. The top three reasons for choosing to work with Rainbow's End are quality of goods/services, employment/training of target population, and reducing community vulnerability. The social mission of Rainbow's End is moderately important to this private business. The interviewee speaking on behalf of the facility management company does not know whether it has any formal policy for social procurement or purchasing as it is part of a much larger conglomerate. Nor is he aware of any other purchases or contracts with other social enterprises.

St. Joe's is also a significant institutional customer, as well as a partner, for Rainbow's End. Hospital departments within the West Fifth campus are encouraged to use Colours Café and the Bistro for all their internal catering. However, some departments may still choose to use outside caterers. The number of catering purchases for Colours Café and the Bistro has increased over time. In the first few years when the West Fifth campus reopened, both the hospital and Rainbow's End put more effort into promoting the foodservices. Now, the two social enterprises are quite embedded in the day-to-day operation of the hospital.

Summary: Lessons Learned

The unique and close relationships between Rainbow's End and its arm's-length parent organization, St. Joseph's Healthcare Hamilton, have a myriad of implications for the success for Rainbow's End. On the financial front, the ongoing funding support from St. Joe's remains critical to the sustainability of the organization. In addition to Rainbow's End, St. Joe's also supports several other non-profit organizations (e.g., housing providers) in a similar capacity to help ensure the continuing care and well-being for individuals who may have once been patients at St. Joe's. Other than the monetary support, Rainbow's End also benefits from the in-kind support from St. Joe's, including the rent-free use of the facilities and space inside the West Fifth campus. Such benefits clearly are not extended to profit-oriented businesses. The social mission of Rainbow's End is the primary reason for St. Joe's to provide such generous support. Although not reported in any financial statements, the extensive in-kind support from St. Joe's contributes significantly to Rainbow's End's ability to break even.

For the team members at Rainbow's End, they have the reassurance that support is there for them, when and if needed, to balance the demands of being independent and working on their mental health recovery. Even though the team members are not patients of St. Joe's, the easy and ready availability of vocational counsellors and other support staff has smoothed team members' employment transition and maintained the sustainability of employment at Rainbow's End.

With respect to customers, St. Joe's has also been instrumental in connecting Rainbow's End to potential institutional customers such as the private facility maintenance company and Mylan Canada. The opportunities to discuss business opportunities with such private businesses may not have been possible without the pre-existing working relationships between these businesses and St. Joe's. Even as far as individual customers are concerned, employees from St. Joe's were among the first to use Mow-Town for residential landscape maintenance. Word of mouth, as seen in other case studies, continues to be an essential part of the social enterprise's marketing plan.

To summarize, the lessons learned from this case include the following:

1. Maintaining existing relationships could be tremendously beneficial, especially with partners and customers who are already familiar with the social benefits that come with their buying decisions.
2. Where possible, additional opportunities could come from leveraging existing relationships. The contracts with Mylan and the private facilitate maintenance company may not have come to be without St. Joe's acting as a referral. The power of word-of-mouth marketing cannot be underestimated.
3. Customers interested in contributing to social benefits through their buying decisions are likely to be willing to pay slightly more for

the goods and services. It is important for them to understand what social value their purchases bring.

4. In-kind support is another significant way partners and customers could support social enterprises, particularly during the early development stages and when taking on new initiatives.

REFERENCES

Crawley, M. (2019, January 17). Ford government poised to dissolve regional health agencies, sources say. *CBC News*. https://www.cbc.ca /news/canada/toronto/lhin-ontario-doug-ford-local-health-integration -networks-1.4980509

Dunphy, B. (2014, April 4). St. Joe's café puts human face on mental illness – and serves good java, too. *The Hamilton Spectator*. https://www.thespec .com/news-story/4448153-st-joe-s-caf-puts-human-face-on-mental-illness -and-serves-good-java-too/

Fragomeni, C. (2018, April 11). Decaying Hamilton church building reborn after purchase by vibrant new congregation. *The Hamilton Spectator*. https:// www.thespec.com/news-story/8386112-decaying-hamilton-church -building-reborn-after-purchase-by-vibrant-new-congregation/

Lang, C., & Ferguson, M. (2012). *Documenting the learning. The rural social enterprise project and the foundation for rural living*. https://ccednet-rcdec.ca /sites/ccednet-rcdec.ca/files/frl_rsep_learning_document_fv.pdf

Lang, C., Ferguson, M., & Harrison, B. (2016). *Rural social enterprise and community ecosystem development: Policy leverage points*. OMAFRA. https:// theonn.ca/wp-content/uploads/2016/05/NewDirections-Research-Report -Final-April-10-2016.pdf

Mitchell, A., Madill, J., & Chreim, S. (2016). Social enterprise dualities: Implications for social marketing. *Journal of Social Marketing*, 6(2), 169–92. https://doi.org/10.1108/JSOCM-06-2015-0043

Muñoz, S. (2009). Social enterprise and public sector voices on procurement. *Social Enterprise Journal*, 5(1), 69–82. https://doi.org/10.1108/17508610910956417

Young, D.R., & Brewer, C.V. (2016). Introduction. In D.R. Young, E.A. Searing & C.V. Brewer (Eds.), *The social enterprise zoo: A guide for perplexed scholars, entrepreneurs, philanthropists, leaders, investors, and policymakers* (pp. 3–14). Edward Elgar Publishing.

OTHER SOURCES

Interviews with Rainbow's End Community Development Corporation, a private facility management company (via email), Eucharist Church, and St. Joseph's Healthcare Hamilton.

Rainbow's End Community Development Corporation, https://rainbowsend
.ca/
Rainbow's End Community Development Corporation – 2016–17 Annual
Report – https://rainbowsend.ca/wp-content/uploads/2018/12/2016-2017
_Annual-Report.pdf

PART 4

The Dilemma of Selling Social Value

At the Centre for Learning, Social Economy, and Work (CLSEW) at the University of Toronto where the editors of this book work, we often purchase our event catering from Common Ground Co-operative – a social enterprise supporting adults with developmental disabilities. Every time we see those who work at Common Ground laying out the food and beverages with care and interacting with event attendees, there is little doubt about the social value of Common Ground's work. However, even when many buyers we spoke with in our study talk about their appreciation of the social benefits generated by their purchases, results from our study show that whether and how to sell social value remains a dilemma for many social enterprises.

In part 4, we use the following cases to discuss the challenge behind the decision to market or not to market social value:

- Let's Work Atlantic and Market Wizards (pseudonyms, Atlantic Canada)
- EthniCity Catering (Calgary, Alberta)
- Horizon Achievement Centre (Sydney, Nova Scotia)
- Calgary Progressive Lifestyles Foundation (Calgary, Alberta)
- Stone Hearth Bakery (Halifax, Nova Scotia)

These cases offer a range of approaches to marketing social value by social enterprises. A few (such as Let's Work Atlantic) are very careful regarding which customers they talk to about their social value. Others, such as Calgary Progressive Lifestyles Foundation, include their support for people with disabilities in all their marketing materials. The unique situation of Stone Hearth Bakery, part of a complex supply chain involving wholesale, distribution, and retail, presents particular challenges for this social enterprise because it may not have any direct relationship with the end consumers, who arguably drive the ultimate preference for social value.

Both our survey results and many of the cases in this book show that price and quality are still primary considerations for customers, which is consistent with previous research by Loughheed and Donkervoort (2009). Social value usually only comes into play when the social enterprises are more-or-less competitive with other types of businesses on price and quality (LePage, 2014). While many customers indicate that social value is important in their purchasing decisions, it remains secondary to the more conventional, economic factors. As the case of EthniCity Catering points out, even highly ethically minded customers have limitations.

In addition to having social value as a secondary consideration, some of the social enterprises featured as cases in this book also have to fight against the stigma attached to the disabilities or challenges facing their program participants. The cases in this section talk about how some of their customers would question the capability of the program participants in delivering quality products or services. The stigma facing program participants can also be transferred to the social enterprises that support them. Questions of stigma may possibly play a part in the decision of Let's Work Atlantic to be only identified by a pseudonym. Calgary Progressive Lifestyles Foundation says that its marketing effort is about not only selling goods and services but also changing people's perception and assumptions about disabilities.

In addition to issues of stigma, some of the social enterprises say they would not want their customers to make their purchasing decisions based solely on sympathy or charity for the program participants. Such purchases, according to the social enterprises, do not help contribute to the sense of self-worth and self-esteem for their program participants. They want the participants to feel their work is just as good, if not better, as any in the marketplace. In other words, the social enterprises want the participants to know their work has merit on its own, despite their challenges.

In this sense, the social benefits generated by the social enterprises are not seen as a value added to the goods and services sold by the social enterprises and even become an impediment to how the social enterprises compete in the marketplace. This is doubly problematic for social enterprises when the programming required to train and support the program participants is likely to incur additional costs that are not part of the equation for other businesses offering the same goods and services. It is not only difficult for the social enterprises to demonstrate that social value should be a critical consideration, but it is also necessary to keep their products and services competitively priced.

Fortunately, many of the programming costs can be offset by funding from governments or foundations. Unfortunately, this additional source of funding could be viewed as giving the social enterprises an unfair pricing advantage, according to Horizon. As a result, Horizon never prices its goods and services more than 5 per cent lower than the going market prices. The competitive pricing offered by social enterprises is also sometimes perceived by their customers and their competitors as a sign that the social enterprises are not paying their program participants market wages, hence reducing the social value created by the social enterprise.

Two of the social enterprises in this section – Let's Work Atlantic and Horizon – have prior experience preparing bids for procurement. However, both make it clear their experience was not one of social procurement. Their experience is that social value is rarely, if at all, a criterion in government procurement regardless of the policies in place. In the few instances when social value may be pitched as a plus, price and quality remain the primary drivers for decision-making.

The cases in this section highlight that the supply chain from the customer side has yet to incorporate social value, which leaves many social enterprises with little to no opportunity to leverage their social value or use it as a differentiating factor in the marketplace. The ongoing negative assumptions about the capability of people who have faced employment exclusions also present additional challenges for the marketing efforts of social enterprises.

Guiding Questions:

1. What are the different approaches used by the cases in addressing the dilemma of marketing social value?
2. What are the marketing challenges that are unique to these social enterprises, especially compared to their competitors in the marketplace?
3. Do you think social enterprises should market their social value?
4. How can social value be marketed by social enterprises without compromising the dignity of marginalized people?
5. Does social value have a place in the market?

REFERENCES

LePage, D. (2014). *Exploring social procurement*. Accelerating Social Impact CCC, Ltd. https://ccednet-rcdec.ca/sites/ccednet-rcdec.ca/files/ccednet/exploring-social-procurement_asi-ccc-report.pdf
Loughheed, G., & Donkervoort, M. (2009). Marketing social enterprise: To sell the cause, first sell the product. *Making Waves, 20*(2), 16–19.

13 Let's Work Atlantic and Market Wizards[1]

ANNIE LUK

Introduction

Let's Work Atlantic (LWA) is a non-profit organization located in one of the major cities in Atlantic Canada, with a mission to support and empower individuals with disabilities. Although incorporated in the late 1960s, LWA opened its doors in the mid-1970s to about twenty clients who needed support due to their disabilities. At the time, the organization operated with fewer than ten staff members and offered day programs.

Susan Smith, the current executive director of LWA, has been with the organization since the mid-1980s and can still remember when "it was a small agency in a residential area." Forty-five years after it first started offering its programs and services, the organization now serves more than six hundred clients with over one hundred staff members. LWA serves clients who are living with developmental, intellectual, psychiatric, and/or physical disabilities. Throughout its years of growth and evolution, LWA has maintained its mandate to support clients through training and employment opportunities and by helping "transfer people into the community to build up their confidence."

Organizational Development

Over the years, LWA has transformed itself from a sheltered workshop to an organization offering a wide range of support and outreach services. In assisting clients to gain employment, LWA provides a variety of training, social, and community services to help its program

---

1 Please note that all the names in this case are pseudonyms as per request by the organization.

participants not only learn the necessary skills to obtain employment but also adapt to different work environments outside the organization.

Currently, LWA consists of five divisions. The employment services division supports program participants who are interested in entering the workforce. Programs within this division include workplace essential skills, job coaching, job search centres, matching employers with potential employees, and building participants' social and workplace confidence. The fifteen-week workplace essential-skills program for up to twelve participants trains those interested in entry-level positions in retail, administration, foodservices, etc. The program for social and workplace confidence runs over fourteen weeks for a maximum of thirteen participants and includes providing participants with workplace experience at LWA or one of the community partner employers. The second division at LWA runs the social and community programs and offers a wide range of activities from art and music to health and woodworking. Another division is specialized in one-on-one support services for individuals with complex needs and acute challenges. The organization also runs a residential division providing assistance for independent living to individuals with complex needs.

The last division within LWA is the social enterprise, Market Wizards (MW), which is one of very few organizations in our collection of cases that has both experience in preparing and submitting procurement bids and also success in winning them. MW is a social enterprise specialized in creating branded marketing and promotional materials such as silk-screened t-shirts, engravings, large-format printing, packaging, and signage. First started in the early 1980s, MW now has fourteen paid employees who oversee the day-to-day operations of the division. Smith says the impetus for MW is the fact that finding jobs is "very, very difficult" for people with extreme disabilities. MW currently works with around forty to fifty program participants who receive job training or are employed in the division.

As one of the divisions within LWA, MW offers job skills training and employment opportunities to individuals with disabilities. Some of those who have received training may end up working elsewhere while others find work at MW. In addition to the programming benefits, revenues from MW also "assist other programs [within LWA] and help with sustainability." Up until 2016, MW operated more closely under LWA's banner. In 2016, the social enterprise rebranded itself to be a specialized supplier of a wide range of advertising, promotional, and marketing products.

Although MW has its own website and a separate name, the social enterprise continues to share a location with its parent organization.

MW also receives personnel, space, and financial support from LWA. For those who are training or working within MW, LWA is also able to provide what Smith calls "wraparound services" for them "to make sure we're providing services that meet all the individuals' needs to find success."

The website for MW lists not only all the different promotional products that the social enterprise could help its customers design, it also hosts a blog offering tips on advertising and promotions. At first glance, the website has little mention of LWA and the social mission for MW. Even though the slogan for the social enterprise emphasizes a sense of community, the slogan may be somewhat cryptic for those unfamiliar with its status as a social enterprise or its connection with LWA. The details with respect to MW's social mission are more apparent in the description of the organization, where visitors to the website learn that all of the profits from MW are reinvested in the programs at LWA.

LWA is a large organization compared to many other cases in this book. In 2018, it reported over $5 million in revenue, of which about 60 per cent was funding from the provincial government. The sales of goods and services account for nearly one-third of the total revenue. Although LWA is a registered charity with an affiliated foundation, the total amount of donations collected by both entities in 2018 was minuscule, representing less than 0.1 per cent of the organization's total revenue.

Between 2014 and 2016, the total revenue of LWA remained relatively stable – around $3.3 million each year with funding from the provincial government accounting for about two-thirds and the remaining one-third from sales of goods and services. Since 2016, the revenue from the sales of goods and services has grown by 25 per cent to 30 per cent each year until reaching $1.6 million in 2018. Similarly, funding from the provincial government during the same two-year period also saw a roughly 20 per cent annual increase. In that same period, the organization increased its expenses on advertising and promotion by over 60 per cent (from spending approximately $16,000 in 2016 to over $26,000 in 2018). Despite the considerable increase, this amount remains small in relation to its sales revenue. Since the organization receives few donations, it is likely that expenses on advertising and promotion were for the social enterprise.

Engagement with Procurement Opportunities

This case is an unusual one among all the cases in this book because LWA/MW has experience submitting procurement proposals to all three types of organizational purchasers – governments, businesses, and other non-profit organizations. Not only that, it has also won contracts from all three types of purchasers. The organization's success is consistent with the survey findings in this study, in that it is a large organization with many employees and substantial revenue. It also rates its own capacity in preparing bids and in demonstrating its social value quite highly.

Although MW mentions the social benefits from its operations in its website, Smith says the division is also "very selective not to put in print or highlight this." Smith further states the rationale behind this choice:

> We do not want our customers to purchase from us because we employ people with disabilities. We want them to understand who we are, what we do, and why they should buy from us. The people that work here are valued employees.

This is a sentiment shared with other social enterprises wanting to emphasize the quality of the program participants' work in order to help boost their confidence, instead of benefiting only because of charity or worse yet sympathy.

Another issue facing MW, Smith points out, is despite paying market wages to participants, she still has to counter the "perception that we do not pay people with disabilities or pay them piecework" in order to keep the prices competitive. Indeed, a common perception of social enterprises, particularly those supporting individuals with disabilities, is that they have an unfair competitive advantage because they do not pay market wages or in some ways exploit their clients (Quarter et al., 2015). As a result, the marketing efforts of MW do not necessarily emphasize competitive pricing but rather prioritize the values from (1) quality of goods/services, (2) environmental impact, and (3) supporting local community. Smith sums it up neatly: "When you purchase from us you are giving back to your community. All proceeds support other programs that fall within our mandate." MW also markets itself online; although customers cannot yet make their purchases online, the division is planning to implement this option in the future.

From MW's experience with procurement, examples of winning bids include a contract with the provincial government for approximately $15,000, another contract in 2017 with a large industrial company for nearly $100,000, and a contract over $10,000 from a national charitable organization. Many of the requests for proposals (RFPs) that MW responds to do not have any specific requirement to demonstrate social value, and yet it is clearly important to some of their organizational purchasers. As Smith says,

> The majority of our business [comes from] corporations and unions. We have customers that buy based on price. We have customers that buy because they want to do something good for their community. The younger people really want to do something great. We're not pitying people with disabilities. When you spend your money here, you're doing something great. That money is going back so we can hire another person. That's where your money goes. We have a couple of big customers in Ontario because they love what we do. They really want to do something that changes the society.

The success of LWA with private businesses confirms how social procurement fits in with the broader trend of corporate social responsibility (Barraket et al., 2016).

The primary reason MW pursues procurement and tendering opportunities is the desire to increase sales. Initially, MW was "doing a lot of small jobs." To get "access to some of the bigger jobs," Smith and the staff at MW and LWA "made a list to identify government tenders [as well as those from] unions and businesses." Smith used to deal with procurement during the early days of MW; now, a sales manager is responsible for it. As a result, MW rates itself moderately high in terms of its capacity to prepare bids and very high in terms of its capacity to demonstrate social value on RFPs and tenders. The sales manager is also in charge of marketing and promotion.

Smith was not surprised to hear that our survey revealed not many social enterprises have experience submitting bids, let alone winning them, despite the increasing prominence of social procurement policies especially among governments. In her own words, "bidding is so much work. It's a lot of work, and you really have to understand how to manoeuvre the terminology." As far as she knows, among the social enterprises in her home province, "only two or three have tried the tendering process."

She also acknowledges that MW's success is unusual and much of it due to its size and capacity: "We're not the norm. We have a management team of eight managers [at LWA]. We can break up the tender to each person."

The parent organization's hands-on support has a significant impact on MW's capability to prepare and win contracts. The capabilities within LWA and MW highlight the importance and the challenge of having all the necessary capabilities to prepare, win, and deliver on the bids.

Although social enterprises could, in theory, join forces to ensure all the necessary capabilities are presented in their bids, the effort required to do so should not be underestimated (Revington et al., 2015). If LWA/MW did not already possess the necessary capabilities it is likely their experience would be more closely aligned with the other cases in this book when it comes to procurement.

Smith also offers a unique perspective on government bidding because she has the experience of reviewing and evaluating bids. On the commitments of governments to buy from social enterprises, she says,

> Verbally they do [support it]. But I've been behind the scene reviewing the tenders. It's only my experience, but 95 to 98 per cent is about the dollars. If it's down to two very similar prices, the social value might tip the balance.

In and of itself, the social value from bids does not appear to be a key or even necessary factor in winning procurement contracts.

Recognizing that social procurement policies may be a start, Smith also pushes for more action from governments with a very specific suggestion:

> Talk is cheap; a lot of these people and governments and organizations want to support it. If the non-profits don't have the capacity to prepare the application, it's so tough to write this. If you miss one little thing, you get disqualified. It's almost like you need a degree to get this together. I went to one information session [put together by a government agency], but the information session didn't address the difficulty in putting bids together. You need smart people and the resources and the time to put the bids together. A lot of non-profits can barely get by. If [the governments] want more non-profits to apply, provide resources. Open an office to provide the professionals to help. Kinda like the training and employment services we offer. Provide the training ground for non-profits to learn how to do this. A lot of non-profits can provide the service, but they can't get past the tender.

In giving us her first-hand experience with bidding, Smith echoes many of the same barriers facing social enterprises and other non-social small to medium-sized businesses when tackling procurement requirements. In particular, these challenges reflect the lack of a wide range of factors: expertise; understanding of the procurement processes, platforms and terminology; capacity to prepare bids that would meet the procurement requirements; knowledge of procurement opportunities; know-how for demonstrating social value; and confidence (Barraket & Weissman, 2009; Muñoz, 2009).

Summary: Lessons Learned

This case demonstrates that the current approach in social procurement policies is still insufficient in helping many social enterprises overcome hurdles. The points raised by LWA are especially pertinent in the sense that Smith knows first-hand the amount of effort and the complexity of the skills required to understand and pursue procurement opportunities. Given the difficulty in leveraging social value as a competitive advantage, social enterprises are faced with unique challenges. It remains unclear whether the social enterprises that have experienced success in procurement such as LWA and MW in this case are successful because of their social value or in spite of it.

The case of LWA and MW provides several lessons:

1. Selling social is not the same as soliciting charity or donations from customers. It is important to maintain dignity and pride in the goods and services delivered by those employed by the social enterprises. This may mean educating customers, especially on large procurement contracts, that while considerations should be given to the social value of their buying decisions, they should not see buying from social enterprises as a compromise on quality.
2. Despite a high revenue level, LWA and MW show that stable government funding remains critical to the viability of social enterprises. The costs associated with the social benefits cannot be offset completely by commercial revenue alone; the social enterprises would not be able to stay competitive in terms of pricing.
3. To push social procurement further, hands-on support is needed for social enterprises. It is not sufficient to simply make opportunities available and expect social enterprises to be able to access them. Governments need to provide training and additional resources to support the development of the skills for procurement.

REFERENCES

Barraket, J., Keast, R., & Furneaux, C. (2016). *Social procurement and new public governance*. Routledge.
Barraket, J. & Weissman, J. (2009). *Social procurement and its implications for social enterprise: A literature review* (Working Paper No. CPNS 48). The Australian

Centre for Philanthropy and Nonprofit Studies. https://eprints.qut.edu
.au/29060/1/Barraket_and_Weissmann_2009_Working_Paper_No_48
_Final.pdf

Muñoz, S. (2009). Social enterprise and public sector voices on procurement. *Social Enterprise Journal*, 5(1), 69–82. https://doi.org/10.1108/17508610910956417

Quarter, J., Ryan, S., & Chan, A. (Eds.). (2015). *Social purpose enterprises: Case studies for social change*. University of Toronto Press.

Revington, C., Hoogendam, R., & Holeton, A. (2015). *The social procurement intermediary: The state of the art and its development within the GTHA*. Learning Enrichment Foundation. https://ccednet-rcdec.ca/en/toolbox/social-procurement-intermediary-state-art-and-its

OTHER SOURCES

Interview with Let's Work Atlantic (pseudonym).
Let's Work Atlantic (pseudonym), website.
Market Wizards (pseudonym), website.

14 Ethnicity Catering

ANIKA ROBERTS-STAHLBRAND

Introduction

This chapter explores EthniCity Catering, a social enterprise in Calgary that runs out of its parent organization – Centre for Newcomers (CFN). CFN was founded in 1988 with the mission to "support newcomers and the receiving community in becoming a diverse, united community, through services and initiatives that create conditions of success for newcomers and that foster a welcoming environment in Calgary." CFN as a whole runs a variety of programs and services such as language lessons, settlement services, and employment services. It is a major newcomer settlement organization engaging with more than ten thousand newcomers each year. EthniCity Catering, founded in 1998, is part of CFN's employment training and integration services. EthniCity helps newcomers succeed by giving them culinary skills, Canadian work experience, and self-confidence. The case of EthniCity highlights the role of niche marketing for the growth of a social enterprise, explores the motivation driving its customer base, and illustrates the significance of strong leadership in the growth of a social enterprise. It also illustrates the dilemma of selling social value.

History

EthniCity offers catering services under the umbrella of the CFN and provides multicultural catering in Calgary. Eric Myers, responsible for customer relations at EthniCity, describes it as another "platform" to support the mission of CFN. Sixteen newcomers, mostly women, are hired for one of four annual ten-week sessions of on-the-job culinary training. The program participants are called "kitchen helpers" during their time in training and then "graduates" after they have finished the program. Kitchen helpers are guaranteed a minimum of fifteen hours of work each week at minimum wage. The goal is to provide newcomers with training alongside Canadian work experience, an introduction to Canadian work culture, and the food safety certification from Alberta Health Services so that newcomers can secure employment in the broader community upon completing the program. In partnership with the educational programs at CFN, kitchen helpers also take courses to enhance their English as well as other life skills, such as financial planning and computer literacy.

EthniCity's evolution into a social enterprise was somewhat of an accident. CFN created a collective cooking social group for women to help alleviate isolation. These women started cooking in a church basement that the board of CFN used for meetings. One day, according to Myers, the two meetings overlapped and "one of the board members said hey, that food smells really good, I would buy that. And then someone else said that's a good idea and it sort of sprung from there and evolved as a social enterprise." That was 1998. EthniCity started as – in the words of Myers – a really "low-key" caterer. It then received funding for a catering truck, and later built an eight-hundred-square-foot commercial kitchen in CFN and developed into the full social enterprise and training program that it is today.

Financial Information

CFN, the parent organization, is a registered charity. In 2018, it had revenues of $10.2 million and expenses of $9.8 million. It has been growing steadily over the last ten years, with the budget more than doubling since 2010 (Charity Data, 2019). Not including the kitchen helpers, CFN currently employs 146 staff, 80 of whom are full-time.

EthniCity itself has four full-time staff members – a delivery person, a kitchen assistant, a customer relations person, and a kitchen manager. In the fiscal year 2019, EthniCity generated $205,653 in revenue. Ethni-City relies on two key external funders – United Way of Calgary and Area and Immigration, Refugees and Citizenship Canada. CFN applies for this funding on behalf of EthniCity. Individuals can also donate to CFN specifically for EthniCity and receive a tax receipt from CFN. Half of the salaries of the four full-time staff members at EthniCity and the wages of the kitchen helpers are covered by the external funders. The rest of the costs are covered by a mix of financial support from CFN and EthniCity's sales revenue. EthniCity receives support from CFN in four key cost areas: personnel, in-kind, space, and financial grants. Myers says that EthniCity pays a portion of the overall lease and utilities of the

CFN building. In all, sales revenue from catering covers approximately 40 per cent of EthniCity's operational costs.

The Kitchen Helpers

Newcomers who come to CFN for support after arriving in Canada can be connected to EthniCity, or individuals can apply to the program directly. According to Ajoy Sehgal, EthniCity's kitchen manager,[1] "99.9 per cent" of participants have never worked in a professional kitchen before, and some have never worked at all. However, a majority of the kitchen helpers do have home-cooking experience, says Myers.

Sehgal teaches kitchen helpers basic kitchen skills to prepare them for work in commercial kitchens. He also shows them techniques to make handcrafted appetizers from scratch in the hopes that "they get those skills and are ahead of other people who are trying to look for jobs in the kitchen." His hope is that graduates are employable in positions above dishwashers and line cooks.

Beyond culinary skills, kitchen helpers also develop other supportive skills for working in commercial kitchens. In contrast to the *Hell's Kitchen* stereotype of a scary head chef, Sehgal is focused on empowerment. He recognizes that many of the kitchen helpers also have to contend with traumatic experiences as refugees. He points out that for some kitchen helpers, at first, "they are in a shell, and we try to put them on a different platform where they can express themselves, where they can open up, where they can gain confidence." He is also quick to point out that knowledge exchange goes both ways in the kitchen:

> I encourage them to come out if they can make something. They sometimes need to express that they also know, and we put them on a platform to get that confidence, that yes, you have some ability, and you have talent. You need to take it out, and we will work together, we will collaborate with you, we will try to inculcate some of that skill.

He has incorporated the ideas and home culinary skills of kitchen helpers in daily training and in the final menus, which helps build their confidence. As Sehgal says, "I definitely feel they bring individualized talent."

EthniCity is proud of the success of its graduates as measured by employment status after graduation. Over 90 per cent of the graduates

---

1 Since the preparation of this case in 2019, Sehgal left EthniCity Catering.

from EthniCity find work soon after completing the program, although this success metric does not capture the type of work graduates find. Sehgal names Tim Hortons and other coffee vendors as the "biggest supporter" of EthniCity's graduates. Many graduates also find work at IKEA, grocery stores, and the new Amazon warehouse. Some have landed jobs in commercial kitchens in local restaurants, and Sehgal hopes this number will grow.

The Customers

Myers identifies non-profit organizations as the largest customer group for EthniCity, accounting for about half its sales. Part of these sales are from CFN itself, a definite perk of being part of a large parent organization. The minimum order at EthniCity is one hundred dollars and eight servings per item. Myers says the other half of the sales are made up of organizational purchasers from governments and businesses, while individual customer sales are "very minimal."

The engagement of newcomers at EthniCity figures prominently in its online promotional materials. Myers confirms that most customers directly reference the social mission of Ethnicity, and that they want to hear stories about the kitchen helpers. However, he also points out that customers do not buy from EthniCity only to support a charitable cause. They also value the diversity of unique flavours.

Donna Yanciw purchased from EthniCity when she was working at Discovery House, a non-profit organization offering housing, counselling, and empowerment training to women escaping domestic violence. Yanciw started working with EthniCity based on a suggestion from the chief executive officer of Discovery House. Overall, Yanciw would purchase from EthniCity four or five times each year, at approximately five hundred dollars for each order. She continued working with it because "prices are very reasonable, Eric [Myers] is wonderful to work with, and they always accommodate me at the last minute."

Yanciw also refers EthniCity to others because she feels that EthniCity is easier to work with than conventional catering businesses, and people enjoy the food. Interestingly, when asked if the social mission of EthniCity is part of her purchase decision, she said, "Honestly I've never thought about it. It's more about the service they provide to me and their reliability." Nonetheless, she names quality, competitive price, and charitable status as reasons behind her purchases from EthniCity. Yanciw states that she prefers to support other non-profit organizations "like ours."

In addition to other non-profit organizations, the oil and gas sector represents an important customer for EthniCity. Myers quickly points out that "the Calgary economy is not great right now" due to the falling price of oil. Even though EthniCity still receives orders from the oil and gas sector, sales have decreased, which has forced EthniCity to look elsewhere for customers.

The Calgary Stampede is also an organizational purchaser for EthniCity: it buys catering for board meetings and networking events for the Stampede throughout the year. Although the Calgary Stampede account does not generate significant revenue, it is a symbolically significant customer since it represents the integration and celebration of newcomers at such an iconic Calgary event.

Two other important organizational purchasers are the Calgary YMCA and the Calgary Kanahoff Conference Centre. Myers says that the YMCAs in Calgary use EthniCity as "their go-to people for any catering that they need." EthniCity looks after about 80 per cent of YMCA's catering needs. Both purchasers work with EthniCity on an order-by-order basis, not through any long-term contract.

Another angle that EthniCity hopes to capitalize on is through "community initiatives spending" in the finance sector. "Last year," Myers recalls, "RBC had this neighbourhood grants pitch event where people were pitching to win to fix up things in their community. And they hired us to cater that event. But that company has a community initiative and a certain amount of money they have to spend per year on that." Since establishing a relationship with RBC, it has been a repeat, but not frequent, customer.

Marketing and Selling Social Value

Even though Myers says that most customers refer to EthniCity's social mission, he also emphasizes that customers are "looking for deals. And if the food didn't turn out, they're gonna complain the same way they would for a private enterprise. I feel like the expectations remain the same." He says that even highly ethical customers have limitations. As with many other cases in this section, price and quality are still the primary consideration for most EthniCity customers. EthniCity may attract new customers through its social mission, but as Myers points out, "you still have to deliver the goods, or the customer is not going to call again."

The customer expectations of both quality and social value are consistent with LePage's (2014) report on the opportunities and barriers presented by social procurement. The report states that customers expect social enterprises to deliver "quality and competitive products and services to meet purchaser business requirements" (LePage, 2014,

p. 3). Or, put more matter-of-factly by Myers: even at a social enterprise, customers "[are] not that, you know … forgiving."

When EthniCity first started operations, a volunteer looked after customer service on a part-time basis. Eventually the volunteer was replaced by a paid staff member. In 2010, EthniCity decided to make the position full-time and now Myers holds the position. Myers hopes to expand the social enterprise to become more financially self-reliant. Although EthniCity does not have a budget for advertising, it markets through CFN's social media accounts. Myers also makes cold calls to potential customers and sends promotional emails. Most EthniCity customers come through referrals and/or direct experience of EthniCity's services.

Another initiative in marketing is developing EthniCity's reputation for catering large events. To-date, the largest event it has independently catered was for three hundred people. Sehgal is working hard to present EthniCity as a legitimate and competitive caterer rather than the side hustle of a charity. Sehgal's work to overcome customer stigma and boost customer confidence echoes one of the barriers to social procurement: "Purchasers often worry that the social enterprise sector cannot deliver the quality of products and services they require" (LePage, 2014, p. 16).

Limited Experience with Procurement

As EthniCity prepares to grow, its confidence is growing too. EthniCity is very interested in developing procurement arrangements, and currently has a few bids in the works. A long-term contract would allow EthniCity to furnish customer needs more specifically while also providing EthniCity with more financial consistency.

EthniCity recently submitted a bid to open a cafe inside another nonprofit organization. Myers describes the process as "very, very detailed. And specific. And it involved everything." It was his and EthniCity's first time submitting a bid, and he had to do extensive work to pull it together. When asked how the bid process could have been made more accessible, he says, "just to simplify the request, perhaps." EthniCity's experience in submitting a bid is consistent with LePage's finding that organizations that want to support social enterprise need to use a "simplified RFP [request for proposals] process" (LePage, 2014, p. 20). It is not enough to choose a social enterprise rather than a business if they are equal; true bidding accessibility for social enterprise requires a restructuring of the bidding process itself. EthniCity lost out on its first bid. Despite the difficulty of the bid process, EthniCity remains relatively positive about the potential for social procurement. However, within the business and non-profit sectors, EthniCity's experience suggests that consistent customer relationships are rooted in social contracts rather than legal ones.

Growth

EthniCity's desire to grow is twofold: to provide more opportunities for newcomers and become more financially sustainable. On the financial side, EthniCity works to adjust prices on the menus to match the actual costs of production. A few years ago, says Myers, EthniCity was "losing money on food costs, so it just wasn't sustainable." Now, EthniCity prices are determined based on market research: according to Myers, "we review and compare our prices to what our competition in the city are charging. We take into account our food cost, labour cost, and aim to have marginal profit made." The fact that EthniCity has similar prices to market competitors aligns with other cases in this section. EthniCity does not use government funding or donations to lower prices for the consumer but rather to offset the cost of providing social value to kitchen helpers. Sehgal adds that EthniCity is still operating on "very sharp" margins, which is typical for foodservice organizations.

How EthniCity Navigates the Market

This chapter outlines how EthniCity creates social value by reducing employment barriers for newcomers and offering them an opportunity to increase their culinary skills and self-confidence. While there have been dilemmas in selling this social value, this social enterprise has been successful in addressing them. Specifically, EthniCity's use of niche marketing and the importance of its strong leadership have been significant factors in the social enterprise's success. As Sehgal points out, "these sorts of social enterprise will take [people with barriers to employment] a long way and we will have a better society in the future."

Find Your Niche: Innovate out of Tensions

EthniCity's goal of growing for both financial and social reasons fits with other social enterprise case study research on growth orientation by Tykkyläinen et al. (2016). They found that social mission can be both a barrier to and driver of growth because it inspires the growth but also sets limits on how it can be achieved. One way to better balance the tensions associated with growth in a social enterprise is to be highly innovative (Tykkyläinen et al., 2016). The case of EthniCity suggests that the social enterprise is being innovative by pursuing niche markets to address the market tensions of being competitive as an enterprise with more than one bottom line. The niche market that EthniCity pursues is that of multicultural foods. Although Myers does not use the word niche to describe this strategy, he is specifically targeting hotels that host weddings of multicultural backgrounds. Many of these hotels do not have the knowledge to cater these meals. The diversity of EthniCity's kitchen helpers is a natural fit within this niche. As Myers says, "In many cases our students are from the countries where these foods came from." Here, the kitchen helpers are being used to market EthniCity based on the strengths they bring in the form of multicultural culinary knowledge rather than through their marginalized status as newcomers, which is a way to market the social-good creation without compromising their dignity.

Strong and Skilled Leadership

The owner-manager's ability and entrepreneurial orientation is tied to the capacity and willingness of a social enterprise to expand (Tykkyläinen et al., 2016). Until his departure from EthniCity, Sehgal provided such strong and skilled leadership. Before joining EthniCity, Sehgal worked as a chef internationally for thirty-five years, managing large hotels and businesses. His experience as a chef gave him the ability to develop the flexible and changing menus that new and regular customers wanted. EthniCity used to have set menus, but Sehgal talks about the importance of flexibility: "I am very, very flexible and that is what I am taking to the program ... we can customize any and every menu per what the client needs."

Perhaps his international experience is one of the reasons why Sehgal had such big plans for EthniCity. He wanted to be able to cater for groups up to one thousand, while Myers put the current maximum capacity at about three hundred people, in reference to a YMCA event of that size. Although scaling up more than threefold may seem an almost unreasonable goal, this ambition distinguished Sehgal as a leader.

As well as having a strategic vision, Sehgal also has an empowering leadership style that is not driven by personal gain. As he points out, "I've got my recognition; I've achieved all those [a] long time back, and now I want to see my participants, my students on the same platform." He says that he has told the kitchen helpers to "make me useless so that you take the chair ... and they can be proud of integrating into Canada and proud of their jobs." Now that Sehgal no longer works at CFN, it will be interesting to see who fills this leadership role and in what direction they will steer EthniCity.

Summary: Lessons Learned

The way EthniCity engages with the market and with its parent charity provides important insights into how to succeed as a social enterprise, as well as the challenges faced by an enterprise with additional goals beyond profitability.

1. It is helpful for a social enterprise to be housed in a large parent charity organization. This gives the social enterprise access to charitable status to receive individual and organizational donations, provides it with in-kind or subsidized infrastructure, and, in the case of a catering social enterprise, means the social enterprise has a built-in significant customer in the form of its parent charity.
2. Consistent with previous research, to make social procurement and responding to RFPs accessible for social enterprises, especially small to medium-sized social enterprises, it is important to adjust the process and the judging criteria. The process must be simplified so that social enterprises with minimal staff can apply. Social value creation must be incorporated into the RFP criteria on par with price and product quality for a social enterprise to be competitive.
3. Social enterprises can benefit from strong and imaginative leaders. Social enterprises challenge business-as-usual, so a social entrepreneur needs to be willing to try the seemingly impossible. In the face of the stark reality that price and quality are the primary considerations for customers, social entrepreneurs need to chart new ground, find niche markets, and be highly innovative in order to determine whether the seemingly impossible – becoming profitable and creating social value – is possible.

REFERENCES

Charity Data. (2019). *Centre for Newcomers Society of Calgary*. Charity Data. https://www.charitydata.ca/charity/centre-for-newcomers-society-of-calgary/100731660RR0001/
LePage, D. (2014). Exploring social procurement. Accelerating Social Impact CCC, Ltd.

Tykkyläinen, S., Syrjä, P., Puumalainen, K., & Sjögrén, H. (2016). Growth orientation in social enterprises. *International Journal of Entrepreneurial Venturing, 8*(3), 296–316. https://doi.org/10.1504/IJEV.2016.10000297

OTHER SOURCES

Interviews with EthniCity Catering.
EthniCity Catering, https://www.centrefornewcomers.ca/ethnicity
Centre for Newcomers, https://www.centrefornewcomers.ca
Centre for Newcomers – Annual reports – https://www.centrefornewcomers.ca/annual-reports

15 Horizon Achievement Centre

ANNIE LUK AND CAROL PENDERGAST

Introduction

Horizon Achievement Centre is a non-profit, charitable organization based in Sydney, Nova Scotia. Incorporated in 1983, Horizon now employs about fifty staff members and serves approximately 150 clients. Like all non-profit organizations, Horizon is governed by a volunteer board of directors, which currently consists of sixteen members. The mandate of Horizon, as stated in its annual report, is as follows:

> The mandate of the society is to promote and enhance the independence, choice, integration and full community inclusion of adults with mental/ intellectual disabilities or those facing multiple barriers to employment through individualized training, instruction and employment opportunities.

Horizon is the largest vocational training and employment organization catering to adults with mental and intellectual disabilities within the Cape Breton area. Carol Pendergast is the current Executive Director at Horizon. She was with Horizon even before it was Horizon, when the centre operated under the name of Sydney Kinsmen Resource, an early-1980s amalgamation of two existing facilities in the area. For nearly forty years, Pendergast has been trying to strike the delicate balance between the revenue-generating and the programming aspects of Horizon. She has seen Horizon through many challenges, including changing many minds about the capabilities of Horizon's clients and managing ambitious fundraising campaigns to build a new facility for the centre.

Financial Information

Horizon reported total revenue of $3.2 million for the fiscal year ending 31 March 2018. Horizon's social enterprises and community donations generated about 30 per cent of this total, whereas the remaining

70 per cent came from the province's Department of Community Services Disability Support Program and Employment Support and Income Assistance Program. Self-generated revenue saw a 7 per cent increase over the previous fiscal year. Of the remaining revenue, the majority was obtained through provincial government funding, with a smaller proportion in donations. In the fiscal year 2016–17, Horizon reported donations slightly under $500,000 and approximately $1.7 million in government funding. It is also worth mentioning that since 2016, Horizon has embarked on a $12 million capital campaign for which it has raised $1.2 million to date through donations and community fundraising events (Roach, 2017).

Government funding is primarily through the Nova Scotia Department of Community Services as an Adult Service Centre under the disability support program. Adult Service Centres provide community-based vocational day programs to adults with disabilities. In Nova Scotia, there are twenty-nine member agencies, including Horizon, which belong to the Directions Council for Vocational Services Society. Directions provides support and leadership for its member agencies to help secure funding and promote the goods and services offered by the various member agencies.

As a non-profit, registered charity operating a number of social enterprises, Horizon reinvests any surplus revenue into its programs. In addition to wages and benefits, which account for the largest expense line item, the remaining expenses are broken down into the cost of goods sold for the various social-enterprise products and services at approximately 23 per cent of expenses, with the remaining 30 per cent mainly covering utilities and building expenses. As of fiscal year-end 31 March 2018, Horizon held nearly $2 million in assets. The majority of these assets are investments earmarked for the capital campaign "Beyond the Horizon" and the remainder is for equipment.

Social Enterprises

Horizon operates two social enterprises as programs or departments: foodservices and general contracts. The foodservices department provides employment-specific training, counselling services, and interpersonal skill development for those interested in the food, hospitality, retail, or custodial industry. Within the department, clients or program participants may choose to work in baking and catering, or maintenance and janitorial services. Horizon's foodservices department offers banquet and catering services and operates a bakery. The banquet services can serve up to three hundred guests in its three-thousand-square-foot banquet facility at Horizon's Sydney location. The catering services support rental events at the banquet hall as well as offsite orders. The bakery at Horizon specializes in diabetes-friendly baked goods, which are sold to retailers, restaurants, coffee shops, and other organizational purchasers in both public and private sectors. The foodservices department also operates three offsite canteens, all of which are located in Sydney. The maintenance and janitorial services within the foodservices department support the catering and banquet-hall rental services. The costs for the maintenance and janitorial services are built into the catering and banquet-hall rental fees.

The general contracts department offers training similar to the foodservices department, but for those interested in customer service, office, and manufacturing jobs. The two services offered by the general contracts department are (1) mail services and printing and (2) assembly and promotions. Through these two service offerings, Horizon assists customers in creating and assembling letter mail campaigns for marketing and fundraising purposes, issuing billing notices, managing municipal billing (for which the centre has a current contract with the local regional municipality) and designing promotional buttons (a specialty that makes Horizon the largest promotional button manufacturer in Cape Breton). Horizon also offers a range of graphic design, printing, and binding services, including business cards, letterheads, flyers, and brochures. The centre also provides assembly services such as soundboard manufacturing.

Horizon has over six hundred customers who have been involved with the centre at one point or another. Horizon makes around $700,000 in gross sales through its organizational purchasers.

Social Mission and Marketing

Among the three types of organizational purchasers, Horizon believes that its social mission is most important to non-profit organizations, but only moderately important to both government agencies and private businesses. The quality of its services is suspected to be the top reason why government agencies and non-profit organizations purchase services from the centre. The second most important reason is Horizon's competitive pricing. In contrast, for its private-business customers, Horizon believes that competitive pricing is the more significant purchasing factor. Supporting local communities counts as another reason for government agencies and private businesses to purchase from it. Horizon also points out that its charitable status is likely to be one of the reasons for non-profit organizations to purchase from the centre.

The importance of social mission presents a dilemma for Horizon. On the one hand, Pendergast points out that it is extremely important for the centre to offer a place of support for its program participants – i.e., individuals who have mental or intellectual disabilities such as Down's syndrome. On the other hand, she would like business relationships to be a reflection of the quality of goods and services provided by Horizon. To her, this would indicate that program participants are fully capable of doing the same work and providing the same quality as employees elsewhere. At the same time, because of the government funding available for Horizon, it could potentially afford to underbid private business when competing for work. In the spirit of fairness to businesses in the same community, Horizon has a policy to never price its goods and services more than 5 per cent below the average prices offered by private businesses.

At Horizon, the responsibility for marketing is shared by programming staff instead of having a dedicated marketing person. The centre has a small advertising budget, and it mostly depends on word of mouth by existing customers. Staff also attend various trade shows. Horizon currently markets online, with detailed information on its services, using its website and social media (including Facebook and Twitter). Although Horizon has limited marketing capacity, the responsibility for managing its social media presence is shared among all staff, who diligently post about Horizon. For example, during the holiday season, Horizon posts its catering menu and reminds potential customers to place their orders early for their holiday parties. By leveraging the staff's personal networks on social media, Horizon has been able to build an impressive following. As of 2018, Horizon had over four thousand friends on Facebook and nearly one thousand followers on Twitter. Despite its online presence, Horizon does not directly sell anything online. Ordering is through telephone inquiries to staff in the office or by email.

Experience in Social Procurement

Horizon has submitted and succeeded in bids to government agencies. However, the centre has never submitted bids to either private businesses or non-profit organizations. Compared to the other two types of organizational purchasers, Horizon notes that government agencies tend to have more bureaucratic requirements. Its success in procurement contracts has led to shifts in the management structure at Horizon, such as adding a formal financial coordinator. Horizon also has experience collaborating with other organizations in preparing social-procurement bids. One example is when Horizon partnered with a printing company in the private sector to submit and win a bid to work with the province on designing, printing, and delivering five hundred thousand tourism booklets in 2013. This partnership allowed Horizon to leverage its existing relationship with Canada Post to handle the mailing and delivery portion of the project while the private-sector partner handled the graphic design and high-gloss offset printing. In coming together as a team, Horizon and its partner managed to offer a competitive price and a high-quality product for the province.

There are a number of challenges facing Horizon when it comes to preparing for and responding to procurement opportunities. Many of these challenges are related to the fact that procurement remains only about procurement, and social procurement is not yet a concept fully embraced by governments, private businesses, or even non-profit organizations. The tendering process stays focused on dollars and cents, leaving out the importance of social costs and benefits from the procurement opportunities. One of the challenges facing Horizon is that the procurement process tends to be rigid, requiring bidders to already have all the capabilities and resources to complete the work being tendered. Horizon's ability to access and secure community resources and to fulfil the customers' needs in less conventional ways not only goes unappreciated but is often left undiscussed. For example, Horizon may be able to connect with community partners to lease a building to increase its capacity for a specific contract. However, the contingent arrangement would usually be deemed as not having appropriate capacity to complete the required work.

Another challenge is that opportunities coming through the procurement process are usually of higher value, which translates to a considerable amount of work. Horizon is not always able to handle the higher volume of work due to existing commitments and lack of capacity. While balancing existing commitments and upcoming opportunities is likely to remain a constant tension, Horizon has been working on expanding its capacity. In 2016, it launched a major capital campaign to build a new $12 million facility. With all three levels of government supporting the project for a combined contribution of $10 million, Horizon has been working hard to raise the remaining amount (Jala, 2018). The new facility will provide a campus of thirty thousand square feet, eliminating the need to lease space from others and consolidating Horizon's operations all under one roof.

Being able to look for opportunities and prepare bids is also a challenge. Since Horizon does not have a dedicated employee for procurement opportunities, the process is somewhat haphazard, depending on whether Pendergast or other staff members happen to find out about potential opportunities. The staff then discuss whether the opportunity is something they could take on in terms of requirements, capabilities, and capacity. One of the recent bids that Horizon submitted and won was a standing offer from the Nova Scotia Government to do printing work. A standing offer, usually spanning three to five years, allows the government agency to create a pre-qualified list of vendors from which the agency could choose from when the need for certain goods or services arises. At the time of writing, Horizon has yet to see any tender coming from the standing offer (unfortunately, it is not uncommon to wait a long time for a request to come through a standing offer or even to never see one at all).

The most significant challenge, however, remains the stigma attached to Horizon's program participants and presumptions about their capabilities to complete the work. Despite that, Horizon has been able to face this challenge successfully. Currently, Horizon handles all the processing of tax and water bills for Cape Breton Regional Municipality – a municipality of just over ninety thousand residents. The work entails printing, assembling, and posting the municipality's bills to residents in Cape Breton. The contract originated in the late 2000s as a bid opportunity, which eventually became an ongoing contract for Horizon. When Horizon initially won the contract, it was presented as a trial. Pendergast recalls the municipality saying, "we'll try you for a couple of months," but Horizon would have to convince the customer through performance. The contract presented some initial difficulties not only because of the negative perception from the customer but also due to the challenge in securing the necessary equipment. Through quality work, Horizon has been able to change the minds of the municipality and build a respectful relationship among Horizon's program participants, its staff, and the purchaser. However, sometimes even after having had the experience of working together, the perception of customers is still difficult to change. In 2000, Horizon won, in Pendergast's words, "a phenomenal project" with Atlantic Lottery Corporation (ALC, a provincial Crown corporation responsible for running the lotteries) to prepare one hundred thousand mailing packages in eight weeks for the holiday season. Horizon was able to successfully complete the project while providing training and employment for its program participants. The following year, Horizon was asked by ALC to provide training to staff and clients in other vocational programs in New Brunswick. Unfortunately, after two years, the person at ALC who was keen to support social enterprises was no longer in the position of decision-making for this contract. So when ALC decided to automate the sealing and the stapling part for the packages, the contract was awarded elsewhere. The most frustrating aspect of losing the contract, according to Pendergast, was that Horizon had not even been consulted to see if there might be a possibility of continuing this successful partnership with modifications. She feels confident that Horizon would have been able to continue working with ALC and the new machines. The perception that Horizon's program participants would not be able to operate the machines meant that Horizon did not have an opportunity to work out a possible solution.

Other challenges include the fact that although the centre feels very confident in its ability to demonstrate its social value in the bids, it is much less comfortable with preparing the bids. In addition, Horizon does not have any formal social-procurement policy to guide its own procurement or purchasing decisions, even though the centre sometimes chooses suppliers that are also social enterprises.

Horizon indicates that it is extremely interested in seeing more social-procurement opportunities with an emphasis on social value. Pendergast points out that although Nova Scotia is one of the leaders for initiating some policies to encourage government agencies to pursue social procurement and social purchasing (including, the sustainable procurement policy in 2009, the Public Procurement Act in 2011 and the social-enterprise framework in 2017), the opportunities for social enterprises like Horizon are still difficult to come by and manage. Policy changes could potentially improve this situation; for example, the State of New Jersey (2014) has a policy to award 25 per cent of the state's contracts and purchases to small businesses.

Social Purchasing

Even though Horizon has never submitted bids to private businesses or non-profit organizations, the centre considers both as regular organizational purchasers. In other words, these two types of purchasers are mainly engaged in social purchasing. To get a better understanding of the social purchasing for Horizon, we interviewed four of Horizon's organizational purchasers – two are private businesses (CBCL Limited and Rotofast Inc.), one is a government agency (Agency CBNS, a pseudonym), and the remaining one is a non-profit organization (Hospice Care Cape Breton). These customers purchase from Horizon at intervals ranging from twice a year to monthly, and purchase sizes from several hundred to several thousand dollars, depending on the services. Two of the customers primarily use Horizon for foodservices, and their orders are in the range of a few hundred dollars each time. However, they tend to place their orders more frequently.

Kelly McKenzie from CBCL Limited, an engineering consulting firm, knew about Horizon because of her brother's participation at the centre's programs for the last number of years. CBCL spends at least $250–$300 on each order of food trays approximately four to six times a year. McKenzie keeps returning to Horizon for food services for several reasons, with the top one being support for local community. More practical considerations are also important to CBCL such as availability, delivery versus pickup, direct billing versus pay-on-pickup, and price. With respect to price, McKenzie says that "if a social enterprise is slightly higher than another 'big' business, we'd still choose the social enterprise as it's a worthier purchase, in our opinion." However, she points out, "While we applaud the mission, the service, quality, and efficiency keep us coming back." McKenzie is so satisfied with Horizon's services that she regularly refers CBCL's own clients to Horizon and helps promote Horizon personally on her social media. In addition to Horizon, CBCL also purchases from Pathways Cape Breton[1] and employs temporary staff from Ann Terry Society,[2] even though CBCL does not have any official policy on social procurement or social purchasing.

Another private-business customer who spoke with us was MacDonald Gillis at Rotofast Inc., a company that produces anchors for wall and ceiling installations. Rotofast has an open-ended contract with Horizon, based on which the company spends approximately $2,500 a month for packaging services. Gillis first heard about Horizon through word of mouth. Although he has not recommended the centre to others yet, Gillis is highly satisfied with the quality of services from Horizon. While he identifies competitive pricing and high quality as being the top reasons for purchasing from Horizon, he points out that Horizon's social mission is a somewhat important factor as well. On the point of supporting local communities, Gillis says, "As the owner, I have contact with the vulnerable populations that work with the Horizon Achievement Centre and I find it to be a particularly rewarding experience."

Agency CBNS, a pseudonym for a government agency, buys lunches and snacks from Horizon for one of its programs. Each order is approximately one hundred to two hundred dollars, and the agency places an order about once a month. Since the agency heard about Horizon

1 Pathways Cape Breton provides an integrated and coordinated range of services and supports to address the recovery of individuals with mental illness and social challenges.
2 Ann Terry Society helps women living in the Cape Breton Regional Municipality enter the paid workforce by providing career development services that are women-centered and community-based.

through word of mouth, it has since made referrals to other potential customers for Horizon. The interviewee from the agency finds "the quality of the work good and believes in the social mission, which is a winning combination." Unlike the two customers from the private sector, Agency CBNS ranks the employment and training work that Horizon does with its participants as the top reason for purchasing from the centre. In fact, competitive pricing is not considered one of the top three reasons for purchasing from Horizon. Despite being a government agency with an interest in purchasing from organizations with social missions, Agency CBNS does not have a social procurement or social purchasing policy.

For Hospice Care Cape Breton, Pam Ellsworth – the campaign director – works with Horizon twice a year on mailing out newsletters and other mail-related services. Each year, Hospice Care CB spends between $1,500 and $2,000 with Horizon. Ellsworth has had past experience working with the centre and has referred Horizon to others. The top three reasons for purchasing from Horizon are the centre's quality of work, competitive pricing, and customer service. Ellsworth is particularly impressed by how quickly Horizon responds to her requests: "They are very good to respond, and I always speak to a person and get answers quickly." Although support for local community only ranks fourth, she rates Horizon's social mission as important. In fact, Hospice Care CB did not choose to shop around to private businesses before selecting Horizon to work with.

Summary: Lessons Learned

Horizon Achievement Centre, operating both as an adult service centre and as a social enterprise, is constantly trying to strike the right balance amid a series of tensions. There is tension among programming for participants, selling services to generate revenue, and offering real-world employment opportunities. There is tension between competing for contracts and not taking business away from other social enterprises and local small businesses. There is tension between seizing the opportunities to demonstrate the capabilities of the program participants and managing all the demands with limited resources. And there is tension between being innovative and entrepreneurial in seeking new revenue sources and having to make do within stagnating government funding, which remains Horizon's main revenue source. Among all these tensions, the staff at Horizon need to maintain their focus on the well-being of the program participants. The experiences from Horizon offer a glimpse at the complexities in running a social service agency and a social enterprise at the same time. If Horizon ends up leaning to one side too much, it could risk losing its balance and its focus on the mission of the organization. The success so far has been built on positive relationships with the Cape Breton community and the many customers. But as the case illustrates, the effort to win over customers is ongoing. Government policies could help, but ultimately, procurement and purchasing decisions are made by individuals, and they need to be convinced of the unique social value brought forth by organizations such as Horizon Achievement Centre.

The lessons learned from Horizon's experiences include the following:

1. There is strength in numbers. Similar social enterprises coming together could promote the whole idea of selling social even though the social enterprises may sometimes compete for similar opportunities.
2. The tension between selling and programming is likely to persist, particularly when the social enterprises are considering expansion. Reliable government funding for programming could help alleviate some of the pressure to sell more to generate revenue.
3. Partnering with other organizations, including private businesses, could make procurement opportunities more accessible.
4. Selling social is only possible when those issuing procurement opportunities are also interested in buying social and thus purposely include social benefits as requirements.
5. Marketing for social enterprises often needs to include much persuasion to potential customers that they would not give up on quality and performance when buying social.
6. In the absence of formal policy on social procurement or social purchasing, buying decisions to include social benefits are often dependent on the specific individuals and their own personal experiences and views.

REFERENCES

Jala, D. (2018, February 9). New facility for Horizon Achievement Centre is on its way. *Cape Breton Post*. https://www.capebretonpost.com/news/new-facility-for-Horizon-achievement-centre-is-on-its-way-185000/
Roach, C. (2017, November 14). Horizon Achievement Centre unveils next step in fundraising efforts. *Cape Breton Post*. https://www.capebretonpost.com/news/horizon-achievement-centre-unveils-next-step-in-fundraising-efforts-161838/

State of New Jersey. (2014). Small business set-aside. https://business.nj.gov
/faqs/how-do-i-participate-in-the-small-business-set-aside-program

OTHER SOURCES

Interviews with Horizon Achievement Centre, CBCL Limited, Rotofast Inc.,
   Agency CBNS (a pseudonym), and Hospice Care Cape Breton.
Horizon Achievement Centre, https://www.Horizon-ns.ca/
Horizon Achievement Centre – 2017–18 Annual Report – http://www
   .Horizon-ns.ca/wp-content/uploads/2018/09/2017-18-AnnualReport
   _WEB.pdf
Canada Revenue Agency – Charitable Organization Returns – https://apps
   .cra-arc.gc.ca/ebci/hacc/srch/pub/dsplyBscSrch?request_locale=en
Directions Council for Vocational Services Society, https://directionscouncil
   .org/

16 Calgary Progressive Lifestyles Foundation

JENNIFER SUMNER

Introduction

Calgary Progressive Lifestyles Foundation (CPLF) is a non-profit charitable foundation that set up two social enterprises – Cookies on the Go and Lifestyles Bistro – both of which create employment opportunities for people with disabilities. These opportunities promote self-esteem, financial freedom, social networking, job-skill improvement, and community involvement. In 2019, CPLF terminated Cookies on the Go to focus on Lifestyles Bistro. This focus includes its support for people with disabilities, which it promotes through relationship marketing that provides a model for overcoming the dilemma of selling social value. As a work-integrated social enterprise, Lifestyles Bistro engages in social purchasing, but not social procurement.

Calgary Progressive Lifestyles Foundation's mission is to "promote self-sufficiency and quality of life within individuals who have a disability … This is achieved through Community Presence and Participation, Skill and Image Enhancement, Autonomy and Empowerment." Its goal is to provide sustainable employment services, with individuals receiving ongoing access to supports while being prepared for real work environments in the community. After thirty years in operation, it has more than 600 staff, 350 participants, and $25 million in revenue, attesting to its growth from humble beginnings. Neal Sabourin is the current chief operations officer of CPLF.

Calgary Progressive Lifestyles Foundation was founded in 1989 by Adrienne Sabourin, Neal's mother, and she is still the executive director as well as the program coordinator. Back in the late 1980s, governments were looking to outsource services, and Adrienne recognized that the support model for people with disabilities, which involved living in government institutions, could be improved upon. Her new model of supporting those with disabilities to live in private homes worked well, reflecting the broader deinstitutionalization movement. The model of using private homes had much better outcomes at a lower cost, which the government recognized and supported, while maintaining institutions for those who had better outcomes in an institutionalized setting. Adrienne's model looks very much like a foster-care arrangement where the people who own the home – the contractors – are responsible for the resident 24/7, much like a foster parent, but do not necessarily work with the resident around the clock. As program coordinator of CPLF, Adrienne also supervises the case management of the organization. Under her direction, fifteen case managers supervise the direct supports their residents receive.

Neal joined CPLF in 2001, when it had only twenty residents. The organization has changed significantly since those early days when its main relationship was with the Alberta government. While originally CPLF did not require marketing to maintain its operations, the establishment of social enterprises in the retail sector meant that it needed to begin focusing on relationship building and reputation. Although Neal evaluates CPLF's capacity to prepare a bid as low, he will be looking to hire a new community business developer to increase that capacity. Neal says that "it's now all about marketing, so we've had to retool our administrative staff and the tools that we use," including the hiring of a business developer. It was an immense learning curve for all concerned.

Social Enterprises

Until recently, CPLF ran two social enterprises. The relationship between them was complex. While they shared the same operating worksite and cross-promoted one another, CPLF tried to differentiate the two social enterprises to its customers.

When Adrienne and Neal were first imagining these social enterprises for CPLF, Neal looked to Europe for models. From Neal's perspective, Canada has done very well in defining what a social enterprise is, but he was unable to find working models for such businesses in Canada: "I find we're about five to ten years behind Europe." He also expresses disappointment that the Alberta government does not directly support social enterprises, regardless of which party is in power, because he believes the government does not want to provide a competitive advantage to social enterprises over businesses in the private sector.

Having said that, Neal feels there are opportunities for social enterprises that are also charities. For example, CPLF's mission statement and charitable status allows the use of volunteers and the ability to accept donations. With its charitable status, CPLF does not pay GST and has a reduction in its property taxes, both of which are indirect supports. It does, however, collect and remit sales taxes.

Through its social enterprises, CPLF provides gainful employment and volunteer opportunities for people with disabilities. On its website, CPLF uses the term DisAbilities with the word "abilities" capitalized to emphasize ability rather than disability. As Neal explains, "We want to focus on the positive – what do these people have as far as abilities, rather than focusing on the disability." Although Neal points out that it is purely a marketing approach, he is also challenging people to think differently about those who are traditionally marginalized, which is what he feels social enterprises in general are doing.

Cookies on the Go

Cookies on the Go began in 1991 when Adrienne used her own kitchen to bake cookies with a particularly challenged resident as a form of engagement. The resident's job was to mix the dry ingredients. They baked together on a weekly basis and over time, Adrienne found the resident began to look forward to this time in the kitchen; so much so that the resident started combing her hair and wearing make-up. Her hygiene improved, and she was smiling. Adrienne decided to expand on this opportunity, which she felt was offering some self-dignity, job-skills training, and empowerment. She thought that if the organization could get out into the community, CPLF could make sales while advocating for people with disabilities.

As more residents became involved, the program moved into church and community kitchens. CPLF rented these kitchens, and very often there would be no storage area, so the CPLF staff had to tow their supplies back and forth from the offices. Sometimes they would even get bumped for occasions like weddings, which was difficult when trying to develop a customer base. So in 2013, CPLF rented their own industrial space with a kitchen. That choice, however, meant the organization started carrying more expenses and also a higher amount in expenses. In essence, rent was five thousand dollars per month and the cookies were only selling for a dollar each. The revenue from the cookies was not enough to meet the expenses, but fortunately funding for CPLF's core services covered the wages of both staff and residents.

By then, it was also clear that CPLF had moved away from a program closer to an arts and crafts club to a full-fledged business – a social enterprise was born bearing the name Cookies on the Go. Neal became directly involved with an aim to make Cookies on the Go profitable, but it continued to have challenges generating enough revenue to carry costs. In 2019, CPLF made the decision to discontinue this social enterprise to concentrate efforts on their other social enterprise – Lifestyles Bistro.

Lifestyles Bistro

Lifestyles Bistro started in 2013 as a possible solution to the financial challenges of Cookies on the Go. Neal realized CPLF could not get by selling just cookies:

> Cookies on the Go really pigeonholes us to selling cookies, and we can't sell enough cookies in a day to pay for our needs and all our expenses. And it also doesn't match our values. I don't want to fatten Calgary up just so we can pay for our lease.

Lifestyles Bistro was created to address some of the shortcomings identified in Cookies on the Go and to allow CPLF to diversify the products offered to customers. While Cookies on the Go specialized in cookies and baked products, Lifestyles Bistro is primarily a public restaurant. Located in north-east Calgary, it achieves the majority of its sales on site. The bistro also provides catering services and sells to retailers in the city who buy the products at wholesale prices and resell them to the general public.

Neal is always on the lookout for possible future opportunities that will complement and enhance the infrastructure and skill sets that have been nurtured over the years at CPLF to support people with disabilities.

Experiences with Social Procurement and Social Purchasing

In terms of social procurement, CPLF has not submitted any bids for government contracts on behalf of its social enterprises. Instead, the organization is engaged in social purchasing with local businesses. For example, at Christmastime, Cookies on the Go sees an upswing in corporate sales. The staff are always being asked for a price quote for a particular contract, which is a form of bidding for work. Lifestyles Bistro is also continually offering price quotes for catering contracts and working to become a caterer of choice, which means getting on the approved list of caterers for some customers. Overall, Neal estimates that 90 per cent of these price quotes are successful, which speaks to the community goodwill CPLF has developed.

Although CPLF does not engage in any formal bidding process, Neal knows that everyone has to eat, and every company has business meetings. So, CPLF cold-calls potential customers to gain contracts. Neal feels that the mention of CPLF's social mission has made these cold-calls easier to convert to sales. Neal's assessment is that CPLF initially wins sales on price and good food; secondarily, the good feeling that customers experience brings repeat business.

One of the downsides to winning such sales is the strain on resources to complete the work orders. Neal explains that each of the social enterprises at CPLF grew out of activities with the residents. Neal provides an example to highlight the importance of careful analysis and planning when converting resident activities into social enterprises:

> If you are taking a loss every time you sell a cookie, then the more cookies you sell, the more loss you have. You need to slow down and get your ducks in order before you start soliciting new business.

With respect to its own purchasing, CPLF sometimes buys socially by giving preference to other organizations with a social purpose. For example, CPLF has a partnership with the University of Calgary whereby CPLF gives its used cooking oil to the university to convert into biofuel. The partnership not only helps the university but also enriches CPLF's story, adding to its competitive advantage. Currently, CPLF is in the middle of securing a partnership with a coffee roaster that only roasts coffee beans that are traceable to the farmer, supporting the farm-to-cup idea – another opportunity for building on the CPLF story. Purchasing products like the specialty coffee means that CPLF would have to pay more for its supplies, which results in higher prices for CPLF's own products. As Neal explains, "You just can't charge a higher price for coffee, without a story. We need to tell that story because the coffee has to pay for itself, but it also has to make the consumer feel good."

CPLF also buys socially by using environmentally sustainable products and packaging material. These products can pose a challenge because they tend to be more expensive, which is fine with Neal, so long as the social enterprise can communicate the value for the higher expenses to customers. However, sometimes it remains challenging, as Neal explains: "To say we use compostable products isn't enough. We have to go further and say we use compostable products, and it saves this many trees per year." In addition, he sometimes finds the environmental outcomes are not always black and white. For instance, a corn-based product might end up being environmentally more costly than a plastic product.

Employment and Volunteering for Residents

Neal notes that 25 to 49 per cent of CPLF's employed workers identify as having a disability. One of CPLF's objectives is to model a formalized hiring process wherever possible by asking for a résumé and doing an orientation to the organization. The residents who are employed at CPLF currently work as promoters (who go around the local area with flyers), dishwashers, bussers, food packagers, sales representatives, and cleaners.

In addition to paid employees, 25 to 49 per cent of the residents at CPLF also serve as volunteers. CPLF also uses volunteers for fundraising activities, such as barbecues or dances, to support the social enterprise. Currently, however, not much volunteering is happening because CPLF does not have a volunteer coordinator. Neal feels that a volunteer coordinator is important because it takes time to train and coach volunteers, coordinate them, and give them meaningful work.

Revenue and Expenses

One of the tangible benefits from landing sales is increased revenue, which currently offsets expenses. However, both social enterprises always had a negative cash flow after expenses. CPLF hopes the remaining social enterprise – Lifestyles Bistro – will soon be in a position to turn a surplus, which could cover the mileage costs support workers incur as they work with the residents at the bistro. In the end, Neal observes, "When we win business, not only are we increasing our revenue, we are also advocating, and we're also creating opportunities for people with disabilities, which is our mandate."

At present, Lifestyles Bistro has total annual revenues of approximately $250,000 per year, of which $210,000 comes from sales. The rest comes from donations, fundraising, and sponsors, although revenue from services is growing (especially once the bistro can offer its catering with servers, bartenders, and rooms for rent).

Neal notes that less than 10 per cent of CPLF's total expenses are allocated to marketing. The main expenses are staffing: a chef, a manager, line cooks, dishwashers, baristas, bussers, promoters, and cleaners, as well as the community business developer, who is tasked with increasing revenue and relationship building. CPLF has also hired a consultant with limited hours to focus on marketing. Neal feels that, eventually, a full-time consultant would be better, but at the moment, he is satisfied with the current solution because money is still tight, and the social enterprise is not yet breaking even. When the bistro can generate a surplus, it will be able to reinvest in marketing.

Marketing Social Good

CPLF markets its social enterprise on its website and in print, which includes packaging labels and a monthly newsletter to some two thousand e-subscribers and twenty-eight businesses in Calgary. The marketing efforts also include a social media campaign, which results in relationship building rather than sales. CPLF's marketing emphasizes its support of people with disabilities and seniors, particularly in its brochures and business cards. In Neal's opinion, this speaks to branding for social enterprises. He asks, "Why are people going to order our bran muffins, because everyone is selling great food?" He goes on to explain that CPLF just finalized a tagline for Lifestyles Bistro that reads "community, food, people." From his perspective,

> That's why people are going to eat our bran muffins – because the proceeds support our community, great food, sustainable food, healthy food, tasty food and it supports people. And when our caterers order our bran muffins, they are going to win friends and allies around that boardroom table because they're showcasing social responsibility, corporate social responsibility.

Neal observes that back in the 1980s, there was really no opportunity for sponsorship – it was more about donations. Nowadays, he believes that traditional cash donations are often replaced with corporate sponsorship. When soliciting for sponsorship, CPLF is looking for potential sponsors to become more directly engaged with the organizations that they support. Neal feels that CPLF is in the position to offer this because "we can offer them value, where people can feel, smell, taste their support."

CPLF also does some mission-centred co-branding with the sponsors. For example, the sponsors' logos are included on CPLF's packaging, social media, websites, and signage. CPLF can also get into corporate challenges. Neal believes that "the sky's the limit," which is what he feels is great about the non-profit sector: "If you can think about it, and you're courageous enough and have the fortitude, you can do it."

Neal contends that organizations like CPLF must learn to react to a more sophisticated marketplace – a marketplace that not only wants products and services to be excellent but also needs the products and services to make customers feel good. In his opinion, one of the ways to make them feel good is through an altruistic set of values: for example, helping the planet or helping certain populations. CPLF continues looking for local partners with common values and tries to source locally whenever possible. He puts forward the example of searching for a new supplier for loose-leaf tea. He found a potential partner, who gives 10 per cent of her revenues to support Indigenous populations. Neal sums up CPLF's marketing strategy:

> In the first place, we need to showcase our great food, we need to win their business with great food. Once we get them in the door, then that's an opportunity to showcase a little bit of our enriching story, and that's how we win our business. We don't lead off with "we're here to support the community." The public just wants a good burger, and enough said. So we sell that burger the way they want it to be sold and then we feed them with further enriching stories.

For Neal, the "feel good" aspect that communicates with a sophisticated marketplace is all about their story, and it is the story that is going to sell the products. For this reason, CPLF is always looking for ways to enrich that story because it affords a competitive advantage vis-à-vis private-sector businesses. A new way CPLF is going to enrich the story is through offering barista training in the bistro and volunteer opportunities as gardeners to support the farm-to-plate initiatives during the summer months. A further enrichment involves an art entrepreneurial program where artists living with disabilities exhibit and sell their artworks through the gallery in the bistro. Another example is that the staff plans to put inspirational quotes on the cookies the bistro sells to showcase the people who support them.

Online marketing represents less than 10 per cent of CPLF's total sales, mainly because the organization does not have a shopping cart on the website. However, online marketing allows customers to see the products and phone to make an order. Although CPLF is currently renovating its website, Neal doubts that the website would include a shopping cart. Instead, the website will have a template order form that people can submit. The website will also offer a place for online donations, likely through a third party such as Canada Helps, that takes a percentage of the donation in return for offering a platform.

Customers

Neal believes there is strong support from customers, first and foremost, because the bistro offers excellent food and service – it starts there. It ends, from his perspective, with supporting local community and local people.

> If you want a thriving business, you have to have a thriving community. If you don't have a thriving community, how are you going to attract the human resources you need and retain those human resources? It just won't work.

Most of the regular customers are individuals from local businesses within a three-kilometre radius. Neal notes that the bistro is not yet a destination because its opening hours are Monday through Friday 7:30 a.m. to 3:30 p.m. In the future, once the bistro is able to hire an event coordinator, Neal may apply for a liquor licence so that the coordinator can host evening events with live music. One of the regular organizational purchasers for the bistro is a municipal agency, which is also within their three-kilometre radius. For Neal, this radius represents their primary market.

Another of the bistro's organizational purchasers is a non-profit organization called Indefinite Arts, which supports arts and creativity among people living with disabilities. Lifestyles Bistro hangs some of the art pieces from Indefinite Arts to sell on consignment. A number of high schools, including Diefenbaker High School, are also organizational purchasers. Neal finds it odd that although CPLF belongs to a service-provider council that represents twenty-eight agencies in Calgary, none of these agencies has supported the bistro, even after he has approached them. Even though CPLF is a charitable foundation, there is still what he refers to as "healthy competition" within the non-profit sector.

Summary: Lessons Learned

In Neal's opinion, people are always weighing the costs and benefits in a social enterprise. In contrast, a for-profit business is all about profit, so it is an easy decision to terminate a program that is not profitable. But with a social enterprise, it can be about advocacy. He finds that social enterprises are more interested in the triple bottom line, i.e., environmental, social, and financial. While someone in the outside world may ask, why do you have an initiative that loses money, Neal argues, "That's not how you make it to the Promised Land. Sometimes the Promised Land is about other things."

This case offers some valuable lessons for those interested in social enterprises:

1. Focus on the positive. Promote people's abilities rather than focusing on their disabilities.
2. Challenge the public to think differently. This is important in terms of change for those who are traditionally marginalized.
3. Make sure you are generating enough revenue to cover costs. Otherwise, debt mounts up continuously.
4. Develop good will within the community. It will help to gain and maintain business.

5. First, win sales on price and quality. Then, continue sales through the good feeling customers experience when buying your product.
6. Tell an enriching story. You can't sell a product or charge a higher price without a story. It is your competitive advantage.
7. If you use environmentally sustainable products and packaging material that add to the price, you need to include this in your story. It's important to communicate the value customers get for the higher price.
8. A volunteer coordinator is important. It takes time to train, coach, and coordinate volunteers.
9. If you want a thriving business, you need a thriving community. Contribute to your community so you can attract and retain human resources.

SOURCES

Interviews with Calgary Progressive Lifestyles Foundation.
Calgary Progressive Lifestyles Foundation – April Newsletter – http://cplf .ca/wp-content/uploads/2019/04/April.pdf
Calgary Progressive Lifestyles Foundation, http://cplf.ca

17 Stone Hearth Bakery

ANIKA ROBERTS-STAHLBRAND

Introduction

Stone Hearth is a bakery and social enterprise located in Halifax, Nova Scotia. It is one of several programs at MetroWorks, originally founded in 1978 under the name Human Resources Development Association (HRDA). MetroWorks has evolved significantly since then and currently operates a variety of job training and employment programs: an urban farm, a high school certification program for adults, skills-based job training for different sectors, a mobile food market, and Stone Hearth, which includes a bakery and a cafe that provides catering. All these programs are united under the mission "to provide meaningful training and employment opportunities for individuals 19 years of age and older who are living with mental illness and experiencing barriers to employment."

Established in 1982, Stone Hearth Bakery fulfils this mission by employing people with developmental disabilities and/or mental illness at a bakery. This social enterprise is unique in this book because it is the only one that functions as a wholesaler and a distributor, as well as a retailer. In 2015, MetroWorks added a foodservice social enterprise to its portfolio called Stone Hearth Café and Catering in Sackville, which serves Stone Hearth products. John Hartling has been Stone Hearth's manager for program and business development since 2014. He explains that the foodservices venues offer work opportunities in "a structured environment for clients that we felt were not ready to be out into the private sector, a step towards that. Just a little bit more support and training in a real-world environment."

In the 1970s, Harold Crowell, then director of social planning for the city of Halifax, was spurred on by income assistance recipients, who wanted to receive wages rather than income assistance, to investigate alternative means of supporting people with barriers to employment. This inspired Crowell to assemble a board of directors to start HRDA; the collaboration between HRDA and the municipality included seed capital and a commitment from the city to hire HRDA services (Perry, 1993). The collaboration with the municipality proved pivotal for the success of this social enterprise. This history shows the power of creative government approaches to supporting citizens and demonstrates that Halifax was an early leader in social procurement.

The funding to start HRDA was first raised through income-assistance transfer payments. Halifax's department of social planning transferred future income-assistance payments to HRDA, on the condition that HRDA would hire people on income assistance so they would no longer need to receive income-assistance payments. HRDA paid wages to these participants using revenue from the sales of goods and services, such as janitorial services or renovations for social housing (Perry, 1993). Halifax also created a fee-for-service model for any private business that hired an income-assistance recipient for one year.

During this period, the city's department of social planning was "encouraged [by the municipality] to engage in any of these activities on behalf of a welfare client so long as it will end up costing less than the standard welfare grant" (Perry, 1993, p. 91). Since the city covered a large part of the cost of income assistance, it was cheaper for the city of Halifax to stimulate the development of social enterprises which hired people previously on income assistance than it was to pay the entire income-assistance cheque. With these contextual factors, Hartling explains that it made more financial sense for the municipality to procure necessary services from these social enterprises than to hire the cheapest service providers and pay income assistance payments. Hartling adds that in this period "different services and businesses [were] set up similar to Stone Hearth that were meeting county needs and different contracts."

However, this changed in 1996 when the province assumed full responsibility for income assistance. This meant the city no longer had access to these funds and therefore no longer saved money by using the services of social enterprises that employed people who would have otherwise been on income assistance. This change demonstrates the problem of siloed budgets and points to the need for coordinated multi-level approaches to social-service provision.

In addition, the recession in the 1990s led to more financial challenges for HRDA. Due to the financial challenges, it was reorganized and rebranded as MetroWorks, an organization that runs a mix of social enterprises and government-funded social programs. Hartling says the social enterprises "enhance [MetroWorks's] capacity to be more stable. All of our eggs aren't in one basket. If there is a project not funded, we don't have to lay everybody off." Social enterprise is now only one revenue stream for MetroWorks and gives the organization more flexibility.

Social Enterprises

Stone Hearth Bakery distributes products throughout Atlantic Canada to retailers and directly to organizational purchasers. Stone Hearth is the only kosher-certified bakery east of Montréal and specializes in bagels. The bakery also makes different varieties of rye bread, challah, sandwich loaves, buns and rolls, as well as specialty breads such as focaccia. Alongside bread, Stone Hearth also produces dessert loafs, cookies, cheesecakes, and cakes. Retailers such as grocery stores and specialty food markets carry its products, while organizational purchasers including cafes, restaurants, golf courses, places of worship, hotels, and institutional residences buy the baked goods from Stone Hearth to serve to their customers.

Stone Hearth Bakery employs four bakers, two packers, and two delivery drivers. They are referred to as the professional staff who are responsible for training the participants and overseeing the overall operation of the bakery. In addition, two more professional staff members work at Stone Hearth: one is focused on participant intake and the other is the program and business development manager responsible for the overall management of Stone Hearth. On top of the professional staff, Stone Hearth employs about sixty participants each year who receive a sliding scale of pay depending on funding eligibility.

Although Stone Hearth is much smaller than an industrial bakery, it is on par with other artisan bakeries that sell through retailers. The bakery floor is about three thousand square feet with an additional three thousand square feet in the loading bay. The bakery has two shifts each day and operates from 4:00 a.m. until 9:00 p.m. with fifteen to twenty-five people on a given shift.

Stone Hearth tries to cycle participants through every ten to eighteen months. However, Hartling highlights that since Stone Hearth operates as a business, rather than a fully funded program, it has "a bit more flexibility to respond, so sometimes we have people who are with us for several years." Hartling is committed to supporting community members "in a way that is practical." If someone is successful at Stone Hearth but not ready to move beyond it, he is happy to continue working with the individual. This allows individuals to have a better quality of life by staying engaged in a healthy routine, which is important for their overall well-being and stability.

Financial Information

Stone Hearth is categorized as a project of MetroWorks. All of Metro-Works is governed by a board of directors. Any grant funding Stone Hearth receives is awarded to MetroWorks, then directed to Stone Hearth. According to Nora Macnee, the chief financial officer at Metro-Works, Stone Hearth reported revenues of $706,600 in 2018, with $232,500 in government grants and $473,600 in sales.

Hartling points out that there is a misconception within the private sector that Stone Hearth is a charity and sells its products at prices below market value. He explains that undercutting other local baker-ies is "the last thing we want to do," a sentiment shared by Horizon Achievement Centre (chapter 15). Instead, he says Stone Hearth aims to cover its operating expenses and is "very much a viable company."

Hartling says the government funding Stone Hearth receives does not give it a competitive advantage; instead, it levels the playing field. He explains that grants do not cover any business costs that a conven-tional bakery would have. Instead, grant money "helps cover the cost of supporting participants throughout their work activities." After all, as a social enterprise, Stone Hearth operates as both a business and a training facility.

Hartling says it can be difficult to acquire general funding for Stone Hearth because "the operational costs do not fit within the parameters of current funding programs." He also points out that the financial indi-cators do not tell the full story:

> If I was solely focused on achieving funding outcomes, I'd have to reject most of the clients that are referred to me because I wouldn't see them as positive outcomes. If I get a referral, and I know this person is not going to be employed in the near future, we will still accept them and work with them, but if I was really focused on "I have to hit this target that 80 per cent of my clients have to be employed" I might be more in a position where I can't bring these people in.

Personal stories and the longevity of the social enterprise reveal the many examples of successful client engagement, says Hartling. Even though some participants may never gain employment outside Stone Hearth, they benefit greatly from the extra support and community at the social enterprise.

In an era of tightened government funding (Quarter, Mook, & Armstrong, 2018) where governments are seeking to tie funding to indicators (e.g., Crawley, 2019; Hajer, 2019), the point raised by Hartling is a cautionary tale revealing a flaw in this approach to funding allocation.

More broadly, Stone Hearth's revenue model raises the question: should social enterprises be seen as government programs subsidized by sales, or businesses whose social value creation is subsidized by government?

Marketing and Branding

Although Stone Hearth is confident of its social value, it does not always highlight this in its marketing. As Hartling says, "In my experience, the buyers that provide us with steady business are not interested in that [social value]." Stone Hearth has little issue selling to customers who are not interested in its social value, who in turn sell Stone Hearth's products under a different brand name. He says, "I'm not attached to our brand, the Stone Hearth Bakery brand, like I don't care if we sell a product under the brand if it really maximizes the bakery and if the revenue that we generate [helps us to not] be losing money at the end of the day, we'll do it because it engages participants." Not only is Stone Hearth not particularly attached to the brand, but when dealing with large organizational purchasers, Hartling suggests that "sometimes you shouldn't promote the program because people will think there is something wrong with the products, that a professional didn't make it." This selective approach in marketing is especially applicable to food products because of the implications of food safety. It also highlights how for some customers the social good Stone Hearth creates is not seen as value added, but actually as a negative because of the stigma associated with employing workers with developmental disabilities or mental illness. Hartling's experience has shown him that the notion that customers care about social value in a meaningful way is "totally inaccurate." Since Stone Hearth deals primarily with wholesalers and distributors, the social value created through these purchases is not the primary motivation behind the customers' purchasing decision. These customers care first and foremost about price, customer service, quality, and reliability.

To understand this lack of interest in social value by customers, it is important to note that Stone Hearth operates both on the business-to-customer (B2C) and business-to-business (B2B) basis. Although Stone Hearth is not the only social enterprise in this collection that sells mostly B2B (e.g., see chapter 7, EMBERS Staffing Solutions, and chapter 20, Challenge Disability Resource Group), it is the only one that does B2B in a retail environment. Hartling's point on the lack of interest in social value is common among medium-sized organizations that do not sell directly to the end consumers (Leek & Christodoulides, 2011; Youssef, 2018). Leek and Christodoulides (2011, p. 832) write that compared to individual customers, business customers are more "profit-motivated and budget constrained," so they are not as likely to look for branded products with an increased cost. In terms of the final purchase decision, Youssef (2018, p. 735) points out that "[Corporate Social Responsibility] engagement is rather evaluated as a plus, but not as the most salient purchase factor." Instead, Youssef's (2018, p. 728) findings indicate that professional buyers "tend to emphasize tangible attributes such as supplier's financial salience, competencies and production, instead of intangible attributes such as brand image and identification, or emotional satisfaction." This points to the importance of government policies that encourage social procurement to also include specific elements to make social procurement appealing to B2B players in the supply chain who do not recuperate extra value from direct customer goodwill, such as the community-benefit requirements in the case of EMBERS Staffing Solutions (see chapter 7).

Nova Scotia is currently seeing a renewed interest in leveraging public procurement to generate social benefits and to support social enterprises for economic development. Looking ahead, Hartling believes government support and organizational networking are important to build the social economy. He says the worlds of non-profit organizations, social enterprises, and businesses need to start meeting "as people, not just organizations." In this vein, Stone Hearth is now a member of the Halifax Chamber of Commerce. In 2017, Stone Hearth was the first social enterprise to win the Chamber's award for innovative business of the year and small business of the year.

Customers

Two organizational purchasers were interviewed for this case to gain their perspective. Samantha Johnson (a pseudonym) is the culinary operations manager at a long-term care facility serving about 4,500 people and is directly responsible for feeding 1,500 people three times a day. The other is Nick Wright, a former manager of The Galley, a small, ethically minded cafe run by the King's Students' Union of the University of King's College. The long-term care facility orders three to four different products from Stone Hearth on a weekly basis, totalling up to 270 loaves per week. This is a small purchase for the long-term care facility. While the facility has a formal procurement arrangement with its main bread supplier, Johnson says that it does not make sense to have formal contractual arrangements with smaller vendors because "it just takes more work. And I don't think it's really needed." The Galley orders from Stone Hearth once or twice a week to fill orders for all their bagels and bread for grilled cheese sandwiches. Unlike the long-term care facility, The Galley does not engage in formal procurement for any of its products.

Johnson chooses Stone Hearth bread for the long-term care facility where she works because of fantastic customer service and because it has a homemade nostalgia that the seniors appreciate. Johnson refers to the creation of social value as both "just a bonus" and as "equally important to us" as quality and price. Working with a fixed budget for meals, Johnson says that "pricing is always a concern for us, but it's always a balancing act too." In choosing Stone Hearth, Johnson is

> willing to pay a bit more for that premium product because we know the residents are going to be happier with it than they would with something else ... we believe in what they are doing. And we really enjoy using them.

The premium quality of Stone Hearth's bread is often featured in specific dishes where the bread is central and quality is most important, such as with baked beans on molasses bread and spaghetti and garlic bread. Otherwise, due to tight budgets, Johnson opts for cheaper, industrially produced loaves.

The purchasing considerations Johnson identifies are consistent with Hartling's analysis that many customers choose Stone Hearth based on quality, price, and customer service, rather than social value. Although Hartling believes the social value of Stone Hearth serves little in creating sales, B2B branding has a positive impact on customer satisfaction and the opinion of brand agreeableness once the customers have made the purchase. This is evident in Johnson's continued support for Stone Hearth: she is "willing to bend over backwards a bit to use their products."

In contrast, Wright rates the importance of Stone Hearth's social value as moderately important compared to Johnson's higher rating. However, Wright highlights that he rates social value as moderately important because The Galley has to juggle multiple and sometimes conflicting mandates. Although The Galley is not guided by an official procurement policy, it is guided by an informal ethical-purchasing policy that compels it to make purchases that are affordable, ethical, local, and nutritious. Wright explains that The Galley chooses to purchase from Stone Hearth because it "met all our requirements." Two of these requirements, local and ethical, are related to social value. Wright appreciates the opportunity to work with Stone Hearth, even above other ethical brands, because he values their commitment to the local community and their work with people who are marginalized, and views their efforts to be more authentic than many others who are riding the ethical-purchasing trend to generate a profit:

> I was pretty dead set on getting away from businesses run by and for hipsters … because I found that while they did use locally sourced foods, they were often prohibitively expensive and had a very narrow view of what "ethical" meant.

At the same time, price is certainly a factor for The Galley – a small cafe trying to provide affordable food to students. Compared to some of the small suppliers The Galley worked with before, Stone Hearth was actually the cheaper option.

From Stone Hearth's perspective, medium-sized organizational purchasers are ideal customers. Hartling explains that selling to smaller businesses requires significant effort to get new customers and deliver small orders, and it does not allow Stone Hearth to operate at optimal financial efficiency and maximize participant engagement. Working with large organizational purchasers can overwhelm Stone Hearth's facilities and participants by pushing beyond the social enterprise's capacity. With medium-sized businesses, Hartling says "you can develop a relationship with their executive chef and look at menu planning and do the kind of customer service at that level that is very much appreciated and is something that is missing."

Macnee confirms that medium-sized purchasers are ideal because "this type of contract is great – good volumes, single products, easy delivery, reasonable payment turnaround." Even though only 3 per cent of Stone Hearth sales came from medium-sized organizational purchasers in 2018, Macnee says Stone Hearth is trying to build sales in this category. In contrast, sales through grocery stores account for 52 per cent in 2018. However, Hartling says this is not an area the social enterprise is growing because grocery stores now have their own in-house bakeries and charge increasing fees for slotting allowance (rent for shelf space). As a result, the sales through grocery stores come with the highest transaction cost compared to all other customer types.

The organizational purchasers interviewed for this case appear to share a similar viewpoint. Drawing upon an example where Stone Hearth collaborated to develop a bespoke herb bread that was "exactly what we pictured," Johnson from the long-term care facility says that it's hard [to work] with big companies to get them to innovate for you. I mean, they just don't have that flexibility because they're working towards pleasing the masses versus one individual company. But Stone Hearth is small enough that they are flexible to make something for us.

Engagement with Social Procurement

Stone Hearth has not submitted any bids to compete for social procurement contracts. Instead of participating in conventional procurement contracts, Stone Hearth often fills gaps in the procurement agreements. An example is the arrangement with the long-term care facility where Johnson has a procurement contract for most of the bread but still chooses to buy specialty products outside of the procurement agreement. Hartling feels optimistic about this type of arrangement and says, "it puts us to a pretty niche place, and generally it's a pretty good place for us to be because of the size of our organization."

In 2018, the province of Nova Scotia passed amendments to the Public Procurement Act. Hartling sees this as a positive development because contractors who source through social enterprises are given a higher score on their bids. He hopes that larger institutional food providers may be turning to Stone Hearth to include specialty products in their offerings to gain points. Macnee also notices that "university food contractors like Aramark are now interested in buying social."

This case reveals that social criteria in procurement tenders can be highly beneficial to social enterprises; however, not all types of organizational purchasers necessarily find social value relevant or even desirable.

Summary: Lessons Learned

Stone Hearth is a unique case in this book of a social enterprise that is a wholesaler, a distributor, and a retailer. Stone Hearth can provide lessons for other social enterprises, as well as governments and funders in the following ways:

1. Government programs that are not organized in siloed budgets are helpful (and perhaps necessary) to support significant social purchasing and procurement. In the case of Stone Hearth, from the seventies through the nineties, government reduced the need for income-assistance supports through the use of work integration social enterprises. Now, it stands to be seen if the Public Procurement Act can again lead to a supportive environment for work integration social enterprises.

2. Work integration social enterprises should be assessed for success in ways other than the number of participants who are integrated into the mainstream workforce after finishing the program. Not all participants in work integration social enterprises will ever be able to work in the mainstream job market, but they and society still benefit greatly from work in a supportive social enterprise context. Funders should recognize that there is more than one way to measure success.
3. When selling B2B, Stone Hearth's edge is in its size and ability to provide bespoke services for medium-sized businesses and organizations overlooked by multinational wholesalers and distributors, rather than in its social value creation. This may be a successful approach for other medium-sized social enterprises who sell B2B.

REFERENCES

Crawley, M. (2019, May 6). Here's how the Ford government will decide university and college funding. https://www.cbc.ca/news/canada/toronto/ontario-doug-ford-university-college-post-secondary-grants-1.5121844

Hajer, J. (2019, January 16). Fast facts: Social Impact Bonds. https://www.policyalternatives.ca/publications/commentary/fast-facts-social-impact-bonds

Leek, S., & Christodoulides, G. (2011). A literature review and future agenda for B2B branding: Challenges of branding in a B2B context. *Industrial Marketing Management, 40*(6), 830–7. https://doi.org/10.1016/j.indmarman.2011.06.006

Perry, S. (1993). The Human Resources Development Association. *Making Waves, 4*(1). http://communityrenewal.ca/sites/all/files/resource/MW040110.pdf

Quarter, J., Mook, L., & Armstrong, A. (2018). *Understanding the social economy: A Canadian perspective* (2nd ed.). University of Toronto Press.

Youssef, K.B. (2018). The importance of corporate social responsibility (CSR) for branding and business success in small and medium-sized enterprises (SME) in a business-to-distributor (B2D) context. *Journal of Strategic Marketing, 26*(8), 723–39. https://doi.org/10.1080/0965254X.2017.1384038

OTHER SOURCES

Interviews with Stone Hearth Bakery, a long-term care facility in Halifax and The Galley.

Stone Hearth, http://www.stonehearth.ca/

MetroWorks, http://www.stonehearth.ca/about/our-programs/

SUPPLEMENTAL INFORMATION

Revenue Sources (2018): Stone Hearth Bakery

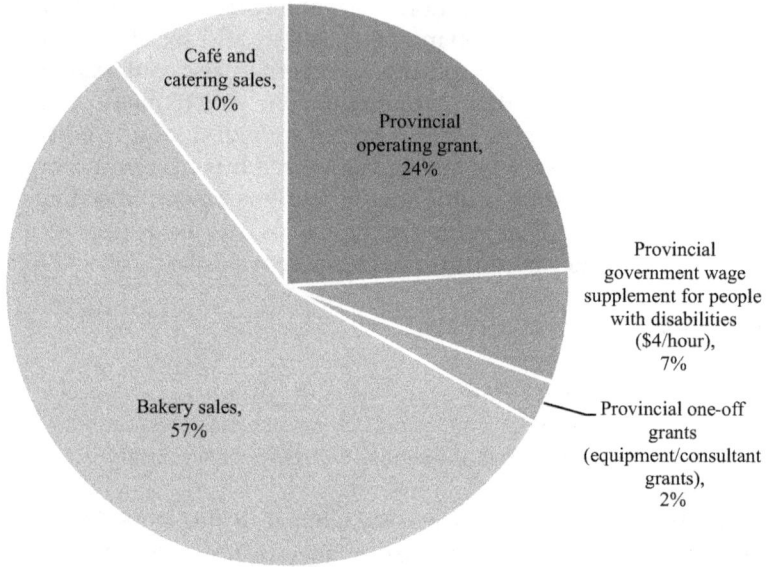

Café and catering sales, 10%

Provincial operating grant, 24%

Provincial government wage supplement for people with disabilities ($4/hour), 7%

Bakery sales, 57%

Provincial one-off grants (equipment/consultant grants), 2%

Revenue by Purchaser Type (2018): Stone Hearth Bakery

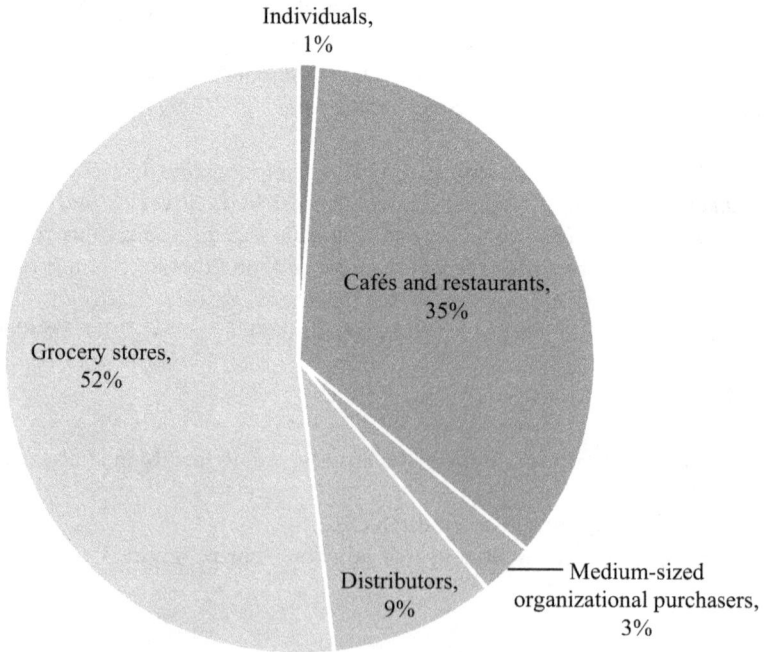

Individuals, 1%

Cafés and restaurants, 35%

Grocery stores, 52%

Distributors, 9%

Medium-sized organizational purchasers, 3%

PART 5

Balancing Multiple Bottom Lines

To many people, the label *social enterprise* is synonymous with the concept of *multiple bottom lines*. These enterprises are mission-driven to create more than economic value; they also generate social, environmental, cultural, or other benefits that contribute to communities. As a type of hybrid entity that can be envisioned on a Venn diagram, WISEs reside where the three spheres of public service, private sector, and social economy overlap (Quarter et al., 2017). Because these organizations straddle three different spheres, some researchers have taken an institutional theory lens to consider how social enterprises may contend with the conflicting institutional logic of the three different spheres (Doherty et al., 2014; Garrow & Hasenfeld, 2012). For instance, tensions and conflicts may arise when the market logic of the private sphere runs against the welfare or humanistic logic of the public and social economy spheres.

In their literature review, Doherty et al. (2014) detail the concerns researchers have raised around the potential social and financial trade-offs to be made in these hybrid organizations with multiple bottom lines. Such trade-offs could result in, for example, the subversion of social goals for financial ones, managerial pressure from conflicting responsibilities, tension between diverse stakeholder groups, mission drift, erosion of legitimacy as organizations with a social focus, and other challenges. Despite these trade-offs, there is also potential for financial and social goals to become mutually reinforcing (e.g., the Fair Trade movement). Also of note from the literature review and with some bearing on part 2 of the book, same-sector and cross-sector partnerships may have particular relevance to the overall strategic management of social enterprises. The following cases illustrate these points:

- Groupe PART (Montreal, Quebec)
- Harbourview Training Centre (Souris, Prince Edward Island)

- Challenge Disability Resource Group (Whitehorse, Yukon)
- Services and Housing In the Province (SHIP) (Ontario)
- LOFT Kitchen (Toronto, Ontario)

How do social enterprises address the challenges of balancing multiple bottom lines while they pursue (social) procurement opportunities? The cases in part 5 all mention some organizational trade-offs. Groupe PART, in Quebec, operates a foodservice social enterprise with people experiencing mental health challenges. Its executive director explains that her commitment to expanding the business aspect of the social enterprise means that less of her attention is focused on its social mission. In order to improve productivity, the organization has also modified its training model so participants would no longer be training directly on the production line. Its strategy appears to be focused on scaling up the business for financial sustainability in order to subsequently scale up its social impact.

The other cases in this part of the book have taken different approaches to manage the tensions among various bottom lines. Harbourview Training Centre, located in rural Prince Edward Island, operates a number of small social enterprises as part of its broad range of programming that supports adults with intellectual disabilities. Harbourview remains adamant that its top priority is its program participants. In the face of trade-offs between delivering on a business contract and supporting participants, Harbourview would choose its participants over its business commitment. For this reason, Harbourview has been somewhat reticent towards the idea of (social) procurement opportunities.

Sometimes, the financial reality makes it difficult for a social enterprise to keep a program running. Challenge Disability Resource Group had to shut down two of its social enterprises for woodworking in early 2019 after years of trying to turn a positive cash flow. Challenge was not able to improve the financial situation for these two social enterprises even after shifting the focus from training to production. The increasing difficulty in securing government funding compounded the problem Challenge faced in maintaining the training aspect of its work.

Services and Housing In the Province (SHIP), a large housing-service organization in Ontario, provides employment and training for its tenants and service-users through its social enterprises. Similar to Harbourview, SHIP expresses a commitment to its participants and has held off expanding its range of cleaning services until it can figure out how to do so without compromising the health and safety of its participants. Although similar to Harbourview in that it makes business decisions based on participant needs first and foremost, SHIP is encouraged by the idea of social procurement and interested in its prospects.

Also in Ontario is LOFT Kitchen, a cafe and catering social enterprise operated by the Christie Ossington Neighbourhood Centre (CONC) to support local youth facing employment barriers and other difficulties. Of the four social enterprises in this part, LOFT Kitchen is the smallest in terms of annual earned revenue. Although it has tried unsuccessfully to submit bids for procurement contracts, LOFT Kitchen sees the value in procurement contracts that would promote financial stability for its training program. Here, the interplay between social and financial goals is not perceived as trade-offs but synergy.

How social enterprises consider their multiple bottom lines may in large part be influenced by their local contexts. Groupe PART is a seasoned bidder for procurement contracts because in the province of Quebec, purchases by organizations regardless of dollar figure are much more formalized. Consequently, by-and-large, all enterprises (social or otherwise) bid for work through competition. Furthermore, one of its major sources of government funding requires "60 per cent of the budget of organizations to be self-funded." As such, Groupe PART is under much stronger external pressure to be financially sustainable through its commercial venture, compared to Harbourview, for example, which as a service organization is comfortable with less than 20 per cent of its total revenue coming from its social enterprises.

When we examine the five cases collectively in order to reflect on the way organizations manage their multiple bottom lines, a pattern emerges that suggests the organizational agency of social enterprises is considerably mediated by their particular set of structural constraints (e.g., context of funding arrangements or urban/rural locale). Reflective of resource dependency theory (Froelich, 1999), organizational behaviour in terms of pursuing government contracts seems to be influenced by whether such opportunities are perceived to be associated with social enterprises' financial survival.

Guiding Questions:

1. How much agency does a social enterprise have in the way it manages multiple bottom lines? In your opinion, would securing government-service contracts help to expand or limit a social enterprise's organizational agency?
2. How does local context influence the viability of social enterprises' pursuit of procurement opportunities?

3. What are some of the ways social enterprises can convert trade-offs into synergy?
4. What are the implications for social enterprises in the face of trade-offs that cannot be reconciled?

REFERENCES

Doherty, B., Haugh, H., & Lyon, F. (2014). Social enterprises as hybrid organizations: A review and research agenda. *International Journal of Management Reviews, 16*(4), 417–36. https://doi.org/10.1111/ijmr.12028

Froelich, K.A. (1999). Diversification of revenue strategies: Evolving resource dependence in nonprofit organizations. *Nonprofit and Voluntary Sector Quarterly, 28*(3), 246–68. https://doi.org/10.1177/0899764099283002

Garrow, E., & Hasenfeld, Y. (2012). Managing conflicting institutional logics: Social service versus market. In B. Gidron & Y. Hasenfeld (Eds.), *Social enterprises* (pp. 121–43). Palgrave Macmillan UK. https://doi.org/10.1057/9781137035301_6

Quarter, J., Mook, L., & Armstrong, A. (2017). *Understanding the social economy: A Canadian perspective* (2nd ed.). University of Toronto Press.

18 The Groupe PART (Programmes d'Apprentissage au Retour au Travail)[1]

RACHEL LAFOREST

Introduction

Groupe PART is a non-profit organization based in Montreal, Quebec, that supports people facing mental health and psychosocial challenges in integrating or reintegrating into the workforce. Its mission is to "promote the socio-professional integration of people with mental health or psychosocial disorders." Groupe PART achieves this mission through two main programs: PART du Chef and PART Cours. PART du Chef is a social enterprise that runs a restaurant and catering service, produces frozen foods, and provides culinary-skills training for its participants. The mandate of PART du Chef is to create sustainable employment opportunities for its participants, mainly in the area of foodservices. Every month, PART du Chef trains between twenty-five to fifty individuals. PART Cours is an adaptive high-school program that works with individuals eighteen to thirty-four years old. More than thirty people a month get their high-school diplomas while receiving ongoing mental health support at PART Cours. Run in collaboration with the local school board, the adaptive high-school program is not a social enterprise per se, although some of the surplus generated by PART du Chef supports activities at PART Cours under the umbrella of Groupe PART.

With an annual revenue from $1.6 million to 2 million, Groupe PART has nearly tripled in size from 2014 to 2019. In terms of total revenue, the restaurant brings in approximately $350,000 a year, frozen-food sales account for about $450,000, and social procurement arrangements through the catering services add another $500,000. The remainder of the revenue comes through various government programs in either

---

1 Translated into English as "program of apprenticeship for the return to work."

employment training or education, which helps Groupe PART to achieve its mission. Groupe PART employs nine full-time and two part-time staff members. The organization has been able to balance multiple bottom lines and grow its operations by professionalizing its business practices and pursuing social procurement opportunities. It now has procurement arrangements with organizational purchasers such as the city of Montreal, universities, and hospitals. These procurement arrangements constitute up to 50 per cent of Groupe PART's revenues through PART du Chef. In its pursuit of social procurement opportunities, Groupe PART has also been supported by a strong network that seeks to accelerate the development of social procurement practices and facilitate collaboration between groups. Martine Thomas is the current executive director, and she was interviewed in preparation of this case.

History and Mission

The idea of providing skills training for residents of Montreal with mental health or psychosocial disorders to enable them to integrate into the labour market first came from a group of social workers in the Centre local de services communautaires[2] (CLSC) in the late 1980s. CLSCs are public agencies that offer health and social services to residents in Quebec. As part of their mandate, CLSCs coordinate access to community resources and, in particular, are responsible for organizing home-support services. The social workers in the CLSC responsible for Montreal realized there were gaps in social services available within the community, especially for the elderly population. They initially decided to launch a pilot project to provide cleaning services for seniors, which could also create a supported employment environment for participants living with mental health challenges to develop their workforce skills and independence. However, the social workers quickly realized that the need for foodservices and catering within the community was even more acute. Since the CLSC ran a cafeteria, the organization already had the facilities in place to prepare meals in-house for delivery, so the social workers shifted the focus of the pilot project to food delivery. This shift enabled the social workers to integrate an employment services component into their mental health services.

As the number of participants in the program began to grow, the social workers realized the model had potential but required a more systematic program structure to oversee the skills development

---

2 Translated into English as "local community services centre."

portion. In 1990, a training program in cooking and frozen meal production was launched: Projets PART. Projets PART began its activities under the responsibility of the Comité de santé mentale (COSAME) – a non-profit organization for community and mental health with twenty years of experience. While independent from the CLSC, COSAME was well known in the community and had an interest in running the pilot program because of its focus on mental health. The program for training and labour-market integration was designed to support participants in learning the job of cook's helper. It also started a home delivery service for people unable to cook on their own and a ready-to-go counter for the general public.

In 1997 the program branched out from COSAME and became incorporated into a separate non-profit entity – PART du Chef. PART du Chef oversees all the job-integration activities from catering to the production and delivery of frozen meals. The program provides a paid internship to participants for thirty weeks, at thirty-five hours a week. In addition, the participants are accompanied by a social worker to provide support through their progress and integration into the workforce.

In the early days of PART du Chef, the staff noticed that many of the participants did not have high-school diplomas and as a result, most of the jobs that participants would be able to seek out were part-time, temporary jobs, which were not conducive to sustainable employment opportunities. The participants could not access the higher-paying, full-time jobs with benefits in public institutions like hospitals. In 2000, the staff decided to launch PART Cours, an adaptive high-school program designed to develop the participants' work-related, social, and academic skills to help them find employment after graduation. In partnership with the Centre de ressources éducatives et pédagogiques[3] of the Commission scolaire de Montréal (the local school board), PART du Chef started PART Cours – a program offering high-school-level French and mathematics courses in the mornings. In the afternoon, the participants meet with their social workers, who provide support services to improve social, emotional, and academic outcomes. The salaries of the two teachers at PART Cours are covered by the school board and at the end of the ten-month program, the participants obtain a certification of studies from the provincial Ministry of Education and Higher Education. The program concludes with a paid three-month internship in foodservices, supported by a funding arrangement with Emploi-Québec.

---

3 Translated into English as "Centre of educational resources and pedagogies."

Given the central mission of both programs was focused on facilitating integration into the labour force, the initial funding source for PART du Chef was Emploi-Québec. This funding arrangement meant PART du Chef was required to report on job-placement rates. There was no assessment of the social value of the program or recognition that PART du Chef was working with a vulnerable population whose employment rates and job tenure tended to be lower than those in the general population.

Another interesting aspect of funding from Emploi-Québec was that provincial grants awarded for labour-market integration programs required 60 per cent of the budget to be self-funded. In order to survive and reach its social mission, PART du Chef had to generate revenue. At first, sales revenue from individual customers purchasing frozen-food delivery and from the ready-to-go counter was enough to cover operational needs. However, PART du Chef had to rethink its strategy in response to changes in the funding environment that began in the early 2000s. Although the overall funding provided to community organizations has steadily increased in Quebec, the available funding has been split among an increasing number of community groups (Jetté, 2008). The impact of this shift is compounded by the fact that funding is not adjusted for inflation, while the minimum wage has increased from nine to twelve dollars. This new financial reality compelled social organizations such as PART du Chef to become more competitive in the market and to professionalize themselves to be more enticing to customers. Suffice it to say, not only did PART du Chef have to grow its customer base, but it also needed to keep its customers happy enough to keep returning.

In 2009, Groupe PART was created to bring PART du Chef and PART Cours under one umbrella, although both programs continue to operate in parallel. The relationship between the two programs is a healthy one, according to the executive director. They share the same board of directors and support staff. They are seen as two avenues towards the same objective: creating integration opportunities.

Groupe PART provides more than employment services; it also provides a variety of employment-support services to help participants build confidence and a social skill set to enable them to have sustainable employment opportunities. With the employment portfolio now under a new Ministry – Ministère du Travail, de l'Emploi et de la Solidarité Sociale – which is also responsible for social-economy initiatives, there is hope that the social benefits from organizations such as Groupe PART may be recognized and the accountability expectations in terms of results will be adapted to the reality of the participants they work with.

It should be underlined that, like many other social enterprises in Quebec, Groupe PART does not rely on volunteers to carry out its mission. Indeed, Quebec generally has the lowest rate of formal volunteering in Canada (Devlin & Zhao, 2016; Statistics Canada, 2014). More interestingly, Groupe PART does not engage in philanthropic or fundraising activities to generate resources to support its activities. Most of the revenue generated, aside from government grants, is through the restaurant, catering, and frozen-food business.

Customers and Marketing

In the early years, the majority of the customers Groupe PART catered to were individuals ordering frozen foods or buying prepared meals from the ready-to-go counter. In 2005, a strategic decision was made to move PART du Chef and PART Cours to the Technopôle Angus site. Technopôle Angus was a flourishing community in the heart of Montreal, which is also home to sixty-two businesses, organizations, and non-profit organizations employing over 2,700 people in such fields as health, life sciences, information, and communications technologies. This relocation offered the organization an opportunity to showcase the essential nature of labour-market integration and the social benefits for the participants in the programs. Groupe PART not only gained recognition and legitimacy, it was also able to access a new market because Technopôle Angus was a strong attraction for potential customers.

With the relocation, Groupe PART opened a new restaurant that was positioned as a friendly neighbourhood cafeteria, involved in the community and committed to offering homemade, healthy dishes at affordable prices. The restaurant leveraged the certification Groupe PART obtained in 1998 from the provincial Ministry of Health and Social Services as part of the Réseau des menus Mieux Vivre.[4] This certification recognizes that the meals provided are lower in cholesterol and fats. It is an important marketing tool across the province for restaurants and hotels.

The restaurant, renamed Caféshop in 2013, primarily employs former participants of PART du Chef. The restaurant markets its services to all the workers in Technopôle Angus and launched a customer loyalty program offering a 10 per cent discount after a certain number of visits. Many local customers are repeat customers who drop in for lunch and then take a ready-to-go meal for dinner. Groupe PART has increased its

---

4 Translated into English as "the network of better living menus."

production from forty meals a day to two hundred, and the restaurant has now reached its capacity level.

Groupe PART uses a three-pronged marketing strategy, emphasizing the quality of goods and services, employment training opportunities, and the importance of reducing community vulnerability. The marketing strategy places the social mission front and centre. Groupe PART is driven by its social mission to foster workforce integration opportunities for people with mental health challenges and psychosocial disorders. The organization also embraces the values of sustainable economic development in its business model noting that "sustainable development is of great importance and requires a special economic, social and ecological commitment." This commitment translates into giving priority to local suppliers in Groupe PART's own procurement practices and to social enterprises when it partners up or buys supplies. Groupe PART also uses 100 per cent biodegradable materials (such as containers, lunch boxes, trays, and utensils). Finally, Groupe PART uses an energy-efficient vehicle to deliver the meals. This commitment to sustainability in all its forms is another example of value-add that sets Groupe PART apart from private-sector businesses. Groupe PART's online presence drives about 11 to 25 per cent of its sales. Currently, less than 10 per cent of its resources go towards marketing.

The most significant challenge for the organization has been to manage growth, professionalize, and build capacity, all while maintaining a focus on its social objectives. In order to do so, Groupe PART hired Martine Thomas in 2016 as executive director. With over twenty-five years of experience in the cooperative sector, she brought a wealth of entrepreneurship and strategic thinking to the organization.

With new leadership in place, Groupe PART went back to the drawing board and re-examined its operational model in order to seek out greater efficiencies and increase productivity with existing resources. It was able to reduce food costs by participating in a social-value purchasing group with other social enterprises. This is an example of how Groupe PART gives preference to collaboration with other organizations that also have a social purpose. Groupe PART also specializes its line of production in order to reduce the production time of each product. Since PART du Chef runs a restaurant, a catering service, and a frozen dish delivery service – all produced by participants in training – PART du Chef works with a training strategy. In order to meet rising demand, full-time staff work on meal production allowing the head chef to focus his energy on the training activities. However, this comes at a cost to the social mission because it means taking participants who were in training off the production line for the social enterprise to be more productive.

When Groupe PART re-examined its core operational procedures in the late 2010s, Thomas found herself with less time to dedicate to the social mission of the organization. She notes that

> there is a part of my work which was dedicated to the social mission and which can no longer be dedicated to it … it must now be centred on the economic part. I have to become competitive and productive to survive.

Now that the organization has grown its operations and is generating a positive cash flow, the executive director is looking to refocus on training and labour-integration programs. Thomas further explains: "Now our mission is to find the balance between production and our mission because to survive, we have to produce, and to survive, we have to produce quality goods." As is typical with many social enterprises, this rapid growth has come with some challenges around balancing the capacity to deliver quality goods, while keeping centred on the social mission.

More recently, Groupe PART has been looking to expand its frozen-food production by developing meals geared for families. Up until now, frozen meals were made only in individual portions. However, Groupe PART now sees a new market that can be tapped into with a growing number of busy families who no longer have time to cook at home. PART du Chef can offer a healthy alternative for them.

(Social) Procurement and (Social) Purchasing

A key part of Thomas's strategy for Groupe PART is to seek out (social) procurement opportunities and to focus her energy on larger customers from both the public and the private sectors. Procurement is seen as a great way to build the catering services, which now account for about $500,000 of total annual revenue. The main organizational purchasers for the catering services are the city of Montreal (which accounts for 15 per cent of the catering business), the provincial Ministry of Health (15 per cent) and the provincial Ministry of Employment and Solidarity (5 per cent). The remainder of the organizational purchasers include the Université de Montréal, McGill University, Concordia University, and the Université du Québec à Montréal (UQÀM), all of which use Groupe PART's catering for conferences; Groupe PART also serves hospitals across the city.

PART du Chef bids on catering contracts ranging from $150 to $6,000. Regardless of contract value, the purchasing process is formalized in the province of Quebec. PART du Chef must put in a bid for the work in a competitive setting (even for small orders). According to its own self-evaluation, Groupe PART rates its bidding capacity as average. The organization does not have a dedicated staff person to apply for these bids. Overall, Groupe PART estimates that it is successful in the bidding process because of its value proposition. Formal bidding processes generally do not include social criteria, although the city of Montreal is working on developing guidelines for assessing such criteria. Nevertheless, according to Thomas, customers find it particularly important and beneficial to be in a position to report their social-purchasing activities in annual reports and statements to stakeholders. A tangible benefit from winning contracts is the recognition and legitimacy for the social enterprise.

Groupe PART also maintains that its success is due to the quality of its products and its price point. An example is a new project currently being developed with a non-profit retirement home that requested bids for a catering service to prepare meals on-site for its residents. Groupe PART's bid came in at half the price of the other private businesses competing for the contract. As Thomas explains, "in addition, because we are not motivated by profits, people know they are receiving quality and that we are not skimping on our quantities." The new collaborative project, which is still in its early stages, is expected to generate an additional $20,000 a month in revenue.

Leadership

The story of Groupe PART illustrates the importance of leadership. The hiring of a new executive director with an MBA and background in the cooperative movement was a critical turning point in the history of Groupe PART. Given Thomas's experience in the cooperative movement, she is aware of the (social) procurement opportunities that the organization needs to take advantage of. Indeed, the long-standing tradition of social economy in Quebec explains why support for social enterprises like Groupe PART is so prevalent (Laforest, 2007). For one, efforts to democratize economic development and allow the community to take greater responsibility for business development has been recognized by the provincial government through funding and legislation (Assemblée nationale du Québec, 2013). Further, the province also mandates municipalities to use social enterprises in their purchasing, thus creating many opportunities for organizations such as Groupe PART to bid on contracts. In fact, all cities must post all contracts of at least $25,000 through Quebec's electronic tender notice system in accordance with the Cities and Towns Act. Although the price range for tendering is far above what Groupe PART works in, the $25,000 threshold is significantly lower than that in other provinces and municipalities across Canada. Such policies promote social procurement as a strategic approach and encourage a veritable culture change across the provinces.

The city of Montreal is now one of the leaders in social procurement. Adopted in 2006, its procurement policy states that when purchasing goods and services, the city will take into account the social, economic, and environmental dimensions of sustainable development. In 2009, the city released a document entitled *Partenariat en économie sociale pour un développement solidaire et durable*[5] to promote the role of social enterprises in its procurement. The city reiterated this commitment in 2013 by signing the *Déclaration d'engagement à l'achat public auprès d'entreprises collectives*.[6] Correspondingly, major institutions in Quebec, such as universities and hospitals, have also started to align their purchasing power with community development.

In order to tap into procurement opportunities, the first thing Thomas did was to join the Conseil d'économie sociale de l'île de Montréal (CÉSIM) – a multi-stakeholder round table – to support Groupe PART in developing connections with public institutions and private corporations in order to grow its business. In the late 1990s, CÉSIM was created in order to promote social procurement on the island of Montreal. It acts as a regional body for the island with its membership of various social enterprises, as well as municipal and provincial government partners and funders. Its mandate is large: to consult and develop partnerships with local and regional players; to promote the social economy; and to support the development and consolidation of businesses and social-economy projects in the Montreal area. Hence, referrals obtained from within the network are an important source of customers for Groupe PART.

Challenges

When discussing some of the barriers to increasing social procurement and social purchasing in Quebec, Thomas highlights two main challenges faced by social enterprises like Groupe PART. First, there is the

---

5 Translated into English as "the partnership with social economy for solidarity and sustainable development."
6 Translated into English as "a declaration of commitment to public purchase from collective enterprises."

balancing act that the social enterprise must achieve between running a viable business generating revenues and remaining true to its social mission, which often involves supporting vulnerable populations or some other social cause. Like many social enterprises, Groupe PART has to walk a fine line between balancing the need to grow its operations and professionalize on the one hand and to stay focused on its social mission to generate sustainable work experience for people facing mental health and psychosocial challenges on the other. Such a balancing act often requires the social enterprise to make choices between these two (oftentimes opposing) goals. We see this when Thomas talks about the challenge of having to put her attention on business models and revenue generation rather than workplace integration.

Second, there is the challenge of demystifying the nature of social enterprises and social procurement in general. One of the members of CÉSIM says that a major part of CÉSIM's role involves sensitizing and educating the public as customers (and public-sector organizations and corporations more specifically) on the importance of the social economy in Quebec. For example, CÉSIM works on clarifying the misconception that social enterprises only cater to those in poverty or have a cumbersome and overly democratic governance structure. The strength of the social-economy movement in Quebec means that Groupe PART is able to draw support from many networks in order to raise awareness on the importance of social enterprises and promote social procurement. Networks similar to CÉSIM exist in all the major regions of Quebec, as does a provincial body called the Chantier de l'economie sociale. All these networks work on the *L'économie sociale, j'achète!*[7] Campaign (CRE de Montréal, 2015), which was initiated by the provincial government in 2013 to support social enterprises in developing links with public institutions and private corporations. The *L'économie sociale, j'achète!* Campaign provides a forum for this dialogue between organizational purchasers on the one hand and the social enterprises as vendors on the other. Between 2013 and 2015, two hundred contracts were awarded to social enterprises thanks to the campaign.

Summary and Lessons Learned

This case provides an overview of the strategies that Group PART has adopted in order to manage its transition in size and scope of activities by balancing multiple bottom lines, tapping into existing networks,

---

7 Translated in English as "the social economy, I buy!"

and seeking out new (social) procurement opportunities. A number of important lessons can be gleaned from this case.

1. The arrival of a new executive director for Groupe PART was an impetus for change and professionalization in order to manage financial pressure. During her tenure, Thomas has implemented important changes to operational procedures and hiring practices. While professionalization can undermine the values of social enterprises, it can also help buttress their vision. Thomas has helped clarify the value proposition and position of Groupe PART in relation to other actors in the field. The Groupe PART website illustrates that every aspect of the various programs is connected to the social mission and the goals of sustainable economic development, which are key pillars of the organization.

2. As it continues to grow, Groupe PART recognizes the delicate balance between productivity and mission may come at the price of a loss of local customers. Nevertheless, it is interested in gaining opportunities to secure new customers through social procurement and social purchasing. Thomas sees opportunities ahead with a rising awareness of the importance of aligning purchasing practices with social and economic development priorities; Groupe PART still has much potential for growth.

3. The context of Quebec's social and political culture in this case illustrates how important it is to build an environment that supports social enterprises in securing opportunities to grow their business through social procurement. In Quebec, social networks and purposive communities are built on fostering collaboration between suppliers and customers to leverage purchasing power for social benefits. This has enabled organizations like Groupe PART, with very little experience, to hit the ground running and quickly tap into social procurement opportunities.

4. It is also important for organizations to develop knowledge in how to strategically use (social) procurement and (social) purchasing to grow and generate revenue for their social mission.

REFERENCES

Assemblée nationale du Québec. (2013). *Projet de loi no. 27, Loi sur l'économie sociale*. http://www.assnat.qc.ca/fr/travaux-parlementaires/projets-loi/projet-loi-27-40-1.html

CRE de Montréal. (2015). Le projet-pilote montréalais L'économie sociale, j'achète!, un succès. https://www.esmtl.ca/nouvelles/article/le-projet-pilote-montrealais-leconomie-sociale-jachete-un-succes/

Devlin, R.A., & Zhao, W. (2016). *Philanthropic behaviour of Quebecers* (Working paper #1607E). Department of Economics, Faculty of Social Sciences, University of Ottawa. https://socialsciences.uottawa.ca/economics/sites/socialsciences.uottawa.ca.economics/files/1607e.pdf

Jetté, C. (2008). *Les organismes communautaires et la transformation de l'État-providence. Trois décennies de constructions des politiques publiques dans le domaine de la santé et des services sociaux.* Presses de l'Université du Québec.

Laforest, R. (2007). The politics of state-civil society relations in Quebec. In M. Murphy (Ed.), *Canada: The state of the federation 2005 – Quebec and Canada in the new century: New dynamics, new opportunities* (pp. 178–98). McGill-Queen's University Press.

Statistics Canada. (2014). 2010 Canada survey of giving, volunteering and participating (CSGVP). https://www150.statcan.gc.ca/n1/daily-quotidien/120321/dq120321a-eng.htm

OTHER SOURCES

Interviews with Groupe PART and CÉSIM.
Groupe PART, https://www.groupepart.ca/
CÉSIM, https://www.economiesocialemontreal.net/programmes-et-activites/leconomie-sociale-jachete/
Chantier de l'économie sociale, https://chantier.qc.ca

19 Harbourview Training Centre

ANIKA ROBERTS-STAHLBRAND

Introduction

Harbourview Training Centre is a non-profit organization and a registered charity located in Souris, Prince Edward Island (PEI). Its mission is to create "opportunities for individuals with an intellectual disability to participate in their community, both socially and economically, by allowing individuals to gain a stronger sense of self and independence." One of the ways Harbourview furthers its mission is by offering employment training and opportunities through social enterprises. Government subsidies and donations enable Harbourview to make a trade-off between its multiple bottom lines and prioritize social value creation for participants over profitability.

Harbourview was started in the early 1970s as a grassroots organization by parents of children living with intellectual disabilities. These parents wanted to create opportunities for their children, so they started an informal program providing social activities and self-care programs in one family's home. Harbourview was officially incorporated in 1972 as a non-profit organization. Soon after, the parents realized they would need a bigger space to accommodate the growing demand. By the late 1970s, the program became formalized and a larger, separate facility was built.

Geographical Context

Harbourview is located in a rural community. Judy Hennessey is the current executive director of Harbourview and has been with the organization since the early 1990s. As she puts it, Souris is "100 per cent rural – we live in a town of 1,200 people." Souris is on the north-eastern tip of PEI, right on the sea. It is small in population, but it boasts one of the most important ports in PEI. It is the base for the only offshore fishing fleet in the province and the ferry terminal to Îles de-la-Madeleine, a popular tourist location. The major industries in Souris are fishing and lobster fishing.

This rural context is critical to the activities of Harbourview. Similar to other social enterprises located in small towns, the rural setting presents both a strong need, structural constraints, and many opportunities for the development of social enterprises (Lang & Ferguson, 2012; Lang et al., 2016). Rural areas are less densely populated, so government services are expensive to provide and may be more efficiently and effectively provided by grassroots social enterprises. Despite this, a report on rural social enterprises in Canada says that "there is a lack of representation of the unique voice of rural non-profits in social enterprise (SE) practitioner and policy discussions" in Canada (Lang & Ferguson, 2012, p. 5). The importance of the rural perspective is particularly evident when it comes to Harbourview's marketing, procurement, and purchasing.

Financial Information

Harbourview's revenues for the fiscal year 2017 were $545,724 and the expenses were $558,184 (with staffing accounting for over 60 per cent of total expenses), resulting in a deficit of $12,460. Harbourview has four main sources of revenue: annual operating funding from the province, donations, grants from other levels of government, and earned revenue from social enterprises.

First, the organization receives the majority of its annual funding from the province's Department of Family and Human Services. According to 2017 year-end statements, it received $255,500, which covered staffing and infrastructure costs. Another major grant comes from the province's Disability Support Program – $118,018 in 2017 – which is specifically associated with the intake of new program participants who receive personalized service plans. The substantial government funding is consistent with other social enterprises in Canada that employ people with intellectual disabilities (Quarter et al., 2015).

Second, Harbourview receives some charitable donations, despite not running any specific fundraising drives. Due to the organic nature of donations, the amounts fluctuate year to year from $27,157 in 2015, to $11,115 in 2016, to $18,928 in 2017, according to year-end financial statements. The third category of revenue is a combination of specific government programs and subsidies. For example, in 2017, Harbourview received $3,225 from the Canada Summer Jobs Program to pay staff at its ice cream stand.

Last, Harbourview generates revenue from the various social-enterprise activities. Hennessey says that the bakery and the woodworking shop are the most significant revenue generators at Harbourview. In 2017, the workshop generated $39,738, the bakery $32,603, and the ice cream stand $27,275. The other social-enterprise activities – mail service, restaurant, and cafe – do not have their own revenue lines.

The modest revenue from the social enterprises reflects Harbourview's use of the social-enterprise activities primarily as a means to support its mission of creating opportunities for adults with intellectual disabilities to participate in the community and gain independence rather than to generate revenue. The social enterprises themselves generate enough revenue to cover the cost of goods, pay the program participants a stipend, and fund programming, such as bowling. Although Harbourview is not financially self-sufficient from its earned revenue, the organization can achieve financial sustainability through a combination of government subsidy, philanthropy, and earned income. Harbourview has been financially sustainable for decades through a combination of different income sources, which enables it to provide social services to a rural area.

Programming and Social Enterprises

Harbourview offers four types of programming and support: (1) social/themed programs, such as fitness, social skill-building, and job skill-building; (2) a day program to support people with intellectual disabilities; (3) facilitation for participants in community activities and part-time employment in Souris; and (4) on-site employment through its social enterprises. Although social-enterprise activities are the focus of this case study, Hennessy emphasized that Harbourview is a multipurpose organization and the social enterprises are "just one aspect of what we do."

Harbourview first ventured into social enterprises with a bakery, a woodworking shop (making everything from door signs to picnic tables), and a restaurant, which all predate Hennessey's tenure at Harbourview. She added an ice cream shop in 2003 to take advantage of Souris's tourist season during the summer. Harbourview also opened a cafe in 2018, which has since been discontinued. In 2003, Harbourview started a small delivery service for six local businesses at a fee of three dollars per day to pick up their mail in town and deliver it to them. Since this social enterprise operates in a dispersed area, this service requires a car that must be driven by a support staff, not a participant. Other than the mail service, all the social enterprises are run out of Harbourview's building.

Harbourview currently works with thirty-five participants, most of whom are involved in at least one of the social enterprises. Program participants are typically referred to Harbourview when they age out of public education or by a case worker when families seek government support to care for an adult with an intellectual disability. So far, Harbourview has generally been able to take in every participant thanks to available capacity. However, Hennessey says that occasionally Harbourview cannot welcome a participant into the program if the organization is not able to match a staff member with the skills to support the specific needs of a certain participant.

Harbourview's participants have varying ability levels, and it is possible to participate in the social and support programming without also working in one of the social enterprises. More typically, participants are involved in overlapping programs and social enterprises at Harbourview. For example, the ice cream shop is seasonal, so those participants may play other roles during the rest of the year, and many participants are involved in social programming as well as working in a social enterprise. The participants who work in one of the social enterprises receive a stipend, which is paid from the sales revenues generated by the social enterprises. Harbourview also connects participants with seasonal or small jobs outside of Harbourview, which typically pay them minimum wage.

Hennessey says that "most [participants] stay in our programming for an extended period of time." Some even stay after reaching retirement age, which Harbourview supports with a retirement model prioritizing safety, mobility, and socializing. Fewer participants rotate through Harbourview, but Hennessey says that "some have moved on to jobs; some leave for seasonal employment in the public sector but come back in the off season."

To run the programs and social enterprises, Harbourview currently has five full-time and six part-time staff members, as well as additional support-staff members who join the organization in direct connection with specific participants. Although Hennessey is open to using more volunteers in the future, she says that "for the most part we do not run our services based on volunteers" because, as she puts it, "we operate kind of like a business." Other than the volunteer board members, Harbourview only occasionally uses volunteers for specific activities with participants such as crafting events and for social outings in the community.

Individuals are the primary customers of Harbourview's social enterprises, comprising approximately 75 per cent of total sales. Organizational purchasers account for the remaining 25 per cent and purchase, for example, coffee break snacks, mail-delivery tasks, or woodwork decorations for special events. The main reasons why these organizational purchasers buy from Harbourview, according to Hennessey, are quality, Harbourview's charitable status, a desire to support the local community, competitive pricing, and a desire to support the employment of individuals with intellectual disabilities.

Marketing

Harbourview devotes only minimal resources to marketing (reporting only fifty-five dollars as advertising expense) and has no staff member designated with the responsibility of marketing. Hennessey rates Harbourview's marketing capacity as low. Hennessey points out that there is no numerical way of measuring or tracking positive social impact so it can be conveyed to customers: "We just know, you know … Good news and that sort of stuff."

Instead of any marketing strategy, Harbourview relies on word of mouth. Although common among social enterprises, word of mouth is particularly pertinent in rural settings, as James Dunbar – a social entrepreneur in rural Scotland and speaker at the Social Enterprise World Forum – says: "Relationships are fundamental … People in rural settings talk to each other, we gossip, and then we talk some more" (Casolari et al., 2013). Harbourview harnesses this rural propensity to build relationships by connecting with customers in person and sharing stories. Hennessey adds the story of how the community was curious when Harbourview expanded the building in 2009–10, so the organization "had a large open house and everybody was invited. People were nosy enough to come, and they come, and they keep coming, and they tell the next person, and the next person comes."

Harbourview not only talks about the social value of its products, but also their functional value which "is as important as social and emotional value" (Choi & Kim, 2013, p. 249). Hennessey is well aware of the tension between social and functional value when discussing the quality of Harbourview products and the reasons why customers purchase them. Hennessey emphasizes that the quality of Harbourview's products is "excellent," but she is also aware that "people always like to support us in a way because they see us as a charity." This highlights how Harbourview's multiple bottom lines work together in synergy to support marketing efforts and to generate returning customers.

Another aspect of Harbourview's marketing that is influenced by its rural context is that its building also functions as a community meeting place. When community members use the space for meetings or craft nights with friends, they can also see what is happening at Harbourview first-hand without having to be told about it. For example, the woodworking shop at Harbourview is visible to all. Hennessey describes the value of this:

> A lot of our products are broken-down into the smallest steps so that every person with some sort of ability gets to contribute in some way ... we don't market it like that, but because we live in a small community we see a lot of family members, public come into our building, and our building is very open, so when they come in they witness it, first-hand.

Customers who see the workshop are attracted to the beautiful woodwork products, but they are also attracted to the fact that people with intellectual disabilities "could be part of a beautiful project, and that [participants] could have a feeling of contribution and feeling of success." The interactions between participants and community members at the cafe, the ice cream stand, and the workshop are how Harbourview makes its work visible and communicates its social impact. In a small-town context, Hennessey believes this is highly effective because Harbourview is well known by the community as a whole.

Harbourview gains knowledge of market opportunities as a result of being embedded within the community. This is consistent with research findings on other social enterprises based in rural settings (Steiner & Teasdale, 2019). Hennessey describes this approach by saying "we feel like we belong to the community and the community supports us. Many of the things that we make here are because we know what the community wants." Harbourview is a social enterprise of and for the rural fishing people of Souris, as Hennessy points out:

> We wouldn't start making, I don't know, a bunch of wine racks, because we're not wine connoisseurs here, you know. But we do make lobster traps and lighthouse crafts because we're a fishing community. Because we feel like we know the community, and so therefore we are making stuff that then we know the community would want, so it's back and forth.

Engagement with Procurement and Purchasing

Harbourview does not participate in any formal procurement; instead, it participates in less formal social purchasing. For Harbourview, both the participants and the customers are understood as being in relationships of receiving from Harbourview – the participants receive support, and the customers receive the purchased goods and services.

Hennessey makes it clear that the participants with intellectual disabilities are not simply producers for the customers; the participants are the most important service recipients at Harbourview. This prioritization of participants over generating financial surplus is also reflected in Hennessey's comment that "we run like a business, but we're not like a business because our number one priority is service to the [participants]."

By prioritizing the participants, Harbourview remains cautious about the benefits of social procurement. As Hennessey describes: "If something happens and our clients need our services more, and our bakery couldn't operate, then we wouldn't be able to commit to a contract."

Having said that, Hennessey points out that Harbourview is not against procurement, but "it would have to be very specific to what we could do and what we could handle and the fact that we would still be able to provide the finished product we are used to doing, which is great." Harbourview is wary of social procurement because the obligation to fulfil a contract, at least the way contracts are likely to be structured, could come into conflict with its primary goal of supporting participants.

Due to the importance Harbourview puts on placing participants first, Hennessey feels that social purchasing is more aligned with its mission. Through social purchasing, Harbourview can choose to take or decline a request in the moment depending on the capacity of current participants and existing production commitments.

Harbourview sells regularly to a variety of organizations. It provides the snacks for the parent council meetings at the local school and is considered the "go-to" place to create decorations for celebratory events organized by the Souris City Council (e.g., for "the Mermaid Tears Sea Glass Festival [the council] wanted specific mermaids cut out and painted and fish made and painted"). For Hennessey, the willingness of the council to collaborate with Harbourview facilitates the balancing of the needs of participants and customers.

While large purchases and contracts may be a way for social enterprises to increase their income and grow, this traditional approach to scaling up may not work for rural social enterprises (Steiner & Teasdale, 2018). For the social enterprises in rural settings, diversification is a more appropriate strategy for growth (Casolari et al., 2013). This is reflected in Hennessey's comment that Harbourview's current programs will not grow, but the organization may start branching off into affordable housing, which serves a specific need for its participants.

At this time, Hennessey is focused on serving the participants and less interested in scaling up the operations at Harbourview. Even though Harbourview has consistent relationships with multiple purchasers, Harbourview actually never intentionally sought them out. As

Hennessey explains, "we aren't that big, that if you spoke out too much, we'd have to say no to people because we wouldn't be able to accommodate. We're growing at a pace that we are creating, not work creating us." Harbourview only wants to grow if the growth remains in its control and in the service of its participants.

It is important to note that Harbourview's agency to define appropriate scale based on participant needs, rather than always pushing for customer growth, is predicated on the fact that a majority of its funding comes from the government, instead of earned income. As shown in this case, social enterprises do not need to be viewed as businesses with a goal of revenue generation, but rather as an innovative and responsive mode of social service provision that must be continually funded by grants like other social services. Government-funded rural social enterprises allow the power to stay at a local level and provide services specifically catered to the community while being funded from a higher level of government with a broader tax base.

As noted above, the social enterprises at Harbourview account for 18 per cent of its total revenue, with government funding making up 68 per cent. Although the surpluses of the social enterprises are very modest, a low level of earned income does not mean Harbourview's social enterprises are failing. Instead, it raises the question of whether social enterprises can or should ever replace public funding for social services in a significant way. This case shows how a social enterprise can be valuable even if it does not generate significant financial value. Harbourview's social enterprises provide many important services to the participants, as well as services to the broader community. The organization is rooted in its community and can therefore provide more efficient, relevant, and effective programming. Harbourview generates significant social value that is important and meaningful, regardless of whether this generates, or can be translated into, monetary value.

Summary: Lessons Learned

The case of Harbourview highlights specific elements unique to social enterprises in rural communities, which require further investigation. The case also brings to the fore the tricky question for rural and urban social enterprises alike of how to balance multiple bottom lines, and indeed, whether this is possible.

1. Canada's social economy movement is rooted in the rural context of the Antigonish Movement in Nova Scotia and the Movement Desjardins in rural Quebec in the early 1900s. However, currently

there is a lack of attention to rural social enterprises in practitioner, academic, and policy discussions in Canada. This case highlights that the local context matters, and we need to reinvigorate research on rural social enterprises, not simply transpose the research findings from urban social enterprises onto the rural context.

2. This case suggests that, in rural contexts, the substantially subsidized social-enterprise model may be a more effective and efficient way to provide contextual and community-integrated social services. Government-funded rural social enterprises allow for the agency to stay at the local level, and this funding means that social services can be provided across the country without the inefficiency of government buildings in small population centres, or long commutes for rural people who need access to government supports. This lesson warrants further study to see if it applies to other rural contexts and social enterprises.

3. If a social enterprise is replacing government supports, this case suggests that this kind of social enterprise needs to be seen as a different mode of government social-service provision, rather than as a different method of social-service provision separate from government. Seen in this light, Hennessey's hesitancy to engage in social procurement is understandable because it requires a prioritization of product delivery over participant support. The way Harbourview has been able to balance its multiple bottom lines is only through significant government subsidy. The growing popularity of social procurement exists within the context of the rise of neoliberal policies and the associated reductions in government spending on social programming (Quarter et al., 2018). This case suggests that social enterprises can provide innovative solutions to social challenges but should not be seen as a way to justify a reduction in a public commitment to support and empower citizens of all abilities.

REFERENCES

Casolari, E., Craig, M., & Dunbar, J. (2013, October 2–4). *Rural revitalization: How social enterprise keeps rural communities viable*. Panel conducted at the meeting of the Social Enterprise World Forum, Calgary, Canada. https://tricofoundation.ca/rural-revitalization-how-social-enterprise-keeps-rural-communities-viable/

Choi, E.J., & Kim, S.H. (2013). The study of the impact of perceived quality and value of social enterprises on customer satisfaction and re-purchase intention. *International Journal of Smart Home, 7*(1), 239–52.

Lang, C., & Ferguson, M. (2012). *Rural social enterprise project: Documenting the learning*. Foundation for Rural Living. https://ccednet-rcdec.ca/sites /ccednet-rcdec.ca/files/frl_rsep_learning_document_fv.pdf

Lang, C., Ferguson, M., & Harrison, B. (2016). *Rural social enterprise and community ecosystem development: Policy leverage points*. The Ontario Nonprofit Network. https://theonn.ca/wp-content/uploads/2016/05 /NewDirections-Research-Report-Final-April-10-2016.pdf

Madill, J., Brouard, F., & Hebb, T. (2010). Canadian social enterprises: An empirical exploration of social transformation, financial self-sufficiency, and innovation. *Journal of Nonprofit & Public Sector Marketing*, 22(2), 135–51. https://doi.org/10.1080/10495141003674044

Quarter, J., Chan, A., & Ryan, S. (Eds.). (2015). *Social purpose enterprises: Case studies for social change*. University of Toronto Press.

Quarter, J., Mook, L., & Armstrong, A. (2018). *Understanding the social economy: A Canadian perspective* (2nd ed.). University of Toronto Press.

Steiner, A., & Teasdale, S. (2019). Unlocking the potential of rural social enterprise. *Journal of Rural Studies*, 70, 144–54. https://doi.org/10.1016/j .jrurstud.2017.12.021

OTHER SOURCES

Interviews with Harbourview Training Centre.
Harbourview Training Centre, https://www.harbourviewtraining.com
Harbourview Training Centre – Financial Statements 2016 and 2017.

20 Challenge Disability Resource Group[1]

ANNIE LUK AND JILLIAN HARDIE

Introduction

The Challenge Disability Resource Group (Challenge) is a charitable non-profit organization located in Whitehorse, Yukon, with the mission to "assist individuals with disabilities to learn life skills and job skills by empowering them to be engaged in the community." First incorporated in 1976 as Challenge Community Vocational Alternative, the organization changed to its current name in 2012. Challenge began as a day program for adults with moderate to severe developmental disability before it evolved into a sheltered workshop offering work activities for participants. In the 1980s, as social acceptance grew to recognize the contributions of adults who have developmental disability, Challenge shifted its focus from day programming to job development and vocational training so adults with developmental disability could work for market wages in an integrated work environment. Since then, Challenge has expanded its support to also include individuals with other forms of disabilities, including those that are not formally diagnosed.

Challenge is situated in the north end of downtown Whitehorse on Front Street, facing the Yukon River and the river boardwalk. Although located downtown, it is slightly outside the main tourist area. As the primary hub of Canada's North, Whitehorse is home to over 60 per cent of Yukon's population. The city has a prominent public sector, hosts a number of natural resource sectors (e.g., mining, oil, and gas), and is home to a vibrant tourist industry. The Yukon Visitor Information Centre is next door to the Yukon Government administrative building, where one of Challenge's social enterprises – a cafeteria – operates in the basement.

---

1 Since the research for this book was conducted, Challenge Disability Resource Group has changed its name to Opportunities Yukon.

Services and Programming

Challenge offers three main lines of service: residential services, employment support, and social enterprises. The residential services and employment support assist the program participants in their active and independent living. The residential services are provided through two facilities. The first, Takhini Haven, opened in 2012–13 and offers five bedrooms for adults who need long-term care. Programming is also available to help residents who are interested in transitioning into an independent lifestyle. The second is the Transitional Treatment Program, located in downtown Whitehorse, which opened in 2015 and is specifically designed to support residents with mental health challenges. The six-unit, ten-bed facility was retrofitted from a building previously operated by the Yukon Building Corporation (Government of Yukon, 2015). The Transitional Treatment Program supports both long-term and short-term stays and offers programming focused on life skills.

The employment services at Challenge provide support to community members who may find it difficult to find a job because of their disabilities. The funding support for the employment services comes from the Income Support Unit, which is part of the Yukon Department of Health and Social Services. Three core services are available to program participants: job coaching, employer supports, and community-inclusion support. Challenge also delivers the EmployAbility Skills Program, which is a fifteen-week training program for up to twelve participants at a time. The program is run by a five-person staff team, including one coordinator, one team lead, and two job coaches. Participants learn both technical and workplace skills, such as time management, conflict management, learning styles, and WHMIS.[2] The staff also help participants connect with other social and community services, such as mental health or learning support, to ensure participants receive wraparound assistance. The program is connected with Challenge's social enterprises, which offer employment training in woodworking, catering, and landscaping.

---

2 WHMIS stands for Workplace Hazardous Materials Information System. It is one of the legal requirements that employers and workers have to comply with in order to protect those who work in places where hazardous materials are used (Yukon Workers' Compensation Health and Safety Board, n.d.). https://wcb.yk.ca /QuestionResults/OHS/WHMIS/Q0297.aspx.

Social Enterprises

In 1983, Career Industries was formed as a social enterprise within Challenge. Career Industries started out selling core boxes to the mining sector. These wooden boxes are used for protecting and transporting boring or core samples. The samples are tested for mineral before the mining companies make the decision to proceed with the mining operation or determine where to drill. Back in the 1980s, Yukon was experiencing a boom in the mining sector (since then, the sector has experienced several more boom-and-bust cycles). Aware of the woodworking shop at Challenge, some of the mining companies proposed a program to help develop participant skills through the production of core boxes. The executive director at the time, in consultation with the job coach at the woodworking shop, believed this could be made into a viable business. From there, Challenge started its ventures into social enterprises. Its customers now include mining companies in Yukon as well as Alaska.

Interestingly, the success of Career Industries attracted competition. Several years ago, the then executive director went on the radio to tell the story of Career Industries making core boxes for the mining sector. Two persons who heard the story decided to open their own business to make core boxes – thus creating competition for Career Industries. However, despite competition and the fluctuations inherent in the mining sector, Career Industries has outlasted many of its competitors. Jillian Hardie, Challenge's current executive director, credits consistency as Career Industries' key to success: "Our product is consistent. Our suppliers are consistent. And our buyers are consistent." It also helps that Career Industries charges fairly to the mining companies. Hardie also believes that the development of corporate social responsibility policies has created incentives for these mining companies to buy from Career Industries.

At Career Industries, the woodworking process is divided into distinct tasks for each participant/employee. For example, one of the participants is responsible for operating the lathe. According to Hardie, "we call him the King of Pointy Sticks and he just loves it. He just [uses the] lathes all day long." Currently, Career Industries runs two shifts of seventeen participants who make core boxes. The core-box operations recently moved to a new location because the social enterprise was running out of space. Those who build core boxes can work at Career Industries for as long as they want after they have completed the training, provided that Career Industries has work for them to do. New participants coming to work at the core-box plant may receive wage subsidies during the first six months of their employment. After that, they are paid entirely by the core-box plant.

In addition to core boxes, Career Industries also operates Bridges Catering and The Ledge. Both are social enterprises specialized in food-services. Bridges Catering, which employs up to seven individuals, is run at Challenge's head office on Front Street. Staff at its commercial kitchen prepare catering orders for customers around Whitehorse. The number of staff varies, depending on the volume of catering orders. Everyone at Bridges, including the chef, lives with disabilities. Similar to those who make core boxes, participants at Bridges can stay working as long as they want and as long as Bridges has work for them to do. Wage subsidies are not available for those working at Bridges.

The Ledge, first opened in April 2013, is a cafeteria located in the basement of the Yukon Government's administrative building on Second Avenue (Government of Yukon, 2013). The cafeteria is also open to the broader public, although signage to the cafeteria is not conspicuous. The Ledge runs an integrative lunch program for those from the Fetal Alcohol Spectrum Society, offering them an opportunity to enjoy their lunch with the general public. Once those who work at The Ledge have gained some confidence, the staff work to find them outside employment on a case-by-case basis. Since The Ledge is designed to provide training, all those who work there receive wage subsidies.

One of Career Industries' success stories comes from a participant who first started out at The Ledge. Until he arrived at Career Industries, he had never been employed a day in his life. When he began, he could only manage to work four hours a day. Career Industries accommodated him for whatever number of hours he was able and ready to work. After a while, Career Industries asked him if he would be interested in working a half hour more. He accepted the offer and started working four and a half hours each day. With gradual half-hour increments, he eventually reached full-time hours. After two years working at the cafe, he entered the culinary program at Yukon College. He successfully graduated from the culinary program and asked to return to the cafe so that, in Hardie's words, "he could get grounded before he goes out into the regular workforce." He worked out so well that Career Industries ended up hiring him as the team lead and supervisor at The Ledge. In the summer of 2018, when the head chef had to take a two-month leave, this former participant looked after the kitchen as well as the front of the house for the cafe.

Until March 2019, Career Industries also operated Twisted Wood Works and Twisted Wood Works Retail. Twisted Wood Works – the custom woodworking shop for individual retail customers – as well as the retail store were shut down because they were unable to generate positive cash flow. This shutdown reduced the number of social enterprises from five to the current three. During its eight years of operation, Twisted Wood Works never managed a surplus. When it was becoming increasingly difficult to secure the government wage subsidies for those working at Twisted Wood because the employees could not stay working there on a permanent basis, Twisted Wood tried to shift its model from training to production. However, it still could not turn its finances around to generate a positive cash flow. Ultimately, the decision leading to the shutdown was financially based.

In addition to the core boxes and foodservices, Career Industries also offers business services including mail assembly and giveaway package assembly for public campaigns such as promotion for smoking cessation and sexual health.

In 2018, more than seventy-five participants at Challenge worked for the social enterprises, which delivered goods and services to over 140 customers, earning over $320,000. As the parent organization for the social enterprises, Challenge provides personnel, in-kind, space, and financial supports. None of the social enterprises is incorporated and they all operate as programs within Challenge.

Marketing

Much of the marketing for Challenge is through word of mouth, including referrals from customers. Many of the business opportunities come to Challenge directly. The organization also has a considerable advertising plan using social media, the local Whitehorse directory, and the Yellow Pages. The marketing efforts are important to Challenge because of the organization's reliance on commercial revenue and the fact that it does not receive any government grants for its operations, as Hardie points out:

> All invoices, advertising and menus have the mission statement on it. Facebook page is attached to Challenge Disability Resource Group page. Marketing to the US is primarily on the social responsibility. Marketing in Canada is not as big on the social aspect. They aren't as interested.

Online marketing includes a website and social media. Although Career Industries does not yet sell online, there are plans for the future. It is estimated that less than 10 per cent of expenses are for marketing. No staff member is dedicated to marketing at this point, which means everyone does some aspect of it. Challenges evaluates its own marketing capability as low. At this point in time, Challenge does not have the capacity to spare a staff person to focus only on marketing. However, Hardie mentions that she would rather have a staff person to help with human resources before even getting into marketing.

Financial Information

In the fiscal year ending 31 March 2018, Challenge recorded over $3.5 million in revenue. The majority (78 per cent) of its revenue is from the Yukon territorial government, approximately $2.8 million. The organization also received over $500,000 from the federal government in 2018. The approximately $300,000 revenue generated from the social enterprises accounts for slightly above 10 per cent of Challenge's total revenue. About three-quarters of the revenue from social enterprises come from the core-box plant and the rest comes from the social enterprises offering foodservices.

Experiences in Procurement and Purchasing

Challenge sells to all three types of organizational purchasers, which are estimated to account for about 75 per cent of its commercial revenue. Examples of its non-profit customers include Yukon College, Fetal Alcohol Spectrum Society Yukon, Blood Ties, and the Yukon Anti-Poverty Coalition. Challenge points out that many of the non-profit purchasers look for donations or free/in-kind goods from Challenge, so while they may be considered as customers, they do not necessarily always actually purchase the items.

Jamie Boyd from Special Olympics Yukon, one of Challenge's non-profit purchasers, agrees that Challenge's social mission is an important factor in the purchasing decision. He points out that even though Whitehorse is not a big city with many options to choose from, "it's nice to give money to another organization that is also in need of money." He also mentions that "supporting another non-profit organization" and "keeping the money in the local area" are important considerations. Special Olympics Yukon works with Bridges Catering about three to four times a year for meetings, training sessions, and sporting events. The catering orders range from $200 to $500 each time. As far as Jamie knows, there are a few social enterprises in Whitehorse; however, Bridges Catering is the only one he knows of that provides foodservices.

Organizational purchasers from private businesses come to Challenge "because they feel good about supporting people with disabilities," according to Hardie. Examples include Behind the Barn, Goldcorp, and other mining companies. Government customers are mainly part of the Yukon Government, and they purchase from Challenge because of the mandate to purchase locally as often as possible. One government catering customer typically works with Challenge about six to eight times a year for catering government training events. Each order would be approximately $1,000. The social value of Challenge was ranked as very important by this interviewee from the Yukon Government. However, Hardie believes that the Yukon Government has not yet clearly understood the concept of social enterprise. She mentions that government officials would regularly confuse social enterprises with sheltered workshops and could not wrap their minds around the market wages that they offer to their participants. Ongoing discussions with government representatives are necessary to bring them onboard with social enterprises.

Challenge believes the employment and training of participants is the most important factor for their government purchasers, followed by the quality of goods and services. The Yukon Government also tries to purchase locally as a matter of policy in support of businesses in Yukon. While this is a plus for Challenge, it also means the Yukon Government has a tendency to spread their orders around to every business in Yukon instead of favouring those with social missions.

For organizational purchases from the private sector, the quality of goods and services is the prime consideration, followed by supporting local community and improving the financial sustainability of Challenge. When the customers are other non-profit organizations, the goal of reducing community vulnerability is a top driver for purchasing from Challenge, with improving the financial sustainability of the organization and the quality of goods and services rounding out the top three reasons. The quality of goods and services is an important factor for all three groups of organizational purchasers although where it ranks varies from group to group.

According to Challenge, the importance of its social mission also varies for the different groups of organizational purchasers, with the government agencies rating it as very important and businesses slightly less so. Other non-profit organizations would be in between these two groups. Challenge points out that the social mission is extremely important for its customers from the US because of the mandates there for social procurement and social purchasing. Jamie Boyd from Special Olympics Yukon echoes Challenge's perceptions. He confirms that the social mission of Bridges Catering is very important. However, he emphasizes that the services from Bridges Catering "are good. We wouldn't use them if the food wasn't good. Just to say that the money goes to a good cause is not good enough. They have to earn it!" Similarly, the customer at the Yukon Government ranks competitive pricing and quality of goods/services ahead of improving financial sustainability for Challenge as the main factors in the purchasing decisions.

Bridges Catering is currently on a one-year contract to cater meetings for the City of Whitehorse. Bridges has had the contract for two years; the contract is open for tender every year. Hardie believes that the flexibility of Bridges to meet the customers' tastes and needs is key to its success. For example, the customers have asked for various options for those following the keto or low-carb diet. The city has been a "big supporter" of Challenge for a long time; however, Hardie is not aware of any formal, written policy for social enterprises. The contracting process for the City of Whitehorse does not include any social mission or value. Hardie emphasizes that the quality of product has to be good and the value for money needs to be there first before the customers would consider any of the benefits from the social mission. Similarly, Jamie Boyd from Special Olympics Yukon says his organization does not have any official policy: "When it works for us, we would do that. We don't have any formal process that would rank different options. If we had more options, we would get good quality with money. Just not that many options."

Summary: Lessons Learned

The success of Challenge is indicative of how integrated the organization is within the community where it works. Even though the cafeteria inside the Yukon Government building may not be a prime location in terms of attracting customers, the fact that Challenge could use the site and the facility to provide real-life work experience for its participants is remarkable. At the very least, the location helps increase Challenge's profile among government employees, some of whom have purchased the catering service from Challenge. Additionally, the way Challenge started making and selling core boxes to the mining industry shows the importance of social enterprises' ability to keep an eye on possible opportunities and to be flexible in adapting to unexpected requests.

The lessons learned from the case of Challenge are as follows:

1. A successful social enterprise, like the core boxes for Challenge,
   may come about through taking a risk and imagining how the skills developed through a program could be extended for commercial or industrial uses.

2. Maintaining a consistent and reliable reputation for the goods and services delivered by the social enterprises is key in keeping the customers over the long term.
3. Although many customers may not have any formal policy for social procurement or social purchasing, their corporate social responsibility policy may encourage buying for social value.
4. Creating a work environment that supports clients in their training as well as employment may mean giving up efficiency and productivity, but it speaks directly to the social benefits that social enterprises bring about.
5. Buying local sometimes works for or against the social enterprises as we see in Challenge's example where the government prefers to spread its buying around to as many local organizations and businesses as possible.

REFERENCES

Government of Yukon. (2013, April 17). Bridges café now open in the main administration building. https://open.yukon.ca/sites/default/files/201304 17BridgesCafeNowOpenInMAB.pdf
Government of Yukon. (2015, December 3). New transitional home now operational. https://open.yukon.ca/sites/default/files/20151203New TransitionalHomeNowOperational.pdf

SOURCES

Interviews with Challenge Disability Resource Group, Special Olympics Yukon, and an anonymous government customer.
Challenge Disability Resource Group (renamed to Opportunities Yukon), https://www.opportunitiesyukon.ca

21 Services and Housing In the Province (SHIP)

ANDREA CHAN AND SHIRLEY HANNIGAN

Introduction

Services and Housing In the Province (SHIP) has championed the fundamental right of housing for nearly three decades. SHIP is a community-based organization that provides housing and supports to those with mental health and substance use issues. As an organization, SHIP promotes the well-being of vulnerable populations and works closely with individuals, empowering them to embrace their full potential. SHIP's approach encourages participation in planning and directing personalized supports to ensure clients receive the best possible care.

Although formally incorporated in 1992, the organization's community development work began in the early 1980s when it established its first supportive housing venture in a townhouse for five residents in Mississauga, Ontario. Over the decades, SHIP grew into an organization serving five thousand residents who range from youth to older adults to families, providing both affordable permanent housing, as well as transitional, recovery, and short-term crisis housing. SHIP owns nine buildings and one ground-lease building. Additionally, SHIP manages head leases for over 1,000 tenants living in ninety-five apartment buildings throughout the Region of Peel, West Toronto, and Dufferin County. This chapter explains why the organization, despite having administrative and procurement experience, is not able to leverage its existing capacity for further entrepreneurial expansion and social-procurement opportunities at this time.

As part of its commitment to facilitate independent, safe, and healthy living in the community, SHIP also provides early intervention in mental illness, counselling, and intensive case-management support, tenant support and eviction prevention, employment integration, life-skills development, and support for individuals living with substance use. Operating from an ethos of collaboration, SHIP works in partnership with hospitals and other community and mental health service providers and engages participants in program development and decision-making as part of its overall person-centred approach.

SHIP reports revenue and expenses totalling just under $50 million for the fiscal year ending 31 March 2022. Of this revenue, 84 per cent came from government funding, and 93 per cent of expenses were incurred through charitable activity, with the remaining 7 per cent for management and administration. In that year, the organization spent $23.4 million on salary for 440 employees, about 83 per cent of whom were full-time staff members. As a service and housing agency, SHIP held $66.9 million in capital assets, expended $8.3 million in occupancy costs, and generated gross income of $6.6 million from rent.

Social Enterprises

SHIP serves as parent organization to three social enterprises under the umbrella of Destination Café: (1) the Social Coffee Bean, a cafe with a storefront in Port Credit, (2) Acorn Café & Catering, and (3) DC Cleaning. Acorn Café & Catering operates within Peel Youth Village, a mixed-use building owned by the Region of Peel and operated by SHIP that hosts a local community centre and a residential program for under-housed youth. DC Cleaning provides cleaning services for commercial and residential buildings, including capital buildings owned and operated by SHIP.

All social enterprises of SHIP offer employment and job training opportunities for their participants (including SHIP's tenants and service-users) as well as others in the community facing challenges to finding and maintaining employment. SHIP's community development manager, Shirley Hannigan, explains that the social enterprises are "community-based business[es] with a social mission to provide all staff [i.e., participants] with a safe, flexible and supportive work environment, competitive compensation, a sense of purpose and the dignity and respect that comes with employment."

Destination Café: The Origin Story

As told by Hannigan:

> The story is ... about fourteen years ago [in the early 2000s], SHIP purchased a couple of buildings down at the lakeshore community of Port

Credit, and in the buildings there were two retail locations … [one of these locations] remained empty [after the purchase] and became a drop-in centre for the individuals we supported in the community. And through the drop-in, there was conversation around, "wouldn't it be cool to make something out of this space that would look like more of an employment initiative?" That was the language back then [as opposed to "social enterprise"] as it was long before people did feasibility studies. It was just – "wouldn't it be great to have a cafe here, so let's do this!" We applied for a grant, involved some community partners, and that's how it started.

Consistent with its person-centred approach, SHIP noticed early on that customer service may not have been the most suitable form of work for participants employed or training at the enterprise. To work in a cafe, there needs to be a certain level of communication skill, an upbeat personality characterized by casual banter that Hannigan describes:

"Good morning, how are you? What can I get you?" … and for some staff that didn't come easily. And that's when we looked at [other job options] … SHIP has a number of capital buildings that we own and require cleaning on a regular basis. And we thought this may be a good opportunity for individuals who aren't comfortable within the cafe model and might appreciate a little bit more independent work.

From there, DC Cleaning was born as a cleaning service for residential and commercial buildings. SHIP continues to leverage its expertise in housing operations with its experience in community-based small business to expand its social-enterprise portfolio. As part of its bid for procurement with the Region of Peel to manage Peel Youth Village, SHIP committed itself to starting social enterprises for youth within Peel Youth Village as part of its contract, proposed on its own initiative. Hannigan explains:

And as part of our proposal [to the request for tender], there was an agreement that we would operate three social enterprises … One was [Acorn] café and catering, the second was cleaning – and that's the cleaning in that building, and the third was security, which we very quickly changed to [residential] painting as security was just a bit more risky.

Structure, Operation, and Sales

Social enterprises at SHIP employ between ten and twenty-four people and provide volunteer training opportunities for four to five people a year. While the social enterprises operate individually and have separate staff, they are jointly managed by Hannigan and her colleagues as part of their broader duties at SHIP.

For fiscal year ending 2017, the social enterprises had a combined revenue in the category of $100,000 to $249,999. Ultimately, one of SHIP's goals for the social enterprises is for them to be financially sustainable through sales income. Hannigan was quick to clarify, however, that while not all the social enterprises are able to break even, as a group of businesses they do. She adds that

> It's not to say that every one of our social enterprises is on the plus side. But overall, and that's how we look at it, overall … So cleaning is an easier one to master because you don't clean unless you have a contract. You get paid if you have a contract. The cafe is very different. You can have sales of ten coffees a day versus one hundred coffees another day. So some days it might cover, some days it might not. But overall, we create enough revenue.

SHIP as a parent organization provides ongoing in-kind support to all of its social enterprises, from space to personnel and administrative support such as payroll and staff recruitment. The social enterprises are not incorporated separately and thus operate under the SHIP umbrella. Hannigan explains there is no program funding specifically to support the social enterprises:

> As we don't receive direct monetary support through our organization's funders, portions of my salary are sourced from other revenue streams to support the vocational and employment program.

Contemplating Customer Intention

By SHIP's estimation, the social mission of its social enterprises has greater sway with organizational (i.e., bulk) purchasers than with individual customers, who may just happen upon one of the storefronts. Hannigan explains:

For those that just want a cup of coffee and choose to come to us because they were walking past us, they don't care. Maybe I shouldn't say that so glibly. Maybe they don't care the moment they walk into the door. They may feel differently when they leave … Not every customer [understands our social mission], but those that do, value it.

Although individual customers make up the majority of those who purchase from SHIP's social enterprises, organizational purchasers account for anywhere between a quarter to a half of sales for all the social enterprises combined. SHIP counts among its organizational purchasers Peel Region; other non-profit organizations such as Georgian College, Indus Community Services, Lakeshore Community Health Centre, and Associated Youth Services of Peel; and private businesses located around Port Credit. Some organizational purchasers have standing contracts with the social enterprises (e.g., to provide daily cleaning service) while others make recurring single purchase orders (e.g., five to ten orders for catering per month).

From the perspective of one of the non-profit organizations that regularly buys from Destination Café, the social mission of the cafe is an important factor in the overall purchasing decision. Aware of how its purchases could bring social benefits, the non-profit organization is willing to pay a premium on the product (i.e., a weekly order of ground coffee that averages around twenty-five dollars): "Although the coffee is more expensive than what we could source through other means [i.e., cans of ground coffee from the grocery store], we purchase to support what (they) do."

This testimony reflects SHIP's own understanding in terms of the importance of its social value to its customers. For organizational purchasers from governments and other businesses, SHIP believes that competitive pricing and reducing community vulnerability are the main influential factors and what makes it unique. Nevertheless, SHIP emphasizes that quality of goods and service is always an important factor in the purchasing decisions of all customers, organizations, or individuals. Despite the regular purchases made by non-profit organizations and governments (and to a lesser degree local businesses), SHIP has not benefitted from any social-procurement opportunities.

Seeking Social Procurement

Although expressly interested in social-procurement opportunities, SHIP has yet to submit any social-procurement bids for its social enterprises and the reason is simple: it has yet to encounter any requests for tender that would be appropriate for its enterprises. "There's just not enough time in the day to do some of the research that may be needed to find some of these opportunities," explains Hannigan. She goes on to give examples of the way municipalities could straightforwardly set up their bids and tendering process for social enterprises. From her perspective, the requests for proposals and tenders could be accessed through an online portal where they would be centralized and searchable, and where potential bidders could register to receive notifications for new tenders that would be of interest to their organization. Against the hurdle of finding the opportunities, Hannigan believes that networking with organizations such as the Toronto Enterprise Fund (TEF, a United Way program that supports employment-focused social enterprises in Peel Region, Toronto, and York Region) can help increase awareness of social-procurement opportunities. TEF-supported networking has also been a strategy of LOFT Kitchen, the social enterprise featured in the following chapter.

Unlike many social enterprises that may hesitate to bid on tenders because of inexperience or lack of capacity, SHIP as an agency is in a unique position in that it sees itself as having tremendous strength in proposal development and tendering. "As an organization, we are RFP [request for proposal] heavy," Hannigan maintains. It is the demonstration of social value required in a social procurement bid that raises uncertainty, as she clarifies:

> I think one of the challenges we've talked about over the years is measuring success of a social enterprise. I find that even within the other work that we do, in community development, it's sometimes difficult to measure things that are more anecdotal than when they are numbers-based. We can look at sales, but that doesn't necessarily reflect the success of an individual person. So sometimes that social value ... in the corporate world, in the business world, it's all about profit. Whereas here, it's about people before profit. And I think that makes a world of difference, and it's just a bit harder to track. You can track retention, you can track people requesting time away, you can track absenteeism, the ability to train, learn new things, and some of those other things, but in the end, sometimes it's hard to put a value on, "did this change somebody's life? Is their life a bit better?"

SHIP is confident in its ability to respond to procurement opportunities and yet admits to facing challenges in its ability to demonstrate social value, which stands in contrast to the results of our survey from chapter 3. The survey found on average social enterprises rate their ability to demonstrate social value on a procurement bid higher than their overall capacity to prepare bids at all. The challenge of communicating social impact is common among social enterprises, but it may be particularly salient to organizations interested in becoming involved in social procurement.

Mission and Marketing

Like the large majority of organizations that participated in our national survey, the social enterprises at SHIP dedicate less than 10 per cent of their resources to marketing. Until now, many organizational purchasers come to know SHIP's social enterprises primarily through SHIP itself, events organized by local business-improvement areas or word of mouth. Currently, the social enterprises have a limited online presence. The website of Destination Café remains under construction, previously having been without a website for some time. At the time of writing this case, SHIP is developing its first marketing strategy, which includes examining ways to increase customer engagement via social media. It also has plans to venture into e-commerce.

The marketing challenges faced by SHIP are not uncommon among smaller social enterprises. Although there is a general increase in understanding social enterprise as a concept, knowledge of specific social enterprises operating in the community may still elude the typical consumer, which is exacerbated by the limited marketing coming from the social enterprises themselves. An example would be the organizational purchaser for Destination Café from the non-profit sector mentioned earlier. While this organizational purchaser supports the café through regular social purchases, this customer has never purchased from and is not familiar with any other social enterprises. Admittedly, this customer rates itself as having low awareness of other social enterprises in the community, and accordingly, does not currently have an in-house social-purchasing policy.

Of its existing marketing, SHIP's social mission has always been front and centre. The brochure for Destination Café states: "Our goal is to build a sustainable business while providing employment opportunities for individuals living with the challenges of mental health." Identifying people as consumers/survivors of the mental health system as part of a social enterprise's identity has inherent challenges. But as Hannigan explains,

We always look for buy-in from the people that we support through employment because they're the face of the cafe, so we need to ensure that they're okay with the messaging. And that's been key, and they really are okay with the messaging.

Centralizing the mission in the marketing not only helps attract customers who wish to support the community, it can also offer workers a platform to speak about meaningful employment. Hannigan points out that "when sharing or promoting our business, [the social enterprises'] staff speak freely around their employment supports, their experience and what it has meant to their recovery." Although the message of its social mission has always been strong in the branding of SHIP's social enterprises, SHIP plans on making it stronger still in any future marketing.

Challenges to Growth

The social enterprises at SHIP express their interest in expanding their operations, and similar to other employment-focused social enterprises, such plans for growth require a delicate balance between financial and social objectives. For example, the well-being and safety of its participants makes it cost-prohibitive to take on cleaning contracts with individual customers in their homes. As Hannigan explains,

Not a week goes by that I don't get that call [about cleaning for individual customers], and it's been on our radar to try and look at how to do that. But there's risk levels in terms of [sending one staff], and it becomes very costly to have two staff. But we get a lot of calls for it.

The limitations to providing cleaning services for residential units mean passing on an additional opportunity to support people with mental health challenges. Hannigan went on: "Within mental health and addiction, those are sometimes the first thing to go, not being able to maintain your home, and that leads to potential issues around your tenancy." Being able to provide cleaning services within homes could be the next form of peer support for those receiving housing support through SHIP.

Additionally, investments that go into streamlining processes or extending the lifecycle of the foodservice business have to be funded primarily through grants. In 2013, the Central West Health Local Integration Network funded the purchase of a coffee roaster that quadrupled the speed with which coffee could be roasted. More recently, Destination Café received modest funding to undertake a makeover of the physical layout of the storefront. For social enterprises such as the ones operated by SHIP, the capital injection needed to increase service capacity or to refresh the brand to maintain and increase its customer base is often hard to come by. On top of which, social enterprises have to contend with the same external threats faced by any other small to medium-sized businesses, such as economic downturn and policy changes. The rise of minimum wage, as Hannigan describes, has impacted the social enterprises' financial situation:

> We create enough revenue, [but] it's gotten trickier, and I'm being very candid, because of the increase in minimum wage. It had a pretty big impact on us as I'm sure it did on many social enterprises or small, medium-size businesses, period.

Despite the above challenges, growth remains a focus for the social enterprises at SHIP. One goal for this year is to increase the number of customers using DC Cleaning from the broader community outside of SHIP.

Locating SHIP among Other Social Enterprises

The story of SHIP and its social enterprises reflects other cases presented in this book. For one, SHIP believes that, irrespective of its social mission, the quality of its goods and services speaks for itself (in line with Horizon Achievement Centre, Let's Work Atlantic, and Ever Green). For another, its social commitment, in this case to ensure a safe work environment for its participants, overrides its impulse to capitalize on market opportunities (i.e., expanding service to include in-home cleaning, which is similar to the discussion on Harbourview Training Centre).

The marketing approaches and constraints of SHIP's social enterprises are also common, not only among the cases featured here but more broadly across the sector; they are consistent with the chapter 3 survey findings and current research literature. Word of mouth as the primary promotional tool among social enterprises has been documented, in part because of their budget constraints, but also because it can lead to enduring relationships and legitimacy that can be fostered with key stakeholders. Furthermore, the penny-wise spirit of word-of-mouth marketing aligns with the normative notion of "social mission first." (Mitchell et al., 2015). SHIP's interest in increasing the social enterprises' presence on social media and participating in sector-relevant networking (e.g., with the Toronto Enterprise Fund) is consistent with the call for social enterprises to embrace a marketing model that is more relationship-oriented rather than product-oriented. The more relational (as opposed to transactional) approach is perceived to be more appropriate, especially for social enterprises engaged in public service delivery like SHIP's (Powell & Osborne, 2014).

Conclusion

When balancing multiple bottom lines, the question of how social value is defined and measured (and by whom) as part of the procurement process remains under consideration (Barraket et al., 2015). The challenge that social enterprises face in defining and demonstrating social value has been raised since early research on social procurement (Muñoz, 2009). Although SHIP stands as a unique social enterprise with confidence and capacity in procurement, it shares many similarities with others that hope to fulfil their mission while balancing both economic and social value.

Lessons Learned

1. Different social enterprises grow at different paces, and their development trajectory is specific to their organizational context. Revenue growth is desirable in so far as it contributes to meaningful improvements in the well-being of people supported through employment. An organization may have to forego market opportunities if there is a risk such opportunities may end up impeding the enterprise's primary social goals.
2. Being part of any local social-enterprise network can be an efficient way to share information on social-procurement opportunities, learn from the experiences of others, and contribute to a peer-support system of practitioners.
3. The formal process of evaluating an organization's social value is costly and time-consuming. Although it may already account for the more readily measurable social outcomes (e.g., number of people employed, changes in absenteeism), more substantive measures on improvements in social and economic well-being are challenging to collect and maintain. Since social procurement requires competing firms to demonstrate their social value, social enterprises need to weigh whether the investment into a formal evaluation process will be worth the potential return on investment.

REFERENCES

Barraket, J., Keast., R., & Furneaux, C. (2015). *Social procurement and new public governance.* Routledge.

Mitchell, A., Madill, J., & Chreim, S. (2015). Marketing and social enterprises: Implications for social marketing. *Journal of Social Marketing, 5*(4), 285–306. https://doi.org/10.1108/JSOCM-09-2014-0068

Muñoz, S. (2009). Social enterprise and public sector voices on procurement. *Social Enterprise Journal, 5*(1), 69–82. https://doi.org/10.1108/17508610910956417

Powell, M., & Osborne, S.P. (2014). Can marketing contribute to sustainable social enterprise? *Social Marketing Journal, 11*(1), 24–46. https://doi.org/10.1108/SEJ-01-2014-0009

OTHER SOURCES

Interviews with Services and Housing In the Province (SHIP).

Services and Housing In the Province (SHIP). https://www.shipshey.ca/

22 LOFT Kitchen

JENNIFER SUMNER

Introduction

LOFT Kitchen is a work integration social enterprise located in Toronto that focuses on serving marginalized youth. As part of the Christie Ossington Neighbourhood Centre (CONC), it balances multiple bottom lines by offering both cafe and catering services to customers in the surrounding area, while also developing the employability of local youth facing barriers. Through LOFT Kitchen, these young people access hands-on training in the food and hospitality industries, along with leadership, mentorship, and networking opportunities, social supports and work-readiness programming. LOFT Kitchen engages in social purchasing but has not been successful in bidding for procurement contracts although it clearly values their importance.

LOFT Kitchen's strength is its strong support of marginalized youth – young people aged sixteen to twenty-nine who are experiencing poverty, precarious housing, mental health challenges, and parenthood. In 2017, 515 youth participated in LOFT Kitchen's training and volunteer programs, and the social enterprise served 90,045 meals and 30,495 snacks. This translates to roughly 300 meals per day to its various programs at CONC, while also catering to external customers, thus creating significant opportunities for employment and job training. Although LOFT Kitchen does market its services, it uses marketing materials that do not mention that participants are in a program. The participants are simply seen as part of the staff teams in order to avoid further marginalization. Instead, LOFT Kitchen emphasizes quality of goods and services, employment/job training, and support of the local community. In preparation of this case, we interviewed Sawyer Pow, LOFT Kitchen's youth and social-enterprise manager. Pow is also responsible for drop-in programs, the culinary program, and other training and programs.

Background

LOFT Kitchen is operated by the Christie Ossington Neighbourhood Centre, which provides free programs, services, and supports for vulnerable community members including children, youth, and adults living in poverty. CONC specifically caters to newcomers, single parents, and individuals living with mental or physical health issues, food and income insecurity, homelessness, or other barriers that prevent them from living healthy lives and participating fully in the community. Founded in 1993 and incorporated as a non-profit organization in 1997, CONC became a United Way member agency in 2001 and a registered charity in 2002. Crucially, its volunteer board of directors is largely made up of local residents who reflect the diversity of the area.

In 2014, CONC developed LOFT Kitchen as its only social enterprise. LOFT originally stood for Learning Opportunities in Food and Technology, but the name is now simply LOFT Kitchen. The three LOFT Kitchen paid staff – Pow, the social-enterprise chef, and the production lead – are CONC's employees. In the beginning, LOFT Kitchen ran a pilot cafe and catered internally to CONC's shelter programs. Over time, the cafe grew into a catering business that supports trainees. Although LOFT Kitchen is sustained through grant funding and earned revenue, CONC supports LOFT Kitchen with staff, space, and administration.

LOFT Kitchen first opened its doors at Bloor and Ossington but moved in early 2019 to the Junction Triangle neighbourhood where the new George Chuvalo Community Centre is located (which is owned by the City of Toronto and operated by CONC). Although this move interrupted some of LOFT Kitchen's services and involved a great many changes in terms of personnel and structures, the staff were excited about the possibilities it brought.

Social Mission

As a social enterprise developed by CONC, LOFT Kitchen operates within the mission of its parent organization, which can be found on its website:

> The Christie Ossington Neighbourhood Centre is dedicated to building upon the strengths and vision of community members to improve the quality of life in the Christie Ossington community and surrounding neighbourhoods. By working in collaboration with residents, community institutions, agencies, local businesses, and stakeholders, we will create a safe and healthy community.

CONC's mission guides the organization's approach to the development and delivery of its programs and services, which are grounded in anti-oppression, poverty reduction, a strengths-based strategy, and an evidence-based practice. This approach works on both the macro level of addressing systemic barriers that communities face and the micro level of meeting the particular needs and priorities of individuals.

Culinary Programs

LOFT Kitchen offers hands-on training in its culinary programs for various participant groups (including LGBTQ2SI+ youth, newcomers, etc.). The training includes menu development, menu planning, administration, recipe development and promotion, and front-of-house experience. LOFT Kitchen has a full-time catering chef and a part-time production lead, both of whom have industry skills and experience. The training includes hands-on workshops and one-on-one support on a daily basis. The chef oversees the participants coming into the program, some of whom are interested in working in the kitchen to pursue employment as a chef or cook while others want to focus on their barista skills to prepare them for front-of-house positions.

LOFT Kitchen's culinary programs engage a range of participants, most of whom are young, but not all. For example, LOFT Kitchen received a one-year grant in 2018 to support newcomers and offered four fourteen-week sessions to twelve newcomers in each session. Within the fourteen-week training, participants spent nine weeks in the classroom learning such things as food handling, first aid, and health and safety in the kitchen. Additionally, they gained practical experience through hands-on workshops in the shelter kitchens two days a week. Participants then had a four-week placement coordinated by LOFT Kitchen matching participant interests with industry partners. At the end of the session, many were hired to work at their placement sites; LOFT Kitchen facilitated volunteering and placement opportunities for those who did not have work permits.

As an organization focused on employability, LOFT Kitchen also partners with employment agencies that offer placements. In this capacity, for example, LOFT Kitchen works with United Way of Greater Toronto and York Region and offers culinary training and work placement for six to eight young participants per session. Many of these participants come from other social- and community-service agencies such as St. Stephen's Community House and Eva's Phoenix. The participants at LOFT Kitchen receive a certificate in culinary training upon completion. There are usually eight participants per session taking training in two segments. The first segment is a structured program at LOFT Kitchen, similar to the newcomer program, for eight or more participants. The structured program runs for fourteen weeks, including eight weeks in the classroom and four weeks in the work placement. The second segment provides participants with further work placement opportunities that range anywhere from eight to twenty weeks. Through work placement, the participants have the opportunity to gain supported hands-on work experience alongside trained and experienced staff.

LOFT Kitchen also has a program that places participants with industry partners, including restaurants and hotels. LOFT Kitchen identifies placements for the interested participants, while also offering ongoing support.

Experience with Procurement and Purchasing

LOFT Kitchen has submitted bids on a small number of procurement contracts tendered by governments and businesses, although it has not been successful. This is in keeping with the survey findings from chapter 3 regarding one of the factors associated with whether a social enterprise would bid on a procurement opportunity: the higher a social enterprise rates its bidding capacity, the more likely it is to submit bids. In the case of LOFT Kitchen, it rates its bidding capacity as very high. However, LOFT Kitchen does not align with the other factor: the higher a social enterprise's income, the more likely it is to submit bids. The income of LOFT Kitchen is on the low side compared to others who participated in the survey in this study, at only $30,000 per year.

Since moving to the George Chuvalo Community Centre, LOFT Kitchen has not submitted any bids. As Pow says, "we need to understand our capacity in the new location. It's something we'll be discussing in the future for sure." When reflecting on what LOFT Kitchen would need to consider before mounting a successful bid, Pow feels that physical space and up-front staffing costs would be the main limitations. In particular, LOFT Kitchen would have to discuss with the rest of CONC whether the social enterprise would need to rent alternative kitchen space because even the newly renovated commercial kitchen at the George Chuvalo Community Centre will not be large enough. At this point in time, LOFT Kitchen does not have the resources or the staffing for large, ongoing catering contracts serving over one hundred people.

That said, there are benefits to be gained by LOFT Kitchen bidding on contracts. As Pow emphasizes, "the stability of contracts is always beneficial." When the social enterprise is training youth, it is helpful to have the stability of steady money coming in. He explains that the norm of one-off catering jobs can be hard for training youth. The stability of a contract, he believes, would allow LOFT Kitchen to put in a routine and a schedule when the social enterprise was training youth.

In contrast to its lack of success in social procurement, LOFT Kitchen engages in social purchasing whenever it can. Now that it is in a new location, staff are actively considering their own social purchasing whenever possible (e.g., when buying coffee). One way to enhance its social purchasing involves being part of a network of social enterprises called the Food Cluster Meetup supported by the Toronto Enterprise Fund (TEF).[1] The network is made up of different social enterprises that meet every other month. Some of the social enterprises in the network are well established while others are new or in the process of renewal, like LOFT Kitchen. Industry professionals also attend as mentors. Each meeting features different social enterprises, different topics, and different challenges. While discussions at the meetings are typically focused on what the attendees can offer each other, they also purchase from each other. By joining the network, the social enterprises can build on their strengths and share knowledge and resources, something that Pow finds to be particularly helpful. As he remarks, "It's not competitive – we support each other. We're all in it together." He senses no tension among the attendees regarding competition because the social enterprises are at different stages of development, are located in different neighbourhoods, and offer different products. For Pow, going to a TEF meeting is "mostly just a really great learning opportunity."

The customers for LOFT Kitchen's catering business include non-profit organizations, private corporations, and individuals. Pow surmises that the non-profit organizations purchase from LOFT Kitchen because they understand what goes on in a social enterprise. In other words, social value is one of the main reasons for them to order from a caterer like LOFT Kitchen.

LOFT Kitchen also works with universities. More specifically, different groups within universities come to LOFT Kitchen looking specifically for a social-enterprise caterer. As Pow observes, "I think the fact that we work with youth is a factor they consider when they purchase from us." Similarly, Pow thinks that private businesses that order corporate lunches are looking for a caterer with a social purpose and

---

1 TEF is a funding partnership of United Way of Greater Toronto and York Region, the City of Toronto, Ontario Ministry of Community and Social Services, and the Government of Canada that supports the implementation of social enterprises providing transitional or permanent employment (or training leading to employment) for people who are marginalized (McMurtry et al., 2015).

giving special consideration about where their money is going when they choose LOFT Kitchen.

Overall, Pow believes that LOFT Kitchen has earned a significant portion of its catering business through word of mouth, especially within the non-profit sector. He points out that customers may be drawn by the social value but return for the quality of service, the food as well as the reasonable pricing. In addition, LOFT Kitchen is very accommodating in terms of what customers need within its set menu while also creating custom menus.

Summary and Lessons Learned

Although LOFT Kitchen is in transition, it is finding synergy between its financial and social goals. Pow is very excited about the future, particularly about what the new location will do for this social enterprise. It will continue the catering business and the cafe, while expanding the youth programs, in a new community that is excited by its arrival. Overall, Pow believes interest in social enterprises is spreading and becoming popular, which will benefit the youth who are served by LOFT Kitchen.

1. Understand your capacity before you submit any bids. This is particularly true if any major changes occur at the organization.
2. Your physical space and staffing costs are the main considerations when making a bid.
3. The stability of contracts is always beneficial. It can enable a routine and schedule when training people.
4. If relocating a social enterprise, find out what the new local community needs.
5. If possible, join a network. This can build on mutual strengths and encourage knowledge and resource sharing.
6. Non-profits make good customers because they know what goes on within a social enterprise. Word of mouth among non-profits also helps to increase sales.

REFERENCE

McMurtry, J.J., Brouard, F., Elson, P.R., Hall, P., Lionais, D., & Vieta, M. (2015). Social enterprise in Canada: Context, models and institutions (ICSEM Working Paper #4). International Comparative Social Enterprise Models. https://sprott.carleton.ca/scse/wp-content/uploads/Canada-national -McMurtry-et-al.pdf

OTHER SOURCES

Interviews with LOFT Kitchen.
LOFT Kitchen, www.conccommunity.org/loft-kitchen

Conclusion: Selling Social: Future Directions

LAURIE MOOK

Introduction

Selling Social offers a glimpse into the world of social enterprises across Canada. Social enterprises are market-based organizations that operate to make both a social impact and a profit. Work integration social enterprises (WISEs) have an extra dimension: they provide training and employment to support individuals in marginalized social groups in gaining meaningful and productive employment that enhances both their income and their sense of self-worth. This adds another layer of complexity to the management and leadership of such organizations, from funding and managing human resources to marketing, purchasing, and procurement.

Governments, businesses, and non-profit organizations are increasingly incorporating a social dimension into their procurement and purchasing policies with the intent of making positive contributions to their social agendas. As David LePage of Buy Social Canada says, "every purchase has an economic, environmental and social impact, whether intended or not. Social procurement is about capturing those impacts and seeking to make intentional positive contributions to both the local economy and the overall vibrancy of the community" (Buy Social Canada, 2018, p. 7).

Procurement and purchasing involve different procedures. In procurement, the organizational purchaser sends out a request for proposals (RFP) or request for tender (RFT), and potential sellers compete to win the contract. In this case, the seller or supplier seeks out the purchaser to make possible sales. In purchasing, on the other hand, the organizational purchaser approaches the seller, and while the purchaser may still require estimates, the onus is on the purchaser

	Social criteria or intent not included	Social criteria or intent included
Purchaser initiates RFP and invites sellers to bid → Social enterprise chooses to bid → Purchaser chooses from those bidding	Regular procurement	Social procurement
Social enterprise creates a market presence → Purchaser seeks out sellers through word-of-mouth or by consulting advertisements, websites, etc. → Purchaser makes purchasing decision and may choose WISE	Regular purchasing	Social purchasing

Figure 23.1. Differentiating (Social) Procurement and (Social) Purchasing

to seek out the seller. Typically, regular procurement bids are for formal contracts of higher value and extensive scope of work which are awarded based on price and quality, and social procurement adds some social criteria or intent to be fulfilled as per social policy aspirations. Like procurement, regular purchasing is also mediated by price and quality though of lower value and smaller scope of work, and social purchasing includes and may even give social criteria or intent a higher weight in the decision to buy. Figure 23.1 summarizes the differentiation between regular and social procurement and purchasing.

Social procurement as a way for organizational purchasers to address social concerns through WISEs is an idea that, in theory, seems reasonable. However, in practice, many social enterprises do not have the capacity to bid for such contracts and deliver the required volume of business. Two factors emerge from our survey results as significant predictors of whether or not a social enterprise would submit bids to government and non-profit organizational purchasers: total revenue and self-evaluated capacity in preparing proposals, both with a positive correlation (chapter 3). In other words, the higher the total revenue for an organization and the higher its self-assessed capacity in preparing bids, the more likely it is to bid. However, only 23 per cent of social enterprises have submitted bids to organizational purchasers whose tender documents included social criteria.

This concluding chapter provides a summary of our findings from the nineteen cases in this book and looks to the future. We start by exploring the question from the perspective of the social enterprises – why are social enterprises not more actively pursuing procurement and social-procurement opportunities? Next, we take on the perspective of the organizational purchasers by delving deeper into the decision-making criteria by individual and organizational purchasers outside any formal procurement framework to conceptualize purchaser profiles for social enterprises. These purchaser profiles offer snapshots for social enterprises to recognize the specific factors underlying purchasing decisions, thereby providing insights into how social enterprises may cater their marketing efforts. The chapter concludes with a discussion on implications of these purchaser profiles for researchers, practitioners, and policy developers, as well as a reflection on future directions in these changing times.

What Facilitates Procurement and Why Aren't More Social Enterprises Bidding?

Eight of the nineteen cases in this book indicate that they have submitted bids on procurement contracts. While these cases represent only their own experiences and cannot be generalized, we are able to identify several key factors which facilitated their engagement with procurement; the policy context of the province where they are situated, the capacity of the organization, and relationship building are all important.

> In Saskatchewan, SaskPower established its Aboriginal Procurement Policy in 2012, and more recently in late 2018, the city of Saskatoon updated its purchasing policy to include social and environmental sustainability as criteria for evaluating bids that would provide "best value" (City of Saskatoon, 2018). (chapter 5)

However, social-procurement policies are not in themselves sufficient to facilitate participation by social enterprises. The capacity of organizations to prepare and submit bids and to fulfil the potential order at competitive pricing and high quality is also necessary, as we see in the example of Let's Work Atlantic (chapter 13):

> Smith also offers a unique perspective on government bidding because she has the experience of reviewing and evaluating bids. On the commitments of governments to buy from social enterprises, she says, "Verbally they do [support it]. But I've been behind the scene reviewing the tenders.

It's only my experience, but 95 to 98 per cent is about the dollars. If it's down to two very similar prices, the social value might tip the balance." In and of itself, the social value from bids does not appear to be a key or even necessary factor in winning procurement contracts.

Finally, relationship building is a key factor in the success of finding and being successful in procurement bids, as we see in the cases featured in part 2 and also in Groupe PART (chapter 18) in the quote below:

> In order to tap into procurement opportunities, the first thing Thomas did was to join the Conseil d'économie sociale de l'île de Montréal (CÉSIM) – a multi-stakeholder round table – to support Groupe PART in developing connections with public institutions and private corporations in order to grow its business.

For those organizations with no experience submitting bids, the reasons for not bidding fell into four categories: lack of production capacity, lack of capacity to prepare proposals, the complexity of the bidding process, and the challenge of demonstrating social value.

Some social enterprises such as Horizon Achievement Centre (chapter 15) overcame the lack of production capacity by partnering with other organizations:

> Horizon partnered with a printing company in the private sector to submit and win a bid to work with the province on designing, printing, and delivering five hundred thousand tourism booklets in 2013. This partnership allowed Horizon to leverage its existing relationship with Canada Post to handle the mailing and delivery portion of the project while the private-sector partner handled the graphic design and high-gloss offset printing. In coming together as a team, Horizon and its partner managed to offer a competitive price and a high-quality product for the province.

In contrast, many smaller social enterprises such as Wachiay Studio (chapter 10) note they do not have the production capacity to satisfy the requirements of procurement opportunities, nor do they have the possibility of expansion:

> Despite a keen interest in the new business opportunities procurement may afford, Wachiay Studio has not yet participated in formal procurement of any kind. MacDougall talks about two of the barriers that make him hesitant in seeking procurement opportunities: lack of human resources and production capacity … There appears to be an inflection point where

a social enterprise reaches a stage of success in the context of its local community but needs significant changes to scale up and participate in the broader economy. (Corner & Kearins, 2018; Lyon & Fernandez, 2012)

While remarking on the complexity of the process, smaller social enterprises also lacked the capacity and time to look for bids and prepare proposals. In the words of Let's Work Atlantic (chapter 13),

> bidding is so much work. It's a lot of work, and you really have to understand how to manoeuvre the terminology ... If you miss one little thing, you get disqualified. It's almost like you need a degree to get this together. I went to one information session [put together by a government agency], but the information session didn't address the difficulty in putting bids together.

Another critical issue hindering social enterprises in participating in social procurement is how to demonstrate their social value, as SHIP (chapter 21) points out:

> I think one of the challenges we've talked about over the years is measuring success of a social enterprise. I find that even within the other work that we do, in community development, it's sometimes difficult to measure things that are more anecdotal than when they are numbers-based. We can look at sales, but that doesn't necessarily reflect the success of an individual person. So sometimes that social value ... in the corporate world, in the business world, it's all about profit. Whereas here, it's about people and profit. And I think that makes a world of difference and it's just a bit harder to track. You can track retention, you can track people requesting time away, you can track absenteeism, the ability to train, learn new things, and some of those other things, but in the end, sometimes it's hard to put a value on, "did this change somebody's life? Is their life a bit better?"

From the survey data and the cases featured in this book, we can see that while social enterprises are able to sell to organizational purchasers on a one-off basis through social purchasing, organizational purchasers are not yet creating social-procurement opportunities on a broad basis (despite considerable discussion around policies). Where we can observe social enterprises being able to pursue social-procurement opportunities, these opportunities have not been created through the traditional competitive tender process. Instead, these high-value, formal contracting opportunities have come through because of the specific organizational purchasers' active pursuit of and long-term commitment to including social value in their purchasing decisions as in the cases of BUILD (chapter 4) and SARCAN (chapter 5). Once the social enterprises can work with champions within the organizational purchasers, the relationships thrive. These champions are able to push for changes not only on an individual level among their colleagues but also at an organizational level, changing how procurement and purchasing decisions are made. The cases in this book show that relationship building between social enterprises and organizational purchasers is primarily how social procurement takes place at this point in time.

From the perspective of social enterprises as sellers of goods and services, organizational purchasers and policy developers need to appreciate the challenges facing social enterprises that run employment and training programs for marginalized groups. The additional cost necessary to create social value through their goods and services means that these enterprises may not be able to compete with private businesses that can offer lower prices. In short, these social enterprises have to contend with the challenges in seeking out and responding to procurement opportunities while balancing the level of effort and resources required to run programs for participants.

The cases in this book show that both the social enterprises as sellers and the organizational purchasers need to come together to make social procurement and social purchasing work. Social value (as well as environmental and other non-economic benefits) needs to be embedded in purchasing decisions in terms of both positive and negative impacts. As long as social and environmental benefits remain secondary to economic considerations, the supply chain is unlikely to see the inclusion of social value on a broad basis. This means that social enterprises will remain unable to tout the social benefits they can add to their goods and services and truly use their social value as a competitive advantage. For these changes to take place, we are likely to need broader shifts in societal attitudes beyond individual and organizational choices. In the interim, social enterprises could focus their marketing and selling efforts more specifically depending on the specific profiles of organizational purchasers.

Profiles of Organizational Purchasers

Purchaser profiles help social enterprises understand the decision-making criteria of individuals and organizational purchasers, pursue future customers, and plan strategically. The decision-making criteria of different types of purchasers can inform marketing strategies too.

Defining different clusters of purchasers helps focus resources and attention on those segments that most contribute to the mission and sustainability goals of the social enterprise. As social enterprises focus on specific purchaser groups, intermediaries such as Buy Social Canada could facilitate relationship building with potential customers. The role of these intermediaries in anticipating future needs of purchasers could also be an impetus for funding and starting new social enterprises.

The purchaser profiles are broken down into different clusters representing individuals and organizational types: non-profit organizations, businesses, and governments. Each of these clusters are analyzed according to primary purchasing criteria, such as price, quality, convenience, customer service, and social mission. As a result, ten categories of purchasers were identified.

Individual Purchasers

1. The category of individuals as regular purchasers includes those who generally do not know that the organization they are purchasing from has a social mission, or the mission is a secondary feature. They are buying based primarily on price and quality. This might be because the social enterprise does not promote the social aspect of the business to protect the privacy of its employees, or because the individual customer finds the establishment by living in the local area or happening to pass by. In the latter case, the social enterprise may choose to showcase its social impact once the purchaser is in the door, as the Calgary Progressive Lifestyles Foundation does (CPLF; chapter 16):

> In the first place, we need to showcase our great food, we need to win their business with great food. Once we get them in the door, then that's an opportunity to showcase a little bit of our enriching story, and that's how we win our business. We don't lead off with "we're here to support the community." The public just wants a good burger, and enough said. So we sell that burger the way they want it to be sold and then we feed them with further enriching stories.

2. Socially minded individual purchasers are aware of the social missions of these WISEs, and this is a key reason they choose to purchase from them. For instance, Let's Work Atlantic (chapter 13) notes that "we have customers that buy because they want to do something good for their community. The younger people really want to do something great." However, while the social mission might get them in the door, the quality and price have to be good enough to bring them back. EthniCity Catering (chapter 14) points out that customers are "looking for deals.

And if the food didn't turn out, they're gonna complain the same way they would for a private enterprise. I feel like the expectations remain the same."

Non-profit Organizational Purchasers

3. For some of the non-profit organizations that purchase from social enterprises, price and quality are the critical factors in their purchasing decisions. The social mission is a bonus and sometimes gives the social enterprise a competitive edge, as in the case of Wachiay Studio and CPLF:

> While the social mission of Wachiay is not a primary purchasing factor for Bruce, it is certainly an added benefit. He is primarily drawn to the quality of the product, its competitive price point, and the benefit of supporting a local business. (chapter 10)

> CPLF cold-calls potential customers to gain contracts. Neal feels that the mention of CPLF's social mission has made these cold calls easier to convert to sales. Neal's assessment is that CPLF initially wins sales on price and good food; secondarily it is the good feeling that customers experience – this is what brings repeat business. (chapter 16)

4. Most non-profit purchasers, however, are very much influenced by the social mission and want to support like-minded organizations. They may even pay a premium if that is within their reach.

> The committee [of the Eucharist Church] decided it would be important to hire someone who could benefit from the employment beyond the paycheque: "The main reason to work with a social enterprise is because we believe in their mission serving folks with mental health concerns." (Rainbow's End, chapter 12)

> Working with a fixed budget for meals, Johnson says "pricing is always a concern for us, but it's always a balancing act too." In choosing Stone Hearth, Johnson is "willing to pay a bit more for that premium product because we know the residents are going to be happier with it than they would with something else … we believe in what they are doing. And we really enjoy using them." (chapter 17)

> Overall, Pow believes that LOFT Kitchen has earned a significant portion of its catering business through word of mouth, especially within the non-profit sector. He points out that customers may be drawn by the social value but return for the quality of service, the food as well as the reasonable pricing. (chapter 22)

Business Organizational Purchasers

5. Businesses as a regular purchaser are looking primarily for price and quality. Same as the regular non-profit purchasers, the social mission is a secondary benefit and could provide a competitive edge, as Wachiay Studio (chapter 10) points out:

> Most of our [business-to-business] customers use us because we are good at what we do, we are friendly to work with, and we use environmentally friendly materials. The fact we are a social enterprise is secondary to the quality of the product and service delivered.

6. A second type of business purchasers are those businesses that have ethical or social sourcing/purchasing policies in place and seek out social enterprises as their suppliers. These business purchasers may even pay a premium as they realize the value of social impact. One engineering consulting firm that buys from Horizon (chapter 15) mentions that

> If a social enterprise is slightly higher than another "big" business, we'd still choose the social enterprise as it's a worthier purchase, in our opinion … While we applaud the mission, the service, quality, and efficiency keep us coming back.

A small, ethically minded cafe guided by an informal ethical purchasing policy to make purchases that are affordable, ethical, local, and nutritious buys from Stone Hearth (chapter 17) because, as a former manager noted, it "met all our requirements."

7. The third type of business purchaser purchases wholesale from social enterprises. As a result, these social enterprises may not actively promote the social side of the business. As Stone Hearth Bakery suggests when talking about larger organizational purchasers, "sometimes you shouldn't promote the program because people will think there is something wrong with the products, that a professional didn't make it."

8. The social enterprises that contribute to larger projects such as construction often sell their services as subcontractors to the construction companies leading the projects – the fourth type of business customer. These social enterprises note that they do not necessarily have the production capacity to produce the quantities needed to submit for procurement or social procurement. However, they would participate indirectly in social procurement as larger companies seek them out to fulfil social criteria. For example, EMBERS Staffing Solutions (chapter 7)

was contracted by one of the large construction and building services companies in Vancouver to meet the city's Community Benefit Agreement (CBA) commitments.

Government Organizational Purchasers

9. The regular government purchasers represent traditional purchasing from a government agency that emphasizes value for money. For instance, the executive director of the Challenge Disability Resource Group (chapter 20) notes that the City of Whitehorse's purchase decisions are based on value for money before any considerations for social mission.

10. As noted in chapter 2, when governments at all levels recognize the possibility of using their purchasing power to contribute to achieving their social agendas, the government organizational purchasers add social value to their purchases. For example, at the territorial level, the Yukon government has a mandate to purchase locally and is a customer of the Challenge Disability Resource Group (chapter 20). Another government agency buys lunches and snacks from the Horizon Achievement Centre (chapter 15).

Implications

For many social enterprises in this study, participating in procurement and social-procurement bidding is prohibitive. However, the organizations are still able to compete in the economic and social markets through the purchasing and social purchasing of their individual and organizational purchasers. Understanding the supply and demand sides in terms of procurement and purchasing criteria has implications for several audiences: social enterprises as sellers, researchers, and policy developers.

For Social Enterprises as Sellers

These purchaser profiles highlight that different types of customers have different purchasing goals. There were differences between the following groups:

- Individuals and organizations, which are further divided into non-profit organizations, businesses, and governments
- First-time customers and returning customers
- The economic marketplace and the social marketplace

The categorization of purchasers into mutually exclusive groups is a type of market micro-segmentation that focuses on factors that influence the purchase decision (Hutt & Speh, 2013). Such segmentation recognizes customers' differences, which is the key to successful marketing, as it can lead to the following:

- Closer matching of customers' needs with the company's propositions
- Niche marketing, when appropriate, where the company can meet the needs of customers in that niche segment
- A concentration of resources in the market, focusing them on where competitive advantage is greatest and returns are high (McDonald & Dunbar, 2012)

Determining dominant purchaser profiles also "checks your logic and your basic assumptions about the market" and can also lead to "uncovering hitherto undiscovered customer needs" (McDonald & Dunbar, 2012, p. 40). If a social enterprise can determine what percentage of its sales are made to each segment, this information can help guide capacity building, marketing strategies, and positioning statements to maximize the impact of its efforts.

For Researchers

The nineteen cases in this book offer insights for students and scholars into the complexities of pursuing both social and economic success through the sale of goods and services. The requirement of operating in both economic and social markets leads to the necessity of developing skills beyond those traditionally taught in business schools, where the main focus is on profit-maximizing firms. The cases in this book highlight the importance of skill development in relationship building, marketing, and procurement. Future research may look into the possibility of incorporating social accounting as part of the procurement process and the challenges in the implementation of social-procurement policies.

For Policy Developers

The cases in this book also bring to light many lessons for policy developers. Governments, businesses, and other organizations developing social procurement and social purchasing policies to create social impact should be aware of the possible limitations and barriers facing these organizations. For larger contracts, the facilitation of subcontracts to satisfy social criteria is one strategy that creates opportunities for small to mid-sized social enterprises. The funding of capacity building in subcontracting may be a worthy investment. This includes building capacity in measuring and reporting social impact.

Future Directions

As we finished editing this book, we were in the midst of a global pandemic. COVID-19 has had unprecedented and profound implications on the health and well-being of individuals, the economy, and communities around the world. It remains unclear what the lasting legacy of this pandemic will be. However, we do already know that on the individual level, those most vulnerable (including the employees and training participants of social enterprises) are disproportionately impacted. Similarly, the social enterprises that were previously surviving on precarious funding are faced with an even more uncertainty with respect to their long-term sustainability and recovery.

As governments at all levels look to rebuild their communities after an economic shutdown, we see both value and opportunity in the triple bottom line social enterprises present. Social enterprises create employment and training opportunities for those who have been excluded from the mainstream labour market. While they do not solve issues of systemic oppression, they do support marginalized groups in finding the kind of work that augments both their incomes and senses of self-worth. As society transitions to a deeper realization of equity and justice, social enterprises play an important role in supporting and bringing awareness to these issues. We hope that the cases in this book help enhance understanding of the complexities of operating a business with both social and economic objectives but also provoke critical thinking about the social issues underlying the presence of social enterprises in the first place.

REFERENCES

Buy Social Canada. (2018). *A guide to social procurement*. https://www
    .buysocialcanada.com/wp-content/uploads/BSC_socialprocurement_R5
    _EN_SCREEN.pdf
Corner, P.D., & Kearins, K. (2018). Scaling-up social enterprises: The effects
    of geographic context. *Journal of Management & Organization*, 27(1), 1–19.
    https://doi.org/10.1017/jmo.2018.38

City of Saskatoon. (2018). Purchasing Policy C02-C45. https://www.saskatoon
.ca/sites/default/files/documents/new_purchasing_policy_c02-045.pdf

City of Vancouver. (2020). Community Benefit Agreements. https://
vancouver.ca/people-programs/community-benefit-agreements.aspx

Hutt, M.D., & Speh, T.W. (2013). *Business marketing management: B2B* (11th ed).
South-Western/Cengage Learning.

Lyon, F. & Fernandez, H. (2012). Strategies for scaling up social enterprise:
Lessons from early years providers. *Social Enterprise Journal*, *8*(1), 63–77.
https://doi.org/10.1108/17508611211226593

McDonald, M., & Dunbar, I. (2012). *Market segmentation: How to do it and how to
profit from it* (4th ed). John Wiley & Sons.

Contributors

Andrea Chan is a research associate at the Troost Institute for Leadership Education in Engineering at the University of Toronto. She was a postdoctoral fellow at the Ontario Institute for Studies in Education (also at the University of Toronto) where she completed her PhD in the Adult Education and Community Development Program. Her thesis research explored the relevance of work-centred social support to the employment outcomes and overall well-being of individuals facing significant challenges to finding and maintaining employment.

Marty Donkervoort is a board member of the Social Enterprise Council of Canada. For over thirty years, he has been a leader in community economic development through his participation in the Canadian Worker Co-op Federation and the Worker Owner Development Foundation, among many others.

Gordon M. Djong completed his EdD in Educational Leadership and Policy at the Ontario Institute for Studies in Education, University of Toronto. His research interests include educational policy, safe schools, and comparative education.

Kirsten Godbout is the executive manager of operations at Diversity Foods Services Inc., which operates as a social enterprise providing foodservices within the University of Winnipeg and beyond.

Shirley Hannigan is the community development manager at Services and Housing in the Province (SHIP), headquartered in Mississauga, Ontario. SHIP is a community organization specialized in housing, and it runs social enterprises in support of individuals living with mental health challenges.

Jillian Hardie is the executive director of Opportunities Yukon (formerly known as Challenge Disability Resource Group), an organization providing assistance to those with disabilities in Whitehorse, Yukon.

Yasmin Hariri completed her master's degree in 2020 in the Child Study and Education Program at the Ontario Institute for Studies in Education at the University of Toronto.

Art Ladd was the Executive Director at BUILD from 2016 to 2020. He is currently employed by Efficiency Manitoba, a Crown corporation dedicated to energy efficiency.

Rachel Laforest is an associate professor and head of the Public Policy and Third Sector Initiative in the School of Policy Studies, Queen's University in Kingston, Ontario. Her areas of expertise include governance and inter-sectoral collaboration. Her current research interests focus on poverty reduction strategies, mental health and addictions, and education policy.

Shelley Lepp is the co-executive director of the Writers Collective of Canada. In 2019, she received her Master of Arts degree from the Ontario Institute for Studies in Education at the University of Toronto.

Annie Luk completed her PhD in Educational Leadership and Policy at the University of Toronto. She also holds an MBA degree with a specialization in non-profit management from Schulich School of Business at York University.

Laurie Mook is an associate professor in the Nonprofit Leadership and Management program in the School of Community Resources and Development at Arizona State University. She is also a research associate at the Arizona State University (ASU) Lodestar Center for Philanthropy and Nonprofit Innovation. Her research focuses on the social economy, social accounting, and volunteerism.

Marcia Nozick is the founder and CEO of EMBERS, located in Vancouver, British Columbia. EMBERS is a temporary labour company established in 2001 with the mission of supporting individuals facing work barriers in attaining full-time employment.

Carol Pendergast is the executive director at the Horizon Achievement Centre located in Sydney, Nova Scotia. Horizon is the largest vocational training and employment organization catering to adults with mental and intellectual disabilities within the Cape Breton area.

Audra Penner is the CEO/president of ImagineAbility, a social enterprise based in Winnipeg, Manitoba, with a mission to provide support services for people living with intellectual disabilities.

Jack Quarter (1941–2019) was a professor at the Ontario Institute for Studies in Education, University of Toronto. His research, often funded by the Social Sciences and Humanities Research Council (SSHRC), focused on the social economy and supported social enterprises for marginalized social groups. He was the founding president of the Association for Nonprofit and Social Economy Research (ANSER).

Anika Roberts-Stahlbrand works in Student Life at University of Toronto and completed these chapters as a graduate student in the Adult Education and Community Development Program at the Ontario Institute for Studies in Education at the University of Toronto.

Jennifer Sumner is an associate professor and the Coordinator of the Adult Education and Community Development Program at the Ontario Institute for Studies in Education at the University of Toronto. Her research interests include food and sustainable food systems, rural communities, the social economy, and the civil commons.

Arielle Vetro holds a master's degree in Social Policy and Planning from the London School of Economics and Political Science and an Honours Bachelor of Arts degree from the University of Toronto. Her research explores how particular design interventions in urban public spaces influence people's perceptions of safety and happiness.

David Williams is the executive director of Rainbow's End Community Development Corporation in Hamilton, Ontario. Rainbow's End runs training programs and offers employment opportunities to individuals with mental health challenges through its social enterprises.

Index